Advance praise for *Warrior Rising*

"At a time when it is sorely needed, *Warrior Rising* inspires hope and offers a road map to raising our young men to more than survive, but thrive as confident and successful community builders and leaders. MaryAnne provides us with a close up and personal story that illuminates the role and impact we as men have on the future of all of our sons, and our daughters as well."
  —Michael Powell, president, NCTA

"As MaryAnne Howland reminds us, 'It takes a village to raise a child.' But it also takes a child to raise a village. How many adults hear and understand the calling of youth today to be initiated? So they learn not only the rights and responsibilities of adulthood, but come to know the psychic death and soul rebirth necessary to accomplish that transition? MaryAnne Howland heard the call, rose to the challenge, and blessed us all with a road map."
  —Frederick Marx, cowriter, *Hoop Dreams*, warriorfilms.org

"They say it takes a village . . . and while that may be true, sometimes it takes an army of men to bring a boy beyond the shadow of adolescence into the harsh daylight and truths of adulthood. *Warrior Rising* is a book for our times."
  —Erika Alexander, actor, writer, producer, entrepreneur

"MaryAnne Howland's poignant and powerful story of the birth, delivery, and raising of her son with cerebral palsy is a milestone in the developmental psychology literature. The range of emotions I felt about her and Max's trials as a mother and son gave me a small glimpse into what a parent of a child with a disability might feel. Read this book once, twice, and then pass it on to parents and educators who want to understand what infinite love is all about. A true triumph."
  —Dr. Raymond Winbush, research professor and
     director, Institute for Urban Research, Morgan State
     University, Baltimore, Maryland

"When MaryAnne described to me the rite of passage she had created for her son, who she is raising on her own, I was moved to tears. I wish I'd given my son a Black Mitzvah. When thinking about all of the incredible men it was an honor to work with throughout my years in the music business, all who could have personally shared their own life lessons with him, I can only think of the tremendous added value it would have brought to the successful man I'm so proud to call my son. I recommend this book for every father, regardless of race, culture, or religion."
  —Jim Ed Norman, musician, record producer,
     arranger, CEO, Curb Records

Warrior Rising

Warrior Rising

How Four Men Helped a Boy
on His Journey to Manhood

MARYANNE HOWLAND

A TarcherPerigee Book

tarcherperigee

An imprint of Penguin Random House LLC
penguinrandomhouse.com

Copyright © 2020 by MaryAnne Howland
Penguin supports copyright. Copyright fuels creativity, encourages diverse voices,
promotes free speech, and creates a vibrant culture. Thank you for buying an authorized
edition of this book and for complying with copyright laws by not reproducing, scanning, or
distributing any part of it in any form without permission. You are supporting writers
and allowing Penguin to continue to publish books for every reader.

TarcherPerigee with tp colophon is a registered trademark of Penguin Random House LLC.

Most TarcherPerigee books are available at special quantity discounts for bulk purchase for sales
promotions, premiums, fund-raising, and educational needs. Special books or book excerpts also
can be created to fit specific needs. For details, write: SpecialMarkets@penguinrandomhouse.com.

Library of Congress Cataloging-in-Publication Data

Names: Howland, MaryAnne, author.
Title: Warrior rising: how four men helped a boy on his journey
to manhood / MaryAnne Howland.
Description: New York: TarcherPerigee, 2020. | Includes index.
Identifiers: LCCN 2019027194 (print) | LCCN 2019027195 (ebook) |
ISBN 9780143129820 (hardcover) | ISBN 9781101993439 (ebook)
Subjects: LCSH: Howland, MaryAnne. | Mothers of children with disabilities—United States. |
Mothers and sons—United States. | Children with disabilities—United States. |
African American single mothers. | African American boys—Conduct of life. | Role models.
Classification: LCC HQ759.913.H693 2020 (print) | LCC HQ759.913 (ebook) |
DDC 306.874/3—dc23
LC record available at https://lccn.loc.gov/2019027194
LC ebook record available at https://lccn.loc.gov/2019027195

Printed in Canada
1   3   5   7   9   10   8   6   4   2

Book design by Elke Sigal

Some names and identifying characteristics have been changed
to protect the privacy of the individuals involved.

*Penguin is committed to publishing works of quality and integrity. In that spirit, we are proud to offer
this book to our readers; however, the story, the experiences, and the words are the author's alone.*

For my son, my superhero! Excelsior!

I'd rather be a mother
With only a mother's name.
Than to gain all earthly glory,
Or be known by world-wide fame.
I'd rather be a mother
And press a little hand,
Than to receive the highest favors
As first lady of the land.
I'd rather be a mother
And caress a little cheek,
Than possess the greatest riches
That folks on Earth may seek.
I'd rather be a mother
And a child's future hold,
Than live in costly palaces
With kings, and queenly gold.

—*affixed to a gift from the High Hopes Center,*
author unknown

Contents

Introduction

For my son's thirteenth birthday, I gave him a Black Mitzvah. It was not just a one-day celebration. It was a rite of passage that lasted six years. My gift to him included four mentors to help him on his journey from boyhood to manhood, and who keep on giving to this day.

I thought it was important to demarcate for my son the moment when it became necessary to take charge of his own life and to find his role in his community. But I also wanted to give him more. I wanted to give him wind beneath his wings.

I have been asked why a Black Mitzvah. After an extended search for rites of passage on the Internet and asking many friends, I found that there were few such traditions available to us where we live in the South that exactly fit our family's background and culture. During my search, I learned of East African and Australian traditions where Barabaig and Aboriginal boys are made men through practices that include scarification, banging your penis with a rock, or having your teeth knocked out. Ouch! Quite frankly, Max would not be having any of that.

I found other, less painful examples of rite-of-passage ceremonies, but none seemed to suit my young African American middle-class boy who dresses in Gap clothes, obsesses over anime, and loves to draw. Somehow I just could not see him embarking upon a Maasai lion hunt or doing a walkabout in our urban community.

However, I did find aspects of different religious and cultural rite-of-passage traditions that I could draw on. For instance, the Native American vision quest involves a boy leaving home for a time and then returning with a newfound sense of purpose as a man. That, I could use. And we did.

One of the most accessible and empowering of all of the ceremonies I researched was the Jewish Bar Mitzvah. It doesn't involve pain, extreme risk, or leaving home, though my son might argue that the discipline of learning moral and religious responsibilities involves mental pain.

I admired many aspects of the Bar Mitzvah and sought to incorporate them into our own plan, but the element that drew me the most was the community celebration for boys as they embark on their journeys to adulthood and spiritual maturity.

I had first heard of the idea of a Black Mitzvah from a friend who used the term to describe how she had enlisted some very special men in her life to mentor her son. I was intrigued and could immediately see the value of this kind of group parenting. No matter whether you are single, married, black, white, Baptist, Buddhist, Muslim, atheist, or however you identify, we are all part of a community, and we can all help one another raise our children and should. As the saying goes, "It takes a village."

So I borrowed and expanded on her idea and what I had learned about the Bar Mitzvah to create a foundation for my son's journey to manhood that included a long-term commitment of love, learning, mentorship, and community.

By its simplest definition, a Mitzvah is a good deed. My son's Black Mitzvah was a good deed that extended over six years, from age thirteen through eighteen, to prepare him for life with a foundation of respect, responsibility, and accountability. Four remarkable men—warriors—performed a Mitzvah when they each stepped up to ensure that he would grow to become a man of principles and values: a global citizen.

The deed was sacrosanct because Max is no ordinary boy. He was born with disabilities. He has cerebral palsy, epilepsy, and attention-deficit/hyperactivity disorder (ADHD) and suffered with chronic migraines through age fifteen. Though he had inordinate challenges, above all he was just a boy yearning to become his own man. These four men understood that and helped nurture his many natural gifts so that he could realize his full potential.

Throughout his adolescence, my son had the guidance of mentors who committed to one-on-one time at least once a year and immediate access anytime he needed them. My role was to inform the mentors of new developments, concerns, challenges, and celebrations.

By the time he reached the age of eighteen, Max was grounded with a moral foundation to become the hero he wants to be. His relationships with these four mentors transformed into man-to-man relationships and, as one of his mentors proclaimed, the real mentoring is yet to come.

In addition to the many lessons, we have all gained so much more from the fellowship, unity, and shared life experiences. I continue to be overwhelmed by the impact of all his mentors' unwavering commitment to Max's lifelong mental and spiritual health and well-being.

Warrior Rising

Chapter 1

Beginning My Life as a Single Mom

Ships at a distance have every man's wish on board. For some they come in with the tide. For others they sail forever on the horizon, never out of sight, never landing until the Watcher turns his eyes away in resignation, his dreams mocked to death by Time. That is the life of men.

—ZORA NEALE HURSTON,
THEIR EYES WERE WATCHING GOD

Life happens.

My life began the day Max was born.

Three years before he kicked a hole in my placenta, a war was raging in the Persian Gulf, causing the economy to stumble and with it my once-booming promotional-writing career. In a sluggish market, one of the first expenses to get cut from a corporate budget is marketing, where I made my living. The threat of mounting bills forced me to consider alternatives for lowering my operating costs, and the promise of new opportunities led to a move from New York to Nashville, a city on the brink of a boom. I had met a soldier, a pilot in the 101st Airborne in Clarksville, Tennessee, when he was visiting New York, on leave. In his uniform, he looked like stability and felt like a cool drink of water in the desert heat. He helped seal the deal. I gave my business a reboot in a new city where I had no connections, and no network, only a dream of a new life.

Coming to Nashville with my high-roller New York City portfolio, I found myself on the guest list of every elite social event—it seemed as if a swanky, embossed, artfully decorated invitation printed on expensive thick stock appeared in my mailbox every day. I tried to go to every event. I loved dancing with my new husband on a ballroom floor dressed in a hot new item I'd picked up on a quick visit to the third floor of Saks Fifth Avenue on my last trip to New York City to check in on my clients.

Things were looking up—I felt that I had regained control of my life. But this feeling did not last for long. It is amazing how quickly things can change. I could never have anticipated how much I would soon be drawing on the support of my new village. Especially after terrifying circumstances raised my inner screams to the volume of a shriek.

After the traumatic birth of our son, the warning signs about my marriage became full-scale reality. What I thought was stability was anything but. We had rushed ourselves into a commitment without enough serious discussion about our expectations from each other. I was not the woman he wished I was or needed me to be. And I learned a little too late that he wasn't right for me. Beyond irreconcilable marital issues, life had also become unbearably complicated with the birth of a child with disabilities. We quickly found ourselves facing critical health decisions for our son. It was clear that we had to spend more time operating as partners and less time trying to figure each other out. Unfortunately, we did not have more time.

My husband and I separated before Max turned a year old. A few months later, he moved away to another city, and I became a full-custodial single parent. I had to face the fact that he would not be able to play the role that I had expected and that I would be on my own.

The world seems to be engaged in an endless debate about the value of having two parents in a household versus the negative impact that a bad marriage can have on children. But we didn't have time for that debate either. It immediately became clear to me that raising a child with disabilities was going to take every ounce of strength I had. From the moment Max arrived, I had to learn about a myriad of medical procedures and developmental therapies—alongside dealing with the insecurities that come with being a mother for the first time. That control thing . . . completely obliterated and would never return. Life controlled me from this moment on.

Max.

It was an ordinary day in mid-September when I went in for my second routine checkup. Five months along in my pregnancy, I looked and felt beautiful. At thirty-seven years old, I was a fit and trim size 4, a vegetarian, and a fiercely passionate entrepreneur simultaneously giving birth to a new marketing business and awaiting the birth of my son.

My ultrasound turned out to be anything but routine. I'll never forget the grave look of concern on the nurse's face during the procedure. I could feel her pause her cold, wet wand on my bump, putting pressure over and around this one spot while she peered at the image on the screen. My pulse quickened, as I could see that something was terribly wrong. "What's wrong?" I could no longer hold back. She stopped, put the wand down, got up from her chair, patted the gown over my knees, and said as calmly as she could, "I'll need to go get the doctor to come look at this." In a moment, my pregnancy went from glorious to critical. I was terrified to hear the news. I wanted to know but didn't at the same time. Then the doctor laid it all out, clean, simple, and direct. "It looks like there is a problem with your cervix. It's opening." He went on to explain that my pregnancy was at risk if I couldn't hold my baby. "What do you mean?" I asked. "He or she could just slip out?" "Well, I wouldn't describe it quite that way," he said. "But yes, there is a risk. So, to be safe, I want you to go straight to the hospital. I will call ahead to your doctor so that he will be waiting for you." Weak-kneed, I walked to the car, got in, and sat with my hands on the wheel, wondering if I should call someone. Then I decided against it. I wasn't ready to answer questions I couldn't, and I didn't want to waste a moment of time, so I turned on the engine and sped to the hospital to meet my ob-gyn, Dr. Generes.

Dr. Generes's receptionist was ready for me when I arrived in a state of quiet hysteria. I was quickly triaged through to a private room to wait for him. "Wait here. The doctor knows you're here," I was told. Beyond that, I have little memory of what he said. I heard words like "your cervix is weak" and "we need to do a procedure to protect your pregnancy." I was in a state of numb confusion mixed with mounting panic. But what I did understand was that I needed an emergency medical procedure called a "cerclage," which is done to bind the cervix closed using a string. It took about an hour, and then I was told that I could go home. My head and my heart slowly stopped pounding. "I want you to stay active. It is better for you and the baby. But don't overdo it. The goal is to get you to thirty weeks. That's the stage of viability, and so we need to focus on the next ten weeks. Now go home and take care of yourself and that baby." Those were my doctor's orders.

Four weeks later, I knew something was wrong. It felt as if the knot of string that was holding my baby inside me was slowly coming undone. I spoke to my doctor on the phone and was told to come into his office immediately.

My eyes were focused on a small slant of light that was hitting the exam-room floor as my doctor informed me, "It's not holding." "What's not holding?" I asked him, my voice shaky. "The cerclage. You're going to need another one, a stronger one. This time, I'm sending you to a specialist. You will likely need to be admitted into the hospital for a few days, so you will want to prepare for that." He looked at me with a gentle warmth in his eyes. He was more than my doctor; he had become my friend. He assured me that the specialist he referred me to was the region's best in his field, with an ob-gyn practice of over thirty years.

When I met the renowned Dr. Gergen, I felt a measure of ease in the midst of what was rapidly becoming one of the most terrifying experiences of my life. "You're otherwise in excellent health and your pregnancy is still viable, so let's just think of this as precautionary," he said. To further reassure me, he showed me the new and improved string—so thick it reminded me of basketball shoelaces—that he was going to use to bind my cervix this time.

"Thirty weeks," Dr. Generes had told me. That was the goal. Thirty weeks would yield a healthy child. I marked it on my calendar and began to count down the weeks. But we didn't make it. Four weeks shy of our goal, I found myself racing to the hospital again.

On November 15, 1994, the ground beneath my feet fell away. My water broke, and with it, my hopes and dreams and everything I knew. I was born to a new life as a new life was born to me. And it was irreversible. The days and nights that followed shifted like the fast-moving wind directions during hurricane season. Anything that was sure and predictable now felt uncertain. I found myself unraveling, and all I could do was pray for the strength to make it through.

Max, my first and only child, arrived far too early. At only twenty-six weeks, he put his foot right through my placenta, and the water of life gushed. Holding my legs together as firmly as I could, I tried to hold the life inside me during a wild twenty-five-minute race to the hospital. At the wheel, my friend Sam was tense, focused on the road ahead, weaving through traffic. His wife, Vanessa, rested a steady hand on his arm, as if to say, "You can do this." No one uttered a word. Only the roar of the racing engine cut through the brutal quiet. As I sat in the backseat, I realized that the fingers of one of my hands were clenched tightly around the door handle, and the fingers of the other on the edge of the leather seat. My eyes stayed glued on my view of the road in front of us. Time seemed to stand still as reflected on the moments of the hour just past. How odd it was that this had been Sam and Vanessa's first visit to our apartment. It had been unexpected but very welcome. I'd been home alone, as I spent most days, while my husband was at work. I was surprised to hear a knock at the door, and then open it to see their smiling faces. I ushered them in for big, long hugs. "What a wonderful surprise!" I exclaimed. "I wanted to see what you looked like barefoot and pregnant," Sam joked. Vanessa elbowed him in the ribs and said, "You look beautiful. Don't pay him no mind." I thought it was all I needed, my day made. Little did any of us know that they were angels sent to perform a divine intervention to save my son's life.

I arrived in the emergency room already in mourning, certain that I had lost my baby. Strange hands and arms moved me to a wheelchair. "What are you prepping me for? What's happening? What are you doing?" I asked the flurry of doctors and nurses frantically at work around me. My head whipped from side to side, eyes wide with a desperate need for answers from someone, anyone. Finally, a nurse turned to me and said, "We're going to try to deliver your baby."

Dr. Generes told me he'd been playing golf when he got a message that there was an emergency delivery. He told me that he knew it was me before they even gave him my name and that he had gotten there as fast as he could because he wanted to deliver my baby.

Every person in the room sprang into action to perform the C-section. Within minutes, another doctor standing at the ready got into line formation for the gentle handoff of my tiny twenty-six-ounce baby. As she rushed out of the room to take him straight to the neonatal intensive care unit (NICU), she paused a split second so that I could see my son. I turned my head to get a fleeting glimpse of him, but the only thing I could see through my swollen eyes was a blush of limp red skin as two people in white coats, who seemed to be joined together carrying precious cargo, rushed Max out of the room. Later, Dr. Generes revealed to me that mine was the smallest baby he had ever delivered.

Within the first thirty-two hours following his birth, Max had a severe brain bleed. I received my first of what would be the many medical lessons to come about the different levels of brain damage that can result from hemorrhaging. They are measured in severity from grade 1 to grade 4. I learned that small bleeds (grades 1 and 2) are not so bad for preemies and can heal over time. In Max's case, 60 percent of the blood in his body went to his head, resulting in grade 3 brain damage on the left side and grade 4 on the right. Grade 4 is the worst. Such severe hemorrhaging can cause nerve cell damage and lead to a range of long-term symptoms, including anemia, low heart rate, apnea, and seizures. Blood clots can form and block the flow of cerebrospinal fluid. This can lead to increased fluid in the brain, a condition known as hydrocephalus.

The neonatologist woke me at 2:30 a.m. to tell me the devastating news. It is impossible to remember the exact words he used to communicate to me that Max had a fifty-fifty chance of living, and that *if* he lived, he might be a vegetable. What do you do when you get news like this? First, you ask what you did wrong. Then you cast blame. You curse and you pray. But mostly, you cry and you sob and you moan. Your eyes and your heart become swollen with fear and vulnerability.

I began to spin wild visions of a future that up until that moment I had seen only on a screen or read about in a novel. This happened in *other* people's lives. Wheelchairs, drooling, feedings, adult diapers, drugs, stares, doctors, more and more doctors—I imagined a life robbed of freedom and bound with uncertainty. A life of burden, worry, struggle, the unknown. A life with severe limitations and low expectations. I prayed some more.

Just as soon as I was able, I rushed down to the NICU to see him, to see my baby. I spoke softly to myself: my baby needs me and he is going to live.

Inside his glass incubator, baby Max looked like unfinished business. His cellophane-like skin revealed the intricate network of veins and vessels beneath. His skin was taped inside the bends of his elbows and behind his knees so that it wouldn't tear. You could see his heart beating in his chest like a tiny fist under a sheet. Tape covered most of his face to hold the tubes steady, one in his mouth and one in his nose, each connecting him to a machine—one for feeding and one for breathing.

He lay on his side. His left knee up, his right leg flat, his hand relaxed over his private parts. Sensing my presence, his soft eyes turned to me and our love cemented—a bond that reached far back in time to our African ancestors. In that instant, I became an African Queen Mother. I decided that if it took the strength and the will of our ancestors and every resource available on the planet, I was going to stomp out every obstacle that tried to stand between my child and his will to thrive.

I was still weak and recovering in my own patient room from an extreme loss of blood during my C-section while Max was in the NICU experiencing his own blood trauma on just his second day of life. It was nearly twelve hours after his brain bleed that I learned that Max needed and got a successful blood transfusion from his father to replace the loss of blood in his tiny body that had flowed to his head. It was a critical health decision that was made for the three of us that required no discussion. The doctor explained that the risk of a negative reaction to the transfusion is higher in the case of an extremely premature birth. However, Max overcame his first life-saving procedural intervention with warrior-like determination.

I could not yet snuggle him in my arms, since he was too fragile to hold. I could mother him only through the barrier of the glass incubator. With the thin, white sterile rubber gloves pulled on snugly, I could ease my hands through the holes on the sides of the incubator, gingerly touching my fingers to his arm, just above the elbow and below the shoulder, so he knew his mommy was there. I spoke softly to him, hoping that he could hear in my voice that he could rely on me to protect him. I told him how much I loved him and how strong he was and that he'd be coming home soon.

I sat beside Max for hours and hours. Often I would find my eyes trailing the movements of a young doctor with a tousle of dirty-blond hair and a pleasant face who appeared to be fresh out of med school. In his strong hands with long fingers, he held a small rotary device as he traveled the rows of incubators, gently inserting the tiny wand into each glass dome, carefully touching the fragile skin of these struggling babies to stimulate the blood flow in their tiny limbs. I watched him as he went from one infant to the next, giving the same sensitive and focused care to each little body. His manner suggested that he truly felt it was a blessing to perform such a small act of kindness over and over with patient, careful repetition. I imagined that he had a contract with each of these tiny souls: if they would keep breathing, he would keep their blood flowing.

Through a tiny tube inserted in his throat, Max was fed my pumped breast milk—liquid gold, the perfect food. We all celebrated the day he consumed more than 2 ounces in twenty-four hours. At one month, he was up to 6 milliliters per hour and weighed 2 pounds and 6 ounces. He gained weight and his skin grew thick enough that the tape could finally be removed from inside his elbows and behind his knees. He grew livelier every day, so much so that he pulled out his own endotracheal tube, which set off all the alarms in his station. After the dust settled from the medical activity triggered by the sound of an emergency alarm and his tube was reinserted, the doctor said, "He's feisty," and suggested that perhaps it was a sign that he was stronger and ready to be upgraded to a small continous pathway airway pressure (CPAP) ventilator. She was wrong. He tried it. He hated it, and so the tube was back for a while longer. My warrior was not yet strong enough to feed on his own without a CPAP.

He slept almost all the time. I tried to be there so that whenever his eyes opened, every waking moment, he would see I was there, that his mother would never leave him alone, that we would fight the good fight together.

When Max was four weeks old, he was finally strong enough for me to hold him. A minute with Max in my arms was a pure shot of adrenaline. My breasts tingled with a motherly sensation, though his tiny jaws were much too weak to nurse. Even if just for a few minutes, a kind and merciful warmth completely enveloped my soul.

At the end of week six, Dr. Long, one of the three on-staff neonatologists, came to me while I was loving on my baby. She quietly pulled me aside and said, "I'd like to talk to you for a few minutes." I immediately tensed in anticipation of what she might say. By now, in lieu of questions, my mind had become an open repository for information that I knew little to do with. I was just anxious for some good news. I tuned out the sounds and activity of the busy NICU and focused directly on her face and listened intently so as not miss a word. What she said was brief but bountiful. "You know, I've been watching him. I don't want to give you any kind of false hope. But I've seen that sometimes babies that come into the world the way he did, too early, and experience a brain bleed like he did, sometimes nature has time to correct an error so early on. I've seen it before. He's not finished yet. He's doing very well. He's thriving and getting stronger every day. Those are very good signs. He's a survivor."

Through a burst of tears, I responded to this beautiful woman, "I know. He is, isn't he? He's mine. He's my little warrior. We're going to win. We're going to win together." If Mother Nature was working for him, then I would work that much harder to do all I could to save his life, for the rest of his life.

At ten weeks, he became strong enough to hold in my arms for longer periods of time. When I wasn't by his side, I was reading books and scouring the Internet for information about how to care for preemie babies. It's how I learned about the technique of skin-to-skin contact called kangaroo care, which has proved to have positive developmental effects. It's a method of holding your baby close that was developed in Colombia as an alternative to incubator care for premature and low birthweight babies. I would remove my shirt and hold him against my bare skin so he could feel my heart beating next to his. Though I could hold him for only twenty minutes at a time, he responded to this new routine right away and stretched out his little arms each time he saw me, ready to snuggle.

I crooned the lyrics from one of my favorite songs by Eddie Kendricks, "Can I have a talk with you? Can I make a dream come true?" in a soft, low voice as we rocked in a chair tucked away in a storage room at the back of the NICU. The nurses had cleared out the old medical tables and equipment so that Max and I could have our own private bonding center. Our unspoken agreement was that while the medical team supported his gestation in his medical pod, I would do my part and wrap him with a reason to live—a mother's love. If I could have, I would have reattached that umbilical cord and pushed him back up inside me until he was ready to come out a big, bouncing baby boy, like the other infants down the hall in the normal natal unit.

After a week of kangarooing with Max, miracles began to happen in rapid succession. One of the nurses told me, "We see some significant progress. He's been feeding better. I hadn't heard of the kangaroo care method before, but it seems to be doing some good. Do you mind if we share it with some of the other parents?" Her words were music to my ears—like the words to Helen Reddy's anthem, "I am strong, I am invincible, I am woman," she made me feel as if I really were a Queen Mother, and yet I was simply doing the only thing I could.

Each day before I left the unit, I walked around and looked at the other babies and wondered, "Who will live and who won't?" I saw parents and grandparents come and go, and a few ministers came to baptize or to give last rites. I also saw the babies whose parents didn't visit and wondered where they were. What on earth could keep them away? Were they too afraid? Had they lost hope? Was it foolish to hope? What did God want for us? For me? For Max?

After sixty days, Max graduated to "step down," an area of the NICU for babies who have stabilized and no longer need to be hooked up to monitors and breathing tubes. The doctors decided he was strong enough for his first surgery, a critical necessity to save his vision. Max has been diagnosed with a condition called retinopathy, due to his prematurity, which can cause blindness; it's the same disease that caused Stevie Wonder's loss of sight. It would be his first of four corrective eye surgeries before he turned six years old. We were lucky. We got Dr. Wentworth, the resident pediatric ophthalmologist specializing in the treatment of preemies at risk of permanent retinal damage. The procedure went well. Max would be able to see!

I will never forget that miraculous Day 72 when I came to visit Max early in the morning, eager to see him, as usual. After the ritual of vigorous hand washing, I donned a gown and entered the ward. My heart began to pound, my eyes laser focused on where I knew he'd be waiting to see me, waiting to hear my voice, squirming to be held. Suddenly I froze. Why were there four nurses hovering over his bed? My breath caught in my throat. But then, one by one, they looked up at me with expressions of pure joy. My pace quickened as I walked over to see what they were looking at with such fascination. "Oh my!" I was awestruck by his transformation. Overnight, Max had blossomed like an early spring flower. It was as though a fairy had touched her wand to his head and turned him all rosy with a crown of golden hair. He looked like a cherubic angel. After nearly three months of steady growth, milliliter by milliliter, he had turned into a bouncing baby boy. They took turns holding him as he kicked and cooed. I giggled with delight, thinking, *Look at him. He's a born ladies' man.*

At eighty-three days old, weighing 4 pounds, 7 ounces, Max was ready to leave the hospital and its round-the-clock care to start his life at home. Typically, when babies are born, parents often bemoan that they don't come with instructions. But when a baby comes into the world the way Max did, they are sent home with their parents with folders of information, a list of support services, and a full load of fear unlike anything the parents have ever known. In fact, I was scared to death. But a Queen Mother does not show her fear. She accepts the responsibility that comes with her position, and she leads.

Amid warm and thankful goodbyes to the medical team who had performed heroic life-saving care for him, I took an extra moment with Dr. Long to let her know how her light shone brightest of all.

"Your words were not false hope—they were my every hope. You and your team are angels. You didn't just save Max's life—you gave me mine. I know that this is what you signed up for and so you will tell me that I don't owe you anything, but I promise you that I will pay it forward. We will live every day in honor of all of you. Thank you so much for all you have done for us," I told her as I held her warm hands in mine.

Dr. Long responded, "Yes, I love my job, but especially when we are able to send our babies home to wonderful families like yours. I know that Max will be fine and you will be a great mom. Bring him back to visit us sometime. We'd love to see him. Or just send us a picture that we can add to our wall," she said, pointing to a wall with photos of the faces of many children who had entered their world of wonder in the NICU.

I promised I would, and we left the hospital with Max's toys, prayer gifts, care equipment, a handful of prescriptions, and very detailed instructions. I was dispatched with three prescriptions for eye drops to be applied twice each day, plus an iron supplement of Fer-In-Sol for every morning feeding and a multivitamin supplement of Vi-Daylin for every evening feeding, with an oxygen machine required during both. Every day was like running my own home NICU. I had to measure his intake at every feeding, note the time of his iron and vitamin supplements, his medication, and his temperature. By his actual due date, he was already three and a half months born, weighed 5.5 pounds and measured 17¾ inches. With up to 3 ounces per feeding every four hours, he was growing a little faster. Two weeks later, at 6.5 pounds, he grew by 1 inch. Test results for his oxygen level at feedings showed that he could breathe on his own, though I'd known that for a couple of weeks already.

I also measured how much his head was growing every day. In the two weeks since he'd came home, his head had grown 3 inches, faster than anything else on his body. I called the doctor, and he told me that, yes, we should be concerned that Max might be entering the stage of hydrocephalus. This condition could lead to a range of serious problems, including seizures, double vision, poor balance, and mental impairment. I knew right away that if there was even the slightest probability of new problems, I wanted to try to take them out of the equation immediately so that I could focus on his feedings and weight gain. We made an appointment for Max to get a ventriculoperitoneal (VP) shunt implant, his third surgery in the four months since he was born. This invasive dual surgery in the brain and in the stomach implanted a tube that connected the two to drain fluid off the brain. It would never be removed and would become a part of his internal wiring.

In the months following his homecoming, it took stores of strength I didn't know I had to bear the weight of the responsibility for caring for my son, but there were also tremendous rewards in witnessing the daily miracles. Each day got a little bit easier as I grew used to the routine chiming of the alarm on my watch, alerting me that it was time for the next feeding, measurement, or checking of his vitals. I added my own mommy therapy of gentle body massages over his back, tummy, and legs, paying particular attention to his feet. He seemed to especially enjoy having his feet rubbed and tickled at the finish. His quick smile and bubbly gurgles made my role in his life feel like less that of a nurse and more that of a normal mom, and the joy in this is impossible for me to describe.

His progress was steady. At four months, he weighed in at 7 pounds, 10 ounces. His weight was good enough for the doctors to perform a successful bilateral hernia repair to the groin muscle damaged during his traumatic birth.

At nine months, Max could barely crawl and was diagnosed with cerebral palsy. Added to a growing list of interventions to improve his quality of life, we began physical therapy. He loved chasing the big, colorful inflatable ball that we used to help strengthen his leg muscles. When he managed to pull himself up, he would slap the ball with his tiny fists and bounce on his knees with joy. If he couldn't make it, he would just eventually fall over, roll on his back, and try to kick it with his feet, squealing with laughter. Any physical movement worked wonders on his legs and also stimulated play, which is how Jennie, our therapist, described her job: "We work with our children in a way that it's not work—it's play."

At two years old, Max was receiving occupational therapy to develop his fine motor skills for basic life skills such as holding a fork, brushing his teeth, buttoning his shirt, and zipping his pants. Around this same time, he developed a severe stutter. It started happening out of the blue. One day he was talking fine and then the next day his words seemed to get stuck like a skipping record. His doctor said it was not uncommon for children with birth trauma to have temporary anomalies like this through stages of development. His brain was still healing. So now we added speech therapy to his regimen.

At twenty-eight months, a year into physical therapy, Max began attempting to stand on his own, if only for a few seconds or just to take a couple of steps. Learning to walk included learning to navigate with his custom orthotics, cast to properly set his legs and feet, while pushing his walker that he used to pull himself up and steady his balance. Once he got the hang of it, he was pretty adept. I had to run to catch him a couple of times after I got him out of the car when he just took off on his wheels and went flying across a parking lot, giddy with joy at his new-found freedom. My yells to "Stop!" just made him laugh harder. He thought it was play. I didn't need the extra exercise.

We had our fun moments too. Despite his challenges, Max to this day will not let anything get in the way of his own goals, especially when it comes to girls. Just as he did with the NICU nurses who swooned over him the day he left the hospital, he stole hearts at the skills center. There was one little girl in particular who was quite smitten with Max. Every time she saw him, she covered him in sloppy kisses and tackled him to the floor so they could roll around together. He loved every minute of it. Her mother told me one day, "He's quite the ladies' man. You know you better teach him good birth control." We both laughed. Little innocents—it was cute for now, so we let him get away with it.

Given his fierce determination and with high hopes, we set a goal for him to walk by his third birthday. To help him reach that goal, Jennie, his physical therapist, suggested we start Botox therapy, which is used to treat certain muscular conditions. "Isn't that a toxin?" I asked, alarmed at the notion of putting a poison in Max's already weak little legs; this was before it became a popular retail cosmetic treatment to remove wrinkles. She went on to explain how its controlled use is ideal for relaxing muscle spasticity caused by cerebral palsy. Jennie was his therapist of two years and had never steered us wrong. I trusted her, and it worked! An injection in each leg allowed him to stand taller and walk with a more normal flex at his knees. After each treatment, which lasted about ninety days, he could pull himself up with the assistance of a wall or chair and walk for as long as five minutes at a time!

We had reason to celebrate big time, and so we did. For his third birthday, Big Bird came to play at his party. It had been a couple of months since his Botox injection and he was as rambunctious as any typical three-year-old. Max actually jumped in the air with glee and grabbed Big Bird's hand to introduce him to all of his friends: "This is *my* special friend!" It was funny when he kept trying to get Big Bird to eat birthday cake. Somehow all of it wound up in crumbs on the floor and Max just thought it was hilarious. "Big Bird make a mess!" he laughed hysterically. The excitement of dancing with Big Bird lasted for weeks, even as the Botox didn't. As it wore off, staying active on his feet became hard again.

Three more rounds of Botox and he was ready. Using his muscles made them stronger, enough for the more intensive therapy that would be necessary after a transformative surgery called selective dorsal rhizotomy (SDR). It is a spinal cord surgery that involves severing the nerves that are sending neural messages causing spasticity. It is optimal for children with some muscle mobility, and ideally it takes place at around age four.

The surgery was performed at St. Louis Children's Hospital.

We spent half the day before his scheduled surgery at the St. Louis Zoo. It was my way of making the trip more fun for Max, to take his mind off the scary day ahead. It was a beautiful, sunny day and all the animals were either basking or romping in their pens. Max loved the baby animals, especially the elephants. "Oooh, Mommy, look at him," he said, pointing to the smallest one, toddling clumsily, bumping into his mother with every step. "He's so cute. I want to feed him. Can I?" He repeated this enough to let me know that we would be leaving with a stuffed cuddle-size version of the mammoth.

Once back at our hotel to rest after a long day and to prepare for the day that had finally come, Max was content watching TV and cuddling his new friend, "my baby elephant," a name the animal would carry forever.

While he began to fade into sleep, fighting it every minute as his lids drooped, I paced, prayed, then made up my mind that we were not going through with it. I had to remind myself every other minute that this was the right thing to do until it became almost a chant: *This must be a decision based on hope, not fear. Max deserves nothing less. How would I ever forgive myself if I didn't let him have his best chance to walk, to maybe even run, to play sports like other children? It would be selfish to deprive him of any opportunity to maximize his quality of life. But what if something goes wrong? What if? It's an elective surgery, and there is the risk of paralysis. I will have risked his life and lost. Is this gamble worth a life of permanent nerve damage, paralysis, or worse? The doctor is the foremost expert in the medical world for this one very special operation. No one has performed more successful rhizotomies on three-year-olds than he has.* "He'll be fine." I prayed, "May God bless his hands."

Like the days and nights during Max's months in the NICU, sleep for me never came. At 5:00 a.m. I was still up and moving without feeling, barely breathing. I sat on the edge of the bed and just stared at him. How beautiful and lovely his face, how delicate his little body; his hair was soft and curly, his breathing, quiet and peaceful. *I love him so truly and deeply,* I thought. *I can't do this. Yes, I can. Yes, we will. This is the right thing to do.*

On a Friday in the middle of September, we arrived at St. Louis Children's Hospital at 6:00 a.m., for his SDR. Max was wide awake, happy, snug in my arms. The nurse came to meet us in the waiting room. Then it was time to give him a medicine to make him sleep for the four hours it would take to open, seek, find, snip, and close. "Can we turn back now?" I wondered.

In seconds, he was asleep, his breath light on my neck as his head rested on my shoulder. Too quickly, the nurse came for him. "Mom, it's time," she said to me with empathetic compassion. When she reached for him, I could see her mother's ring with green and pink gemstones dangling on a princess necklace. Her soft eyes held mine while I couldn't help resisting as she pried him from my arms. I nearly fainted. "Let me take you to the waiting room," she said as, weak-kneed, I rose to follow her. I went there to wait, feeling like a defendant awaiting the verdict—guilty or not guilty—knowing that our whole future, our lives rested in the hands of someone who didn't know me, or my son, or the promises I had made to him, or our tumultuous journey to this moment.

There was a beige phone on a table that connected to the operating room. When it rang, it meant there was news. It rang about every thirty minutes, but felt more like every thirty hours. Each call was an update with information such as "He's resting very well" and "The doctor is about to begin now. I'll call you when he's in." The latter meaning that his tiny little back had been cut open and the doctor had entered his insides with tiny precision instruments on his mission to search for and destroy the spastic nerves that were in the way of Max being able to walk on his own.

Another thirty minutes. "Everything is fine. He remains stable. The doctor is searching for the correct nerve, a long and careful process. I'll let you know when he's found what he's looking for."

Another thirty minutes. "He's doing just fine. Do you have any questions?" I could only nod, but not speak, so she couldn't see my lips move to try to ask, "Are you sure he's warm enough?" I couldn't think of anything else except him lying on a cold table with his back wide open. When all she heard was silence on my end, she said that she'd call again in thirty minutes. After I heard her click off, I wished that I had asked, "Can you hold his hand?"

Another thirty minutes. "Good news. The doctor has found one of the nerves. It shouldn't be long now. I'll call you when he has found the second one."

My heart leapt at "good news" and I hoped that meant it was over, Max was completely fixed, and we could go home now. "Good news" sounded like a miracle. It meant playing in the park, climbing trees, riding bikes, running as fast as we could. The second half of her message—that there was another nerve and the severing had not even occurred yet—was mind splitting.

Another thirty minutes. "Okay, he's found the other nerve. Now that he has identified the two nerves, he will perform the rhizotomy. I'll let you know when it's over." "When it's over" sounded ominous. I felt sick to my stomach. I could no longer breathe. I thought I'd have a nervous breakdown at that very moment.

Another thirty minutes. It was going on three hours now. "The doctor has completed the procedure. Your son is doing fine. He looks good and is still sleeping comfortably."

Another thirty minutes. "We're closing now. The surgery went well."

Another thirty minutes. "We're taking him to post-op now to watch him for a little while. You can see him soon. We'll call you when he awakes."

I can see him! My whole body sighed. Suddenly I was aware that the sun was shining through the window in a room that, up until this very moment, seemed to be all walls.

But no one could have prepared me for the sight of my little Max just after his surgery, looking limp, exhausted, and beat up, as if he had been in the fight of his life.

"Mommy, take this off," he whimpered over and over again, while trying to pull at all the tape holding all his IVs and other tubes and wires. "Carry you, Mommy, carry you," he cried. It was his cry for me to pick him up when he would tire of walking with uncomfortable leg braces while gripping the arms of his aluminum walker with wheels. It came from him hearing me ask him, "Do you want me to carry you?" whenever I saw that he was distressed. I knew that his words, "Carry you, Mommy, carry you," meant "Pick me up, hold me, Mommy."

My heart ached. The next twenty-four hours in his hospital room were just as excruciating. The nurses kept close watch to make sure that he had no pain and that there was no infection. I slept next to him, holding him close, comforted by his soft breath on my face.

Just two days after his surgery, to my nervous joy, Max was crawling around his bed and even trying to get out of it. How could this be? Not even forty-eight hours ago he'd had his back cut open and somebody fooling around with his innards! A little apprehensive that he might just tear a stitch, I called for the nurse to come see what was happening. "Is that okay, him moving around like that?" I asked her with my eyes squinched.

"He's fine. It's good that he's moving around. That's a good sign," she said calmly. Still a little skeptical, I watched him carefully to be sure he didn't (Oh, Lawd!) rip his back open.

The next day, Monday, he had his first day of therapy. He was wheeled down to rehab, where the nurse stopped and locked the wheels. Then without any direction, he got up out of his chair and took several steps—fully upright—without his walker! "Whoa!" the therapist gasped. "I didn't expect that to happen quite so fast," she said. He even shocked himself and sat back down! Needless to say, I was ecstatic. Max's reaction said it all: "Look at me! I can walk! I can stand on my own two feet!" God is good.

By Wednesday, he was walking around the hospital floor spreading cheer everywhere he went. "Hi! What's your name?" he greeted everyone he met as if he were running for mayor. Meanwhile, several of the floor nurses fell in love with him, especially Rochelle. Max always cheered her up. "He makes me love my job," she told me. Lucky for me, Rochelle loved spending time with him, and so she let me get a couple of mommy breaks to go outside, get some fresh air and exercise, and explore the city outside the window from the chair next to his bed.

As I strolled outside to catch my breath, I was able to rediscover a little of my old self. While my son's life was being changed inside the medical world of St. Louis Children's Hospital, I was reclaiming my own.

I took in some St. Louis jazz and blues, Euclid Avenue, and the famous Gateway Arch. I found my way to the botanical gardens and took in the rows and rows of brilliantly bright flowers, meandering in a trance as I reflected on the latest stretch of road on a journey that had begun four years before. There was still no obvious or predictable end in sight. And yet my thirst for life—as well as my son's own fierce determination—buoyed me, allowing me to enjoy the St. Louis Art Museum, one of the seven best in the country. I love the mysteries, the dreams, and the textures of the world of art. Beautiful hand-carved wooden masks from Africa; antiquities that tell stories of people and cultures from nearly every part of the world; the hard, smooth crested swirls of acrylic paint in a dusk-colored painting; the dark, rough, scratchy edges of ancient etchings—all the abstractions, distractions, order, chaos, and illusions that art can reveal. Typically, I am very anxious, not wanting to miss a single item. However, this day that I visited the museum, I surrendered to the ambience and, instead of trying to take in every piece, I lost myself in the energy of creation, the intensity within each and every moment it took to make each piece of art I pondered. I absorbed all the emotions expressed in exquisite art forms and made them my own. I was rejuvenated. I needed it.

Back at home, Max was now walking on his own, and while I experienced "alleluia" joy, it came with knee-bending fatigue as I tried to keep up with my new hands-free four-year-old who seemed to want to make up for lost time.

The next thing that happened was straight out of the luxury catalog of silver linings. It came out of nowhere. Max was sitting, enjoying his favorite TV show, *ER*, when suddenly he turned and looked up at me to pronounce, "I'm going to be great!" He was so matter-of-fact about it that without hesitation I affirmed, "Yes, you will!" I now had my mandate to do everything that I could to support his greatness.

My challenge was helping him realize that gift, make it manifest, and use it to achieve a rich and rewarding life. One of the toughest challenges was that I was on unfamiliar turf.

Max's first twelve years were about full-scale, unadulterated mothering, juggling doctors' appointments, medical treatments, prescriptions, therapies, and a home routine that required keeping up with medical equipment, supplies, and pharmaceuticals that I'd never heard of. I didn't expect that motherhood would include testing rounds of experimental stimulants or learning how to administer a dose of diazepam to stop a grand mal seizure.

Through Max's early years, I somehow mustered the strength to overcome all the unexpected challenges of his physical limitations, academic challenges, and systemic human rights issues on top of the typical ones for a first-time mom. However, when it came to the uncharted territory of raising a young boy to become a man, I felt helpless. I knew that the next six developmental years, from ages thirteen to eighteen, would be just as critical as the first twelve. Who would teach my son the things I couldn't? How was I, a woman, supposed to teach a boy how to handle situations that I knew nothing about? What do you do when your peepee gets hard? Or, what exactly *is* men's room protocol? Is there any at all? In the face of mano-a-mano confrontation, when is it best to fight or just walk away? And when is the last time I can step in to handle the situation before he gets called a "mama's boy"?

What matters most to me beyond his health and well-being is his independence and self-confidence, that he believes in himself. I want him to have the confidence to pursue the career in animation that he dreams of. I want him to learn to love himself so he can find and marry the love of his life and raise a family. I want grandkids. I want to maximize his potential to be anything and everything he wants to be. I have never lost hope that one day the ship filled with wishes will come in with the tide.

Chapter 2

I Can No Longer Do This Alone

Can a woman teach a boy to be a man?

It is said that we love our sons and raise our daughters. I like to think that I have done both for Max, but there was a moment when he was twelve years old that I became acutely aware of my shortcomings in raising my son alone. Max came into this world needy, and my inclination was to marshal all my resources to tend to his every need. Deep down, however, I knew that it was my job to teach him to fend for himself, to be strong and self-sufficient, so that he would reach his highest potential. At the same time, I recognized that some things were simply beyond my individual scope and capacity. More and more mothering wasn't the answer.

Since he was sidelined by his physical challenges, I knew I would never be a soccer mom. Max was never going to make that march of pride up to the podium to accept an MVP trophy. He wasn't going to know the rush, the sense of celebrity, the admiration from girls that many young men feel when they excel at basketball or track or football. But his instincts are acute; he knew he'd need to forge his own path to feeling accepted, to earn the kind of attention that young people crave. And his observations from the sidelines were that the guys garnering the most thrilling energy off the field were the bad boys. They were the exhibitionists, masking their insecurities with aggressive behavior.

Max chose to enter the bad-boy arena with the face of a warrior. He wanted in on the battle for glory, but his vulnerabilities were as pronounced as ever, and that's when the bullying began. He no longer wanted to wear the braces on his legs that helped him walk taller because they actually made him feel smaller. The awkwardness with which Max's legs functioned was the equivalent of having a target on his back.

There's nothing crueler than children making fun of other children who are different, whose deficits make them objects of confusion, unsettling anomalies. They don't understand that the impact of their cruelty lasts long after all the kids have left school. And to the recipient of their cruelty, their motives are irrelevant. A child like Max leaves an attack with scars of public embarrassment and the lingering sting that he just isn't like the other kids. His uniqueness is the kind that no child ever wants. Max fought back with great vengeance, and given that he couldn't overcome his enemies with force or might or speed, he launched his battle in the form of words. The school halls had become a theater for open war.

I knew things were going off the rails when one day, from the mouth of my lovable boy I heard, "If he keeps fucking with me, I'm gonna punch him in the face." *What?* Trying for the moment to mask my shock at the profanity, I asked, "*Who* are you talking about?" "Ricky. He's an asshole," Max said. So I had two issues to deal with: my son felt completely free to swear like an angry football fan on the losing side in front of his mother, and he also wanted to slam his fist into the face of a classmate. Which to address first?

"First of all, I don't ever want to hear you talk like that again, young man. It is disrespectful to me and to yourself. You know better, so do better. I am not raising a heathen."

His tone grew soft as he apologized. "I'm sorry, Mommy. I didn't mean to say a bad word. I'm just so mad. I won't do it again," he promised.

But he did do it again, and often. It was always followed by an apology, but his swearing became more frequent, more colorful, and more and more soaked in anger. I wasn't sure what to do about it. My son had always been respectful in his interactions with other people. And yet neither of us was prepared for a situation in which other people were hurling attacks at him. I knew that what I was seeing now was the outside world pushing its way into the cocoon of safety, civility, and respect that I had woven for my son.

"Second, I don't want you fighting anybody. That's just what this Ricky wants you to do. Don't let him win by getting you to stoop to his level. You're better than that," I told him. "Besides, all that is just going to get you suspended. And if that happens, then I'm going to be angry with you, and you don't want that," I threatened.

I was careful not to let him know my real fear: that because of his physical disadvantage, he could get really hurt. I knew that, with his fragile ego, it was exactly what he didn't need to hear. But I also knew that my advice and threat of punishment were not what he needed either. He needed ammo that he could use to win his next battle, the kind of ammo that I do not have in my arsenal of calm and restraint. In fact, I really wanted to confront Ricky myself and beat his ass!

And it was not just the cruel boys hurling cruel comments at him. Max was suddenly consumed by the strange creatures with multicolored fingernails, carrying smart little purses to match their tight shirts and short skirts, who constantly threw shade at the boys and giggled in groups. He drowned in envy at the sight of these girls draped on the arms of his competition, snuggling against lockers or stealing kisses in corners. There were none for him.

"No one likes me," he said with downcast eyes and a frown that reflected the misery of a hundred nos. "Today this girl nearly knocked me over in the hallway. She didn't even say, 'I'm sorry.' I know it's because I'm different and I walk funny," he said.

His confidence and self-esteem began to wilt like cut roses on a hot, dry day. All I could do was hug him, but I knew that it didn't help much. A mother's hug can salve the sting, but the open wound is still there.

At a time when all boys struggle to be comfortable with their changing bodies, Max had the extra challenges of seemingly small things being extremely difficult for him to do, like tying his shoes and buttoning his shirt. Putting on a tie and buckling a belt were nearly impossible. He hated that he had to ask for my help. It made him feel like he was weak and unattractive. He became unsure of himself and overly self-conscious. When he looked in the mirror, he did not like what he saw. His spirit was deflating. You could see it in the way his shoulders drooped and his glasses sat lopsided on his nose. He simply stopped caring. It broke my heart.

Besides the bullies, girl problems, and struggles with putting on his clothes, Max stumbled academically. His individualized education program (IEP) included accommodations for longer testing times, tutors for math and English, and behavior modification techniques to curb his enthusiasm for attention. "Put your hand down. Wait until I finish, and you might get the answer to your question," his teacher would have to say much too often.

Despite Max's urge to become his own man, sometimes after a particularly hard day, he would sheepishly ask if he could sleep in my bed, wanting the comfort and protection of his mother's warmth. Since he was too old, too big, and too fidgety, I'd let him sleep on the floor beside my bed, and he settled for that so we could talk some in the dark.

"Are you awake?" he would ask when I would slip into a light snore.

"Yes, I'm awake," I would mumble, and he would talk some more until he fell asleep.

I knew it was time for him to become his own man. I also knew he needed the kind of guidance and support that I was unable to provide. He needed to learn the secrets of success among men.

"He's just in fifth grade!" I bemoaned to one of my close momma friends. "I don't know if we'll make it through this year, forget about high school!"

I knew I had homework to do. Leaning in, I started paying closer attention to men, the ones I knew and the ones I didn't. I observed them discreetly, paying close attention to the smallest details. I studied their "mannetisms," as Max calls them. I watched how they moved. I listened intently to the way they expressed themselves. I smelled and drank them in like warm sweet tea. I became more astutely aware of the importance of ego, status, and conquest. I also noticed the unspoken negotiations they had in order to come to an acceptance of each other: "As long as you're cool with me, I'm cool with you."

Next I applied my laser focus to the distinct differences between men and women, the ways we react to situations and interact with each other. Where women may take pride in getting things done, men take more pride in you noticing what they have done, good or bad. Where women talk, men seem to have an unspoken language. One afternoon at the gym, I noticed several scenarios where one guy walked up to another guy and asked,

"Can you spot me, man?"

And without hesitation, the stranger would move to hold the weights so as to steady his lift.

Then, "Thanks, man." Respect given, nothing else needed.

Never, in all the years that I've been going to the gym, have I ever even once thought to walk up to another woman and ask her to spot me. In fact, if I communicated to another woman at all, there was always a note of envy in my words of encouragement.

"You're looking good, girl. Keep it up."

I began to recognize that there was a special code of understanding and expectation that exists between men, and especially between men and boys.

I paid particular attention to the men who impressed me most. I realized that my admiration often stemmed from seemingly small things— the way they carried themselves or handled a situation or spoke to others. These were the kind of men I most wanted Max to grow up to be like. Kind, confident, forthright, and respectful.

It was a friend, another single mom, who gave me the idea of a Black Mitzvah when Max was just six years old. It struck me as brilliant when she told me all about how, for her son's thirteenth birthday, she had created a circle of male mentors to help guide him on his journey to manhood. So when Max turned thirteen, I dusted off my friend's idea and decided to use it as a platform that I could build on to create a support system, a lifeline not only for my son but for myself.

I knew that my young mariner prince was set to embark on a heroic adventure of self-discovery and he needed male co-captains to help him navigate this journey. So I turned to our trusted and supportive inner circle of family and friends to find ready and willing warriors to stand by his side.

I had never been to a Bar Mitzvah and still haven't. All that I know about the tradition is from what I've heard others describe and what I've seen in movies and on television—big celebrations with lots of extended family, lots of food, dancing, and the young celebrant dressed in a black suit as he reads from the Torah. Through my conversations with Jewish friends, I learned that the Jewish rite of passage offers Jewish families so much more than the opportunity to throw a lavish party for their sons. The Bar Mitzvah helps to build a strong spiritual foundation for boys and to engender a sense of responsibility. Jewish boys also emerge from the ceremony with the strength of a promise that they have a village to support them throughout the rest of their lives. I thought it admirable, something that any young man could benefit from.

With the Bar Mitzvah serving as a template, I set about planning Max's Black Mitzvah, a rite of passage that was not just a day, but a journey that would last for the next six years of lasting relationships with mighty men on whose shoulders he could stand. I wanted to build a community for Max—a reliable circle of men he could emulate so that he would have a roadmap for becoming as brave and exceptional as they were. As it turned out, this all happened and so much more. Max became an apprentice to four masters of their own universe. Like a unicorn that can be taught only by a virgin, my son learned from these men how to unleash his own magic.

Having found in the Torah a primary model of faith, community, and accountability for my son's rite of passage, I replaced it with the Bible and began planning Max's opening ceremony for his Black Mitzvah.

Max enjoyed reading the Bible like a storybook, starting from page one and making his way through all the colorful tales. He preferred Genesis, particularly the "who begot whom" story line. I asked him to choose a favorite Bible passage—one that he most connected to. I explained to him that he would share this with everyone at his birthday celebration, so he should choose carefully. Given his love of Genesis, I was surprised when he chose a verse from the Book of Isaiah, and even more surprised when he told me it was Isaiah 40:29–31.

He connected with the promise of the Lord giving power to the weak, the way Stan Lee, creator of Marvel and god of the comic world, so successfully imbued superhuman powers in his iconic characters, something Max wished for himself.

Next, we set about choosing our Black Mitzvah mentors, by far the most important decision we had to make and one that I felt we needed to make together, since they would essentially become a part of our family as his collective dad. We had to seriously consider their qualifications. Whom among our male friends and family did Max admire most? Whom did he look up to? It was important that each man was someone Max trusted and felt completely comfortable with. It sparked a very interesting conversation about many men we knew. I learned a lot about how we viewed people differently and how a personality trait that I found appealing conflicted with how Max experienced the same trait. I was surprised at Max's reaction to my suggestion of a dear friend, Ari, a trophy-winning athlete in any sport he tries and with a hug that lingers on you even after you've been released from his arms. Max said Ari was totally not cool! He chose Ronnie, an older cousin, because every time we saw him he was sporting a fly jacket with a different superhero or one of his favorite artists—Usher, Michael Jackson, or Prince—emblazoned on the back. I think Max was hoping he would give him one. Whether he did or would, I knew that Ronnie, who seemed to jump from job to job, wasn't exactly the kind of influence that I had in mind. After we considered a few others, we narrowed it down to four "uncles" who we mutually agreed were the best of the best: Lawrence, Chris, Kevin, and Jay.

Lawrence is the youngest of my three brothers, three years older than me. He himself is a father and also a mentor to the sons of other men in and outside of our family. His annual "backyard barbecue with the boys" is a tradition that has developed quite a long repertoire of comedy and trash talk served up at family events. Uncles, nephews, cousins, and friends from DC to Dallas, New York to New Orleans, and places in between fall in for a "not to be missed in case you get dissed" event. Max was truly looking forward to his first big "hang."

Like my father, Lawrence is a man's man—a Mandinka—a force of will, career focused, financially astute, and a sportsman. At six feet five, he makes his presence felt on whatever court or course he plays, or even in the aisles of Home Depot, where he relishes intimidating many a Home Depot guy. He is a mechanical engineer with a passion for fixing things himself, which makes him everybody's go-to guy for questions or opinions about what the car repairman advised or how to set up an entertainment center or home broadband system. When he's not playing golf, he's tinkering. He can install a sprinkler system, clean a pool, plant a tree, and hook and tow a boat. His do-it-yourself wizardry is the envy of neighbors and friends. And while his favorite kind of humor is to joke about the helplessness of women, his wife completely owns him. "What do you know about a computer? You're just a woman," he says. He loves to provoke an eye roll or a swift comeback from his queen. "That's why I married you—you know how to fix things. My personal handyman," she'll say, to which he will always throw in the towel with a grin. He's a beautiful man to watch.

Chris is the husband of my dear friend Ramona. Knowing what I know about Ramona told me a lot about him from the moment we met. He must be righteous, respectful, and a man of worth. You see, I've known Ramona since first grade. After our graduation from elementary school, we went our separate ways to pursue our dreams of a life outside the low-income neighborhood that we grew up in. We loved our friends and our community that raised us, but we were both spoiled by the images on glamour-dripping TV shows like *Dallas* and *Miami Vice*, and in the ads for upscale lifestyle homes with attached garages, big lawns, and shiny cars in the pages of the magazine *Time for Kids*, which we flipped through during social studies class. I wanted to be Marlo Thomas in *That Girl* and Angela Davis at the same time. Ramona wanted to own three homes, a big dream for a 'round-the-way girl from the hood. We both went to private all-girl prep schools, then on to the best private universities, landing in two of the biggest and most competitive US urban markets, she in Chicago and I in New York. While I was getting early on-the-job training in corporate America that led me to entrepreneurship, Ramona earned her doctorate in child psychology, started her own very successful practice with both private and government-agency clients. Thirty years passed, and then one night we bumped into each other in L.A. at a private party for the Essence Awards. I felt a tap on my arm and heard a familiar voice that I had not heard in a very long while say, "Aren't you—" and before she could finish, I screamed, "Ramona!" We hugged as if we had to make up for so many years apart, ready to pick up right where we left off when we ourselves were just Max's age, thirteen years old, and graduating from eighth grade.

When Ramona went to introduce me to her new husband, Chris, I was surprised when she brought over a white man with a ponytail and a square, stocky build who didn't look quite comfortable in a suit. But then, with a smile as wide as his face, he took my hand into both of his and said, "Nice to meet one of Ramona's sisters." I immediately liked him. It was clear that he absolutely adored his wife and that he absolutely belonged in a room where the only reason he stood out was because of the color of his skin. He fit right in with the all-black party in the room.

Everything about him seemed to be her dreams come true. One of the three homes Ramona dreamed of as a little girl is now their own in Maui, near where Chris grew up. Their *'ohana* (family) extends to their homes from Hawaii to Michigan to Chicago. The first thing I came to appreciate about Chris is how quickly and easily he welcomed me and Max as members of his own family. Like the Hawaiian "aloha," he is relaxed, warm, and friendly. His wry sense of humor, he says, he gets from his mom.

"I have a tattoo on my butt. Wanna see it?" he'll say. It cracks Max up every time. I must admit, it is kind of funny.

Chris also may be the only person I have ever known who can actually play the harmonica, and he plays it very well. Max and I have watched him at many an open mic blowing into his harmonica while foot stomping with a band of his friends. Besides music and jokes, his great passions are politics and social enterprise. Together, he and Ramona are a power couple on a mission to change the world. Being around both of them is always a lesson in generosity, community, and respect—important values that I knew Chris could teach Max better than anyone.

Kevin is one of my best friends of fifteen years. With a disarming personality, he is one of the few men who can pull off a naturally curly puff in a rubberband that sits at the back of his neck. He's a fast, energetic talker, and we instantly bonded over the phone after an introduction from Andrea, a colleague who knew I would be interested in his new business magazine. By then, my small business included media-buying services for our corporate clients that were interested in targeting urban professionals. She sent me his launch issue with a note that said simply, "I thought you might be interested," and I was not just interested but astounded. The quality of the editorial and photography in his first issue was very impressive, especially considering the fact that he did it without one advertising dollar, which was unprecedented and a bit crazy. I had to know him, so I called him. After two hours of conversation with no periods in between sentences, I knew I had found a perfect match for our clients' target demographics, but I had also found a soul mate, a friend for life.

The magazine is just one of his businesses. Kevin is a serial entrepreneur, always in one phase or another of developing yet another business to add to his entrepreneurial portfolio. Of all the people in the world I know, he is perhaps the most ambitious and the most driven. He is the owner of several businesses that also include a children's book business, a patent-owned plastic dinnerware business, and an event production business for urban professionals. His dogged determination is inimitable and his optimism is infectious.

Kevin is also one of the funniest and most social people I know, which makes him a magnet to people of every ilk and persuasion. No matter the subject or how controversial it might be, he has a viewpoint on it that will make you laugh.

"He may be homeless, but he's single, so he doesn't have to hear about it," he can say in a way that makes you say, "Ugh," and laugh at the same time. He and Max share an ability to win people over with their charm, wit, and big hearts. Anyone who knows Uncle Kevin respects and admires his unwavering devotion to two people: his grandmother and his daughter. His deep respect for women is rooted in the love and wisdom he received from his grandmother, whom he credits for lifting him morally and spiritually from rags to riches. His inauspicious early years of struggling to survive the streets turned into an incredible success story. The fire and fight in Kevin is not unlike that in my Max. So who better to nurture and guide a young man determined to do things his own way than an older man who has made it his life's work to be true to his purpose?

Jay is a financial planner who made his first million by the time he was twenty-seven and wears it well, with his dapper style and signature wide-legged stance. He has earned every financial certification possible and has offices in Nashville, Detroit, and Charlotte, with several churches and municipalities as clients. A man with starched Christian values and financial stewardship as his ministry, he guides his clients to "a path of spiritual growth through financial peace and prosperity." I am lucky to be one of his first clients. Mine was an investment in him personally as well as an investment in our financial future, because I believed in his mission and trusted him implicitly. He has served us well, and it's how I came to know how good his heart is.

Jay grew up without a father in his life, and in some ways he believes he is a stronger man because he was forced to be the man of the house from the time he was a little boy. He had to take care of his mother and figure things out on his own. He promised his mother that one day he would buy her dream house filled with everything she could ever need or want. Because he watched his mother do with so little while raising him on her own, he vowed that he would never have to struggle to make ends meet. He has more than lived up to both promises. He devoted his career to helping others build their own strong financial foundation. And after ten years of managing portfolios to secure retirement futures for people like his mother, he bought her a beautiful home and handed her a credit card with instructions to go shopping for anything she wanted to decorate it.

It is easy to see why I was excited that he agreed to be a mentor.

"Uncle Jay, please teach Max how to save and invest so that I can look forward to my own retirement in my dream house like you gave your mom," I told him, facetiously.

As I was confident it would be, Jay's ministry to Max has been a great deal more about life than about money. With Jay's help, my dream retirement includes the kind of peace of mind that comes with seeing your child mature into a healthy, grounded, responsible, and caring adult.

Our asks are answered.

I confess that I was nervous to ask each of these four men to make what I thought was a huge commitment to a child who was not theirs, especially one with disabilities. For weeks, I tried to find the courage as I mentally rehearsed the words I would use. What if they all said no? Fortunately, we hit the jackpot. Turned out, they all were willing, and even honored, to be asked.

I knew there would be months of planning for my son's Black Mitzvah, and I had to get to it. There was no time for dwelling on my hectic schedule, which included running my own business, working with my clients, volunteering on boards, managing our home life, and taking care of my growing boy. Max's birthday, as always, was my top priority, and this was going to be a very special one because it was also a preparation for his Black Mitzvah. So, with my heart in my throat, I picked up the phone and called each one of the four men and let the words fall out of my mouth without ceremony or preamble: "I really need your help. I think I may be screwing him up. Would you be willing to be a mentor to Max?"

I was overwhelmed by the immediate reactions. When they were asked to step up, their responses were everything.

Uncle Lawrence: "Of course I will. He is part of our proud family legacy. He should know that, and I'll be sure that he does."

Uncle Chris: "I'd be honored to be his mentor, and I am honored that you even asked me. I've raised two sons who are now grown. If I could, I might have done some things differently, and now I get a chance to do a better job. I look forward to that opportunity."

Uncle Kevin: "Yes, absolutely, in a heartbeat. It means a lot to me that you even asked me. I could have used a few mentors when I was coming up. Going it on my own taught me a lot, but it would have been great to not have had to learn so many lessons the hard way."

Uncle Jay: "My little buddy? For him? For you? Anything." Choking back his emotions, he added, "I was raised by a single mom. I watched her struggle. I know how hard it is. I'll do it for you and Max, and I'll do it to honor her too. I hope to teach him how to handle himself and handle his money. I'd love to see him become everything you want for him. If I can be a part of that, I'm in."

I was overwhelmed, awash in human kindness and a huge sense of relief at the same time. And so began a tremendous journey in which the love, trust, admiration, and respect Max and I already had for each of these men deepened into utter awe and tremendous gratitude. What further underscores the character of these four men is that they were all completely aware of the full circumstances of what they were committing to when they signed up for the long road ahead with Max. Max is no ordinary boy.

A dear friend of ours said it best: "Max brings out the best and the worst in people." For as often as he is warmly embraced, he is just as often coldly shunned or mocked or even abused. It is a tragedy for all of us that it so difficult for some of us to accept people just because they are different. As an African American male with cerebral palsy, and socially awkward because of his ADHD, and a firehose of honesty, Max is a human conglomerate of differences. He is not for the faint of heart, and if you have one, he'll steal it.

I believe this is why when his mentors were asked to be in his life to help him develop into the man we all wanted him to become, they agreed without hesitation. They recognized the rocky road ahead and wanted to help smooth as many bumps as possible, paving the way for Max to learn to minimize his weaknesses and maximize his strengths, to find his own stride, and to develop his own swagger the way they have. In short, these four men were exactly the kind of warriors that could help raise one.

As part of the preparation for his Black Mitzvah, I gave Max something new and exciting to focus on to take his mind off the problems he wasn't able to solve and put it on the blessings he could count on. I charged him to write a personal letter to tell each of his chosen mentors what he admired most about him and what he hoped to learn from him.

"We can put them in each of their gift bags," I told him. He brightened at the idea.

"That's easy! I can do that," Max said, his spirit immediately uplifted.

The hardest part for him was putting his thoughts on paper since his lack of fine motor skills makes handwriting so exhausting and time consuming. But he was delighted to do it because he knew exactly what he wanted to say.

It was a simple idea, but as it turned out, it was also very profound. Before he sealed each envelope, I asked if it was okay if I could read the note he'd put inside. Through each of his personal letters, I learned some things I never knew before, including what he cared about most and who he wanted to be. At just thirteen years old, he wrote messages that were honest, simple, and direct.

Dear Uncle Lawrence,

I admire that you have a good career and take good care of your wife. You are a great husband. You are also fun to hang out with. I know that you love me and care about me and I'm glad that you are my uncle.

I look forward to learning from you more about what it is to be a man and what I need to do be successful like you and to be a good husband one day. I also want to be a good father and I think you can help me with that too.

Dear Uncle Kevin,

I like that you are funny and have a sense of humor about everything. You make me laugh when I need to. I also like that you are creative and that you created books for children. I really like cartoons a lot and would like to create better stories for kids who watch them.

I would like to learn from you to be funny too. I also want you to teach me about photography.

Dear Uncle Chris,

You are a really great husband and a generous person. Even though you are sometimes harsh, I like that you are straight with me even when it is hard for me to hear. I know you care about me and want me to grow up and be strong. I really like that you are a good listener too.

I think you will teach me how to make good decisions.

Dear Uncle Jay,

I admire you because you are so good with money and you take such good care of your mom. You are always dressed real nice too. I like that you are fun and like to play video games with me. I'm going to beat you next time.

I hope to learn to make a lot of money like you and take care of it so that I can take care of my mom like you do.

As I read each letter from Max, I imagined what the expression on each man's face would be as he read it. I knew that each of them would feel mighty proud about how they were seen by my son, who was completely free of stigmas, innocent, and brutally honest. I saw what Max saw too and might have said something similar. But these words of admiration from a thirteen-year-old boy who saw these men as embodying everything that a good man truly is were spoken with such an open heart and mind. Max was willing and ready to learn from these men, and it filled my heart and soul with joy.

I was not the only one to give Max a writing assignment. In preparation for the Black Mitzvah, Uncle Lawrence asked Max to write an essay answering the question "What does it mean to be a man?"

"I want you to put some thought into it, Max," he instructed. "In order to be a man, you have to think like one."

It was the first time Uncle Lawrence had spoken to him in a manner of one man to another becoming one. Max took his assignment seriously, with every intent to meet his uncle-turned-mentor's high level of expectation. He wrote:

> *Being a man means I must persevere in life and school.*
>
> *Being a man means not feeling sorry for myself. When I woke up after my last surgery I was in pain. It made me realize that many other people also have pain. I have some friends that have some bigger problems than I do. My friend Andrea can't talk and Bizzy B. can't walk as well as I can. I am very blessed.*
>
> *Being a man means be fearless. Adventure teaches me to try new things. Tokyo was a big adventure. I saw anime outside of the United States. I went to origami class and learned to make a cat and a penguin. I also tried all kinds of sashimi. The squid had tentacles. I also tried fish that had fins and gills. It was strange but I am glad I tried it, so now I know I don't like it.*
>
> *Being a man means face your fears. On our last trip to Hawaii, we went on a snorkeling cruise. I was afraid to get into the water. I had been knocked into the pool when I was much younger, maybe five years old. It traumatized me. But, the dive instructor who led the cruise coaxed me into the ocean. She helped me swim from the back of the boat to the front. It felt so good that two days later on another snorkel cruise I went into the ocean again with Diver Dan. Instead of a snorkel he gave me a view box and I could see all the different colors of fish. It was so interesting that one hour later I got in again. I faced my fear of water and learned to enjoy the ocean.*
>
> *Being a man means helping others. Last summer I volunteered at a center helping deliver lunches to senior citizens. The days were hot and*

sometimes I did not feel like doing it but I knew it was important to the "young" ladies. That's what I call them. At the end of the summer I received the Volunteer of the Year Award. I was very proud, but more importantly I got the satisfaction of helping others.

Being a man means accepting responsibility without complaining.

Being a man means taking care of the environment and my health.

Being a man means fighting your own battles and standing up for yourself and being ready to fight for people you love. It means taking care of your family and protecting them.

Being a man means being a good father and husband.

Being a man means treating women with respect.

What do you know? At thirteen, he was already a family man.

"That's a fine essay, Max. You have the makings of a Kappa man," said Uncle Lawrence. "If you do all of the things you wrote, you will do us all proud."

"What's a Kappa?"

"I'll explain it to you when you are ready."

"I'm ready."

"Not yet. You have to prove it. I'll let you know when you are ready."

It's time to Mitzvah!

Planning and participating in Max's celebration was fun—and unencumbered with expectations, since we had never done anything like it before. So it was all the more rewarding when it came with so many instinctive moments and surprising revelations, starting with the generosity of our hosts, who were excited to be a part of creating a new tradition that they could share with their own son when he came of age.

Uncle Chris and Ramona offered their lovely lakefront summer home as the location for our Black Mitzvah celebration. It's nestled in a private community on the shore of Lake Michigan, where residents enjoy boating, a nine-hole golf course, bike riding, and gorgeous sunrises and sunsets. In the early evenings, neighbors take casual strolls through the narrow winding streets filled with beautiful homes, greeting each other warmly. It's a tight-knit community where dinner parties and church on Sunday are opportunities for close fellowship.

Chris picked us up at the airport in his big, beautiful blue-and-white 1955 Chevy Bel Air.

"Ooh, nice! What kind of car is this?" Max asked. "I've never seen anything like it before."

"You don't see many like these anymore," Chris said with a mix of pride and joy.

Then Uncle Chris wrapped it up with a bow: "One day I might let you drive it."

Max's eyes got as big as saucers. "Whoa! Cooooool!" He was clearly already dreaming of that day.

We hopped in and cruised toward his house, taking in the beautiful view of small-town streets lined with tiny shops selling organic food and handcrafted goods, along with a couple of farm-to-table restaurants and the one local gas station. In between the buildings and trees, I had peeks of sparkling Lake Michigan.

As we got closer to the house, Chris's phone rang. "Yeah," he said. "We're right around the corner."

When the car pulled up to the house, Chris looked at Max through his rearview mirror, and I turned around in my front seat to watch Max's face. As usual, it was buried in the latest edition of his favorite manga magazine, so he didn't see what was waiting for him just outside the car.

"Look, Max!" I had to say twice to get him to look up.

When Max finally looked up, he immediately pulled himself up in the seat and plastered his face against the window, eyes wide open. Posters featuring Max's handsome smile with the tagline "VIP" written in large letters lined the driveway leading to the front of the house.

Max couldn't get the door open fast enough. As we spilled out of the car, a beautiful young lady, about Max's age, emerged from the side door and approached him with her hand outreached to welcome him.

"Hello, Max. I hear it's your special day! I'm Mya," she said, smiling brightly.

I'm certain that Uncle Chris was behind this brilliant move.

Max melted, grinning ear to ear, completely lost his cool, and blurted out, "Wow! You're beautiful!"

She smiled back with a knowing look and took his hand. Then, without so much as a glance back at his mom, Max, like a puppy, followed the sweet, svelte brown-skinned girl with long legs down the driveway to the next big surprise awaiting him.

Amused to see Max so swept away, I followed the pair to a backyard with a spectacular view of Lake Michigan. A lush carpet of lawn was all that separated the house from the rocky shoreline. Clearly a lot of love had gone into the preparations for this important day. The Crayola-green lawn was festooned with huge colorful balls the size of small children, as well as a tall, inflatable yellow waterslide. Picnic tables with bright table-cloths were scattered about and the mouthwatering smell of food on the smoking grill made me realize that I was hungry.

We were greeted by Mya's parents who had also come in for the weekend, and Chris and Ramona's friends from the neighborhood, many of whom had children young enough to enjoy any reason to play outside and eat cake, while their parents were more interested in being part of something they had never experienced before, a Black Mitzvah cele-bration. They were curious to meet the very special guest of honor and his mother. It had also turned out to be an absolutely beautiful sunny day, perfect for a backyard party.

While Max and the other kids slipped and slid, we adults moved as little possible as we lay in comfortable lounge chairs, our sunglasses tilted toward the blue sky and our bodies slathered with sunscreen. I was con-sumed by the warmth of the sun and the fellowship.

"Ramona, I could not have done this without you. Together, for Max and all of us, we are creating a moment of history for our family, our com-munity. You are amazing," I told her. "And this whole thing here . . ." I said, waving my hand like a wand over the whole setting. "You have outdone yourself, girlfriend."

Everyone agreed, with a round of "uh-huhs," and raised their glasses to give a group testimonial: "Girl, your event planning is so exceptional that you even got the gods to deliver perfect weather."

Then, as if on cue, a clown suddenly appeared and strolled onto the lawn—another little surprise Ramona had planned for Max. Heads turned, eating and drinking stopped midair, and the kids paused mid-romp and rushed to crowd around the clown. For the next hour, he performed a delightful repertoire of magic tricks and corny jokes that made everyone laugh, applaud, and sometimes moan in good humor. The whole afternoon was filled with magic.

I had never seen Max so happy. Uncle Chris and Ramona had made the start of Max's Black Mitzvah celebration a joy-filled birthday bash to rival any birthday party I'd thrown Max in his first twelve years of life.

In the three days following the opening party, we had planned a full schedule of male-bonding activities, including a boat outing, golf, and a backyard barbecue. Unfortunately, our timing coincided with an annual local music festival, which included an appearance by the filmmaker Michael Moore, and travel into the nearby airport was impossible. A lack of available flights left Uncle Kevin stranded en route, unable to get a connecting flight. Uncle Lawrence had learned about this ahead of time, when he could not find a flight out of Dallas. Uncle Jay had booked early, and so he was the only out-of-towner who was able to be there in person.

Determined that all Max's mentors be included in mind and spirit if not in body, we scheduled phone calls with Uncle Lawrence and Uncle Kevin for the Mitzvah dinner and ceremony. Our hearts were joined across time zones and hundreds of miles for one of the most fulfilling moments in all our lives: Max's rite of passage into the promise, power, and purpose of manhood.

On the first day of Max's welcoming into the fraternity of men, I set a gift bag by each mentor's place at the breakfast table and one at Max's place. I also put bags by two spots at the table to acknowledge Uncle Lawrence's and Uncle Kevin's presence in spirit.

Red is Max's favorite color, and so, of course, the bags had to be red. Each bag contained a red baseball cap with THE BOYS printed in white letters on the front of the crown. Matching red polo shirts proudly displayed MENTOR on the front, except for Max's shirt that read MENTEE. Each goody bag also included two items tied to the specific activities Max would do with his male mentors: a red apron embroidered with KISS THE

COOK and a set of Nike golf balls. Also inside each bag was a white envelope that held the carefully folded, handwritten message Max painstakingly scribed to each of them on his personal letterhead.

I learned only while writing this book that these items I had created or selected were called PROPS (puberty rite of passage sensory), an idea explained in the excellent book *Boys Becoming Men: Creating Rites of Passage,* by Lowell Sheppard. He defines PROPS as tools to mark moments of immersion in a multisensory experience designed to overcome a challenge, rise to the occasion, or teach a lesson. He also explains how the noun "props" and the verb "prop" can mean to enhance performance, provide support, propel forward, or provide a safeguard for a successful journey.

The first activity was designed to teach Max about having purpose. Uncle Chris announced that Max was going to be schooled in the game of golf, a sport that demands great patience, focus, and integrity. It is also a sport that Uncle Chris and Uncle Lawrence share a passion for, and there was no way Max, as their mentee, wouldn't learn the game and earn a name, or at least learn to appreciate it!

At first Max thought he was there just to ride around the course in the golf cart. Oh, that was big fun! Until Uncle Chris made it clear that he had something else entirely in mind. Aside from my getting him to hit a few balls on a tennis court and the horseback riding he did as part of his physical therapy, Max had never played any sport at all, or wanted to, and he certainly wasn't interested in golf. So when Uncle Chris asked him to get his 5-iron, Max just looked at him like he was crazy.

The look on Uncle Chris's face said it all: "You are not out here just to be hanging with grown folks. You ain't grown!" With his "I'm not playing around" voice, he carefully explained how to find the golf club he'd asked for and waited patiently—well, sort of. Max, always melodramatic, made a big deal about not knowing which club was the 5-iron, pulling each club out of the bag and asking, "This one?" and then putting each wrong one back in clumsily and out of the order in which they had been so carefully arranged. You could see the impatience withering into the lines on Uncle Chris's forehead. He was clearly not amused.

Then, at the moment of voilà, Uncle Chris held his hand out in a way that clearly indicated, "Now, please." I thought Uncle Chris might hit him with it. But of course he didn't. To be honest, I might have. Instead, Uncle Chris said only, "Thank you, Max," as he strolled up to the tee.

This was just the first activity and I was already having misgivings. I wasn't sure how much of this both of them could take. God forbid Uncle Chris take back his promise before we even get to the ceremony. I had already begun thinking of a plan B if this did not go well. Fortunately, I didn't have to. Uncle Chris proved to be "smarter than the average bear," as they say.

"Now watch this," Uncle Chris said as he set up, addressed his position, settled into his concentration, and powered through his swing. Like a pro, he hit the sweet spot—*crack!*—and sent the ball sailing in the air to within inches of the hole. He smiled and looked at Max with a twinkle in his eye. Funny how a well-hit shot in any game can make an ego soar above the storm. The whole mood changed. "That's how you do it," he said. And just like that, they were "boys" again.

"Thanks, Max. That was exactly the right club. So you and me, we both made that shot. And it was a good one, right?" said Uncle Chris cheekily.

Max's face lit up with a slow smile, and he hopped back in the cart. When they arrived at the next hole, he leapt out of the cart to keep in stride with Uncle Chris as he walked up to the tee. By the end of the round, Max did not share with Uncle Chris a great love for the sport of golf, but he learned a lot about the pride, preparation, and sense of power that come from even being a partner in the process of holing the ball.

With egos adequately massaged after their afternoon of golf, the trash talk resumed until it was time for the next activity, "Real Men Cook." Chris and Max donned their KISS THE COOK aprons, items we women had thoughtfully designed and demanded they wear, if only because we knew we would get some great pictures out of it. We were pleased that they agreed to put on the aprons but anticipated it might take a little coercion to get the two men into the kitchen. Turns out, it didn't take much effort at all.

Uncle Chris considers himself a man of culinary skill and was totally into it. In anticipation, he had even gone shopping to get the necessary ingredients for his special guacamole.

"Grab that onion for me," Uncle Chris said to Max. "Now watch me.

I don't want any finger bits in my guac, so I'll show you how to do it, and then you can try. This is how you hold the onion, and this is how you hold a knife," he began.

With Max as his sous-chef, Uncle Chris chopped, mixed, and seasoned with precision, all the while giving Max lessons in measurement, handling a knife, working as a team, and taking pride in whatever you do.

I have to admit that I winced when Max seemed to enjoy wielding that knife a little too much, like boys do. You could just see it in his eyes and the twisted curl of his lips that he was thinking, "Ooh, a weapon!" When Uncle Chris grabbed another knife and challenged him to a duel, that's when I had to leave the kitchen. Oh, Lawd! I couldn't watch another minute. I told them I would be in the next room ready to call 911.

Fortunately, there was no need for an ambulance, and we were all rewarded with what was honestly the best guac I've ever tasted. Best of all, Max now knew how to make it for me anytime I wanted it. Mother's Day has been taken to a whole new level now, thanks to Uncle Chris! Although, I must admit, I still cringe a little when I hear the knife drawer open.

Over the course of the weekend of activities, Uncle Chris continued to be patient, intent on connecting with Max, giving him instruction and thoughtful feedback on his sometimes awkward, sometimes defiant, sometimes silly remarks. A theme began that weekend that has continued throughout Uncle Chris and Max's relationship: Uncle Chris will tolerate only a certain amount of nonsense, especially when there is much ground to cover. And at the top of his list is responsibility to community, something that Uncle Chris has devoted much of his life to.

What it means to be part of a community is something Max had not yet had an opportunity to truly appreciate, given that he was the sole focus of the mission and purpose of his mother. Max never had to share or never really had much responsibility beyond being expected to pick up his clothes or put his dishes in the sink. Chris immediately recognized that Max was spoiled rotten and had his mother wrapped around his finger. Chris had also grown up as an only child raised by a doting single mom. So Chris was empathetic, but he also knew exactly what he needed to do. Teaching Max how to use a knife for something as basic as opening an avocado was more than a kitchen skill; it would help him build confidence and independence. I had been too afraid to, been too fearful that he might hurt himself. But coddling is exactly what Max didn't need. He needed to be self-reliant and capable of contributing, not just taking. While teaching him to properly and safely use a knife for food preparation, Chris also explained to him that men also have a responsibility to help prepare the table and that they are not to just be served but expected to help serve.

At first Max resented being tasked with new chores and retaliated with indignation, stubbornness, and petulance to the point of being obnoxious.

"Why do I have to do it? I don't want to," he would retort to nearly anything that he was asked to do.

But his mentor never lost his cool. He knew what he was dealing with, and he was sensitive to how Max's ADHD-related behavior required an extra measure of patience and accommodation. He was persistent and drove home point after point, recognizing that he needed repetition and constant redirection to get the response he was looking for and a change in his attitude. Some of it took immediately, and some still requires more work.

Uncle Chris definitely made his imprint over that weekend, and Max developed respect for his "no BS" rule. He got affirmation that Uncle Chris knew him better than he knew himself and that he accepted him for who he was and loved him for it. Max knew that another man cared about him and, even more, that he had confidence in him, despite all his challenges. He knew that Uncle Chris had high expectations and that he also had his back.

Max was pumped up by the time Uncle Jay arrived.

"You should have seen the airport! It was packed!" were the first words out of Uncle Jay's mouth when he walked through the door. "Smells good in here," he said, breathing in the spicy aroma of the marinating guacamole.

"You can have some after I kick your butt," Max said, before giving him a big hug.

As Uncle Jay put his bags down, he lingered to meet Max at eye level and responded, "Oh, we'll be eating soon then, because it won't take long for me to take you down."

Max smiled and said, "I have something for you," and handed him his gift bag. "My mom made these," he added. It was nice to be included, and I gave Jay a warm hug.

Then he turned to Chris and said, "This is my Uncle Jay. He came here all the way from Nashville to come to my party."

Of course, Chris knew this already, but that didn't matter. Max was in his element and wanted to show off his friend and the fact that he was very special. It was the first time Chris and Jay met. Chris still had on his KISS THE COOK apron, and, as he shook Jay's hand, said, "Hey, man, I'm not into that. But if it's that good, then maybe," Jay said, directing his eyes to the words of invitation emblazoned on Chris's apron. They both laughed heartily. They liked each other instantly.

Then the three of them, Uncle Chris, Uncle Jay, and Max, donned their matching caps and shirts and posed for silly photos and high fives. Max, for the first time, was part of a team, a special club of distinguished gentlemen, and he made sure he was front and center in every shot.

Max was quick to jump in and claim back Uncle Jay for his own. Impatient to engage in his favorite activity, and in need of attention, Max tugged him into the game room, where the two collapsed on the couch and got in position. So, with his controller in hand, Max's gaming nemesis was ready for battle, and the trash talk revved up to high gear. While Uncle Chris took a break to get the grill ready, there was unbridled testosterone in the game room, until the coals were hot and the smoke was perfect for some first-class barbecue action.

On Chris's cue, the crew took their places grillside. Max was the only thing Chris and Jay had in common, so it was up to him to make the connection. Whether he fully understood what or how, Max did what he does naturally, and that is to say whatever is on his mind.

As I stood inside the kitchen door, I heard Max say, "Uncle Chris, do you even know what you're doing?"

Oh, why did he go there?

Jay backed up with a "Whoa! Oooh! That's rough, man."

Then it was on. I laughed out loud and all three looked at me, and I knew that was my signal to disappear, so I did. But not without a glance back to see that the mentors were enjoying the verbal sparring with

Max as the main the target. Max pouted a little, but he loved every minute of it.

The next day started bright and late with the first order of business after breakfast, to hit the outdoors and take advantage of a perfect day for boating on Uncle Chris's white Boston Whaler, sitting in the dock ready and waiting. Richard, a friend of Chris's, had dropped in the night before for a weekend visit with Chris, unaware of the ceremony to begin Max's Black Mitzvah, but delighted to be able to be a part of it.

"Who's coming?" Uncle Chris polled all in the room with his eyes trained on Max. "Can I drive?" Max asked in a way that seemed to be an ultimatum. "If I can't drive, then I'm not interested," seemed to appear in a thought bubble above his head. "Can you?" Uncle Chris challenged him. "I can drive!" Max responded to what to him sounded like a "yes" to his question. "We'll see," Uncle Chris said, not yet completely giving in without first making clear some important expectations to receive such a reward.

"Did you tell your mother and Aunt Ramona 'thank you' for preparing breakfast?"

"Yes, sir."

Uncle Chris looked at both of us to make sure we were satisfied with that response. We both smiled and gave the thumbs-up.

"Did you help clear the table?"

"Yes, sir."

Uncle Chris, once again, checked in with us. We both nodded in approval.

"Did you do it like you wanted to?" Uncle Chris said, mimicking checking off a checklist.

"Yes, sir," Max said with a chuckle. We all laughed.

"All right, let's hit the deck," Uncle Chris said to all who were on board for an afternoon cruise on his boat. Max, Uncle Jay, and Richard immediately stood to head out the door. Mya looked at her parents as if to say, "Can I go too?" All the grown-ups realized that we were in an awkward position. It was supposed to be a "boys only" bonding activity. However, no one, especially Max, could say no to the beautiful brown-skinned girl. Her parents turned to me with a look of hopelessness. "Of course, you can," I said, knowing there was no other appropriate response. Besides, there was a lesson to be learned about how to behave in front of a female you want to win over, so perhaps he would learn to be a gentleman. Mya could not care less about being the only girl and leapt out of her chair to join the boys.

Ramona and I took up residence in two lawn chairs to relax as Uncle Chris handed out life preservers and assisted Max with his to make sure it was secure. Giddy and anxious, Max climbed into the boat. "Get out of the boat," we could hear Uncle Chris say from where we sat several yards away. "You have to hear the rules before we go out so we don't lose anybody once we leave the shore," he said in all seriousness. We could see heads nodding as his instructions followed. "Now, I'm going to get in first, then Max you can help Mya in and be sure she's sitting down, then Jay," he ordered. He turned to Richard, who already knew the drill, and after he got in, untied the rope to set them free to go. Once everyone was in and seated, Uncle Chris started the engine and moved out slowly into the water. Ramona and I waved as they sailed away on the calm waters sparkling under the bright sun. It was an absolutely beautiful day for boating.

Two stress-free hours slowly ticked by as Ramona and I were enjoying quiet girl talk, when we were interrupted by the sound of Max calling, "Mom, I drove the boat! I drove the boat!" He was waving his arms with a smile so wide that it put the period on the conversation between the two of us as our attention was diverted to taking in every moment of Max's utter euphoria.

By the time we were all ready for the birthday dinner, we had grown into a big family that included several friends of Chris and Ramona's who had come to join us. I was concerned that we might not have enough chairs for everyone to fit at the table. "I got you, girl," Ramona said, leading me to a closet where more chairs were stored. While we were alone for a minute, I took the opportunity to let her know what was on my heart.

"Ramona, I can't thank you enough. After being apart for nearly thirty years, you have come back into my life as if we never skipped a beat. We go back a long way, since first grade, and I have had many new friends since, but no one has ever been a truer friend than you. You stepped up immediately to help me at a level that no one ever has. It only took a couple of months for you to come all the way to Nashville just to take care of me and Max, just to give me just a few days of much needed rest. Then you saw me trying to tame my hair with a wig because I had no time for it anymore and you said, 'Oh no, girlfriend. You can't hide all that beautiful hair,' and gave me the gift of freedom from the daily ritual of hair care with my new locs, which have changed my life forever. And then you do this. You heart is so big. I'll always love you for that," I told her, unable to control the tears.

"We're sisters. We have to take care of each other. You know I got you, girl," Ramona replied as she always does.

We kissed and rocked in a long and warm hug, ended with a sigh and a smile, and then went back arm in arm to rejoin our friends and family. It was time for the big event!

The sumptuous meal of roast turkey, vegetable lasagna, grilled veggies, whipped potatoes, and Max's favorite dessert, a chocolate three-layer cake, was served family style. After everyone had their fill, it was time for the moment of solemnity—an exchange of a promise between men. We cleared the table, and at its center I placed a bowl with smooth stones, one for each mentor and one for Max—like the five smooth stones that David used to fight Goliath.

Max opened the ceremony with his carefully selected Bible verse. Though he was very well prepared, having researched and practiced for weeks, he was nervous. He fumbled a little until he finally opened to the right page, smiled shyly at all of us, and then began to slowly read the passage he had chosen for the occasion, careful to enunciate every word:

Isaiah 40:29–31

> He gives strength to the weary
> and increases the power of the weak.
> Even youths grow tired and weary,
> and young men stumble and fall;
> but those who hope in the LORD
> will renew their strength.
> They will soar on wings like eagles;
> they will run and not grow weary,
> they will walk and not be faint.

Max finished with an "Amen" and then looked up at me as if to ask, "How did I do?"

Through tears, I smiled, overwhelmed by one of the proudest moments I have known. "Amen," I echoed.

Uncle Chris and Uncle Jay both nodded to affirm that the passage was a good choice, and the three of them talked for a while about what it meant.

"Why did you choose that particular passage?" Chris asked.

"Because I want to be strong and sometimes I need help," Max answered.

"We all do, Max. I will always be here for you, as will your mom, your family, and everybody else here in this room. But know that the Lord is always with you too."

Uncle Jay paused for a moment as if to measure his words and then said, "It's okay to be weak. You can't always be strong. It's okay. Sometimes we all are. Just trust in the words you chose to speak today, and thank you for reminding me too."

The three lingered for a while on the topic of what it meant to be strong and steadfast. Max's mentors, each in his own way, explained how essential these two qualities would be for Max, that his life and all he would make of it would depend on how strong and steadfast he could be.

When the last word on the subject was uttered, the three of them all seemed to exhale in the same breath and fall into a moment of reflective silence. Max's prayer seemed to hover in the air around us. Then Uncle Chris looked at the stones as if carefully considering which one to reach for. He chose the green one. He placed it in his hand and slowly curled his fingers around it, addressing Max directly.

"Do you know Matthew 25:31–46? The key phrase in that scripture is 'whatever you did for one of the least of these brothers and sisters of mine, you did for me.'

"In essence it's saying we serve God when we take care of each other. Given that God is the almighty creator of the entire universe and is beyond comprehension, what can we do for God? Jesus tells us in this passage that we do for God when we do for one another.

"And we are charged not so much to do it for friends, family, and those who can repay us, but to do it for 'the least of these brothers and sisters of mine.' In this passage, those in society who are considered among the 'least' are elevated to familial status by the Son of God.

"I believe that we are called to see ourselves in others. In so doing, many of the horrible ways people treat each other would begin to stop. It is an extension of the Golden Rule: Do unto others as ye would have them do unto you. Ultimately, when we see ourselves in others and we see God in them, we finally see God in ourselves."

When he finished, he passed the stone to Max, closing his hands around Max's hands, as if to indicate it should be held with a firm grip.

"Hold it like it's an energy force," he continued.

Max seemed to know exactly what this meant and the warrior in him lit up his face.

"Do you know why I chose the green stone? Because it represents the earth, natural growth, and life. It also represents our responsibility to this earth," he explained.

"I like your personal letter you wrote me," Uncle Chris told him. "You said some nice things about me. I hope I can live up to them. But I can promise you that I'll always be straight with you as long as you're straight with me."

He described to Max his vision of the man he dreamed Max could be. He promised he would always be there for him and told Max of his expectations for him as he grew to be a righteous young man.

"Do you know what are the three Rs? Righteous, respectful, and responsible. Remember that. I will always hold you accountable for the three Rs. You have to ask yourself of any decision or any action you take, does it withstand the test of the three Rs? If it doesn't meet all three, then it is not the right decision," he said in a voice that seemed conjured from the ancestors as he locked Max in a stern man-to-man, eye-to-eye grip that would make any man sit up straight and straighten his tie.

Max mumbled a "yes, sir," and then instinctively knew that wasn't sufficient. Without prompting, he sat up straight, cleared his throat, and repeated, "Yes, sir."

It was Uncle Jay's turn. He chose the blue stone, a heavenly color that is a symbol of responsible wealth. He invited Max to open his gift from him, his first watch. In fact, there were two in the handsomely gift-wrapped box—one digital, one analog. Max oohed and aahed, struggling to choose which one to put on first. Max loved them both so much that he couldn't decide which to wear, so he wore them both. Uncle Jay helped him put one on each wrist.

Along with the Swatch timepieces, Uncle Jay imparted wisdom about the importance of time and money.

"It's important not to waste either."

He explained that his own grandfather had given him a watch and that it had great meaning for him in his life.

"He used it to motivate me," Jay told Max. "He taught me that time is the true measure of life, and unlike a watch, we can't roll it back. There are no do-overs, so make the most of every minute, moving forward, not back. Appreciate that we have this great gift called the present."

He paused as if to consider his own words and then said, "No matter what we have gone through, the obstacles we face, God has allowed time to shape us, make us better, and hopefully we use it to grow closer to Him. Through Him all things are possible."

I believe that Uncle Jay must have recognized something else about Max that inspired his choice of gift. If you spent any time around Max, it was easy to see that Max had an obsession with time, as if somehow it would run out on him or he might miss something. He had a compulsive need to ask repeatedly, sometimes within a matter of a few minutes, "What time is it?" At times, it could be exasperating.

Because of his ADHD, planning and routine were survival techniques critical to reducing his stress and anxiety. He needed to be reassured over and over that he was still on course. He didn't respond well to change, and surprises could cause a complete meltdown. Uncle Jay found a way to channel his compulsion into an advantage. Now he could keep track of time on his own to help calm his nerves—and not wear out mine. Why hadn't I thought of that? (Though Max would still often ask about the time, I'd always remind him, "What does your watch say?" And then one day he stopped asking. Uncle Jay's gift to Max was a gift to me as well.)

Max asked Uncle Jay to give him his stone and then held up both his arms like a champion to show off his new adornments before crossing them over his heart and saying, "Thank you, Uncle Jay. I will wear them every day."

Uncle Jay reached out to give him a double pound, a black man's handshake. "What time is it?"

Max answered, "It's my time." Yes!

On that note, it was time for me to give Max my present. It was what he most wanted. It was the perfect gift to give to him at this moment. It had a special purpose, and he had been begging for it for over a year—a cell phone. Max couldn't believe it.

"My own cell phone!" he squealed with delight. "I can't believe you got me a cell phone!"

He jumped out of his seat and even did a dance move, waving his new phone in the air.

"Okay now, don't make me regret this," I told him. "This phone is for you and your mentors. I have programmed all their numbers in it for you to call them whenever you want. I don't need to know your conversations. What you share is between you and them."

That was my mandate. I thought it was important to establish a code of trust, a bond between men.

I also reiterated the promise to each of his mentors that they only need to share with me on a "need to know" basis. This has proved to be invaluable, as there is so much I can't know about what it's like to be a young man, and there are times when Mom just won't understand. And to be honest, in most cases, I'm sure I don't even want to know or try to understand.

"That's between y'all," I like to say to them.

Uncle Chris's friend Richard, the unwitting guest for this auspicious occasion, had been quiet throughout the ceremony. After each mentor had their say, and all the gifts were opened, and the givers sufficiently thanked, Richard asked if he could share his thoughts about what he had just witnessed.

"Of course," we all chimed.

I invited him to choose one of the remaining stones. He chose the amber-colored one, representing God's brilliant and immediate presence.

He then turned to Max and said to him, "It is abundantly clear that you are very loved, young man. It is so beautiful to see men valuing men and sharing their feelings so openly. I am so glad that I am here to be a part of your celebration. In fact, I wish I'd had a Black Mitzvah."

Everyone laughed. It sounded so funny coming from a white man.

He went on to tell us that he was very moved by the power of Max's Black Mitzvah and the commitment of the newly coronated mentors. He also saw something he had never seen before in his best friend, Chris, whom he had known for decades.

"Chris, I've known you for a really long time and never knew you could be so deep, man," he said, ribbing his friend. "Much respect, man. It's beautiful."

Then he turned back to Max.

"Max, you have a bond with him for life now. That's really cool. But remember, that doesn't mean you should listen to everything he says. Trust me," he joked.

Becoming serious again, he told us that he felt that as valuable as a Black Mitzvah could be for any young man, it would also be of great value for Max's mentors.

"What a tremendous opportunity not just for you but for your mentors. It goes both ways, my man," he said to Max. "You get to teach these old boys a few things too."

Max grinned and nodded enthusiastically to know that he was more than just a student, that he could be a teacher too.

For the rest of the weekend, Max relished every minute spent talking with each mentor, receiving full respect and undivided attention from the circle of men. The impact was amplified by the village that surrounded them.

As more friends of Chris and Ramona's dropped by to say hello and to meet Max, the house filled with parents and children of all ages, role-modeling mutual respect and social behavior. I could see him taking it all in, appreciating that he had found his tribe.

No one judged him or asked him why he walked funny. Anytime he asked for something and said "please," it was given. "Thank you" earned a "you're welcome." When going to the kitchen for a glass of juice, he learned to ask, "Would anybody like something?" He seemed especially happy if someone said yes, so that he could demonstrate good manners and be rewarded with a "thank you." He learned that sharing and giving were ways to get the attention he craved, but in a positive way.

Though not able to be there in person for the Black Mitzvah weekend, Uncle Lawrence and Uncle Kevin called and spoke to him privately. I could hear Max's enthusiastic account of the dinner celebration, the gifts, his golf outing, making guacamole, driving Uncle's Chris boat, riding in Uncle Chris's cool car, and best of all being met by the cute girl when he arrived the first day. I also heard long pauses in between. I knew they were sharing their own wisdom, expectations, and promises to be there for him in any way that they could. I could tell this from Max's occasional "Uh-huh," "Yes, sir," and "I will."

Having just given my word to Max that his conversations with his mentors would be private, I immediately broke my promise and asked to hear what they said. I thought that since we all got to hear from Chris and Jay, that it would be okay this one time. Max paused to think about it for a minute. He really liked the idea of his newfound freedom inside his circle of men and really appreciated the fact that I had created it for him. So he decided to share with me, just this once, the highlights that he knew I would like best.

"Uncle Kevin reminded me to 'respect your mom.' He told me to take care of you like you take care of me. He said I was lucky to have a mother like you and that I should always remember that." That's so Kevin.

I hugged Max and told him, "I am lucky to have a son like you, and I will always be here for you, no matter what."

He kissed me on my cheek and hugged me back hard.

"Thank you, Mom. I know. I love you," he said.

That moment alone made all my efforts to create my son's Black Mitzvah worth it.

Uncle Lawrence armed Max with a message of courage through prayer and a poem. It was not at all what I expected from the man I knew as my brother, whom I had never heard wax poetic. However, he was as precise and intentional as I did know him to be, choosing the perfect psalm.

>*Psalm 23:4: Even though I walk through the darkest valley, I will fear no evil, for you are with me; your rod and your staff, they comfort me.*

Beyond his favorite prayer, Uncle Lawrence also shared with Max an honorable tradition among the men of our family.

A second generation Kappa Alpha Psi fraternity brother (our father also pledged), he proudly passed on to his nephew the words of the poem "Invictus" by William Ernest Henley, held dear by Kappa men:

Out of the night that covers me,
Black as the pit from pole to pole,
I thank whatever Gods may be
for my unconquerable soul.

In the fell clutch of circumstance
I have not winched nor cried aloud.
Under the bludgeonings of chance
My head is bloody, but unbowed.

Beyond this place of wrath and tears
Looms but the horror of the shade,
And yet in the menace of the years
Finds and shall find me unafraid.

It matters not how straight the gate,
How charged with punishment the scroll.
I am the master of my fate:
I am the captain of my (KAPPA) soul.

Max was mesmerized by the power in those words.

"Wow, that's really awesome!" he said, his eyes wide.

"Yes, it's what makes a man a Kappa man."

With that, Max became a lifetime pledgee to the man Uncle Lawrence would steward him into becoming.

When we returned home from the weekend of celebration, there were two gifts waiting for Max. One was a package from Uncle Kevin. His gift to Max was a camera and a digital printer. It had special meaning because photography was the gateway to Kevin's own career success. That camera represented a tool to unleash Max's own creative instincts.

"Success comes from learning to leverage all that you have available to you. Even if you don't have much, if you have a passion, that's a great place start," he told him.

"I love to draw," said Max.

"So you're creative. So what are you going to do with it? To achieve your dream, you have to have a vision," he told Max. "What's your vision? What is your purpose?"

He knew Max loved to tell stories with his drawings and to share them with everyone and anyone, even strangers. That camera would allow him to see and connect to people in a new way, the way his drawings always did. He could use it to capture reflections of real life to include in his story lines to help him with his mission to tell better stories.

"I look forward to seeing a better world through your eyes, young man," he told Max.

In addition to the gifts, each of the mentors agreed to spend quality one-on-one time with Max, give him 24/7 access, and be there to cheer every milestone. This translates into mano a mano visits for three to four days to a week at a time for as many as five times a year.

The second gift was a round-trip ticket from Uncle Lawrence to spend his first mentoring week with him. It would be his first solo flight and his first experience in "boot camp," as we would all laughingly come to refer to it.

Since the weekend celebration of Max's rite of passage, together we have shared so many moments of joy and laughter and just as many of tears and the pain that comes with growth and maturity during his tumultuous teen years. Max has received the benefit of the kind of influence, insight, and guidance that paved the path of success in front of him. In turn, the mentors have benefited from the exposure to the unique challenges and experiences of a young man whose journey to manhood included a few more minefields than they'd ever dreamed of or anticipated. There was room for growth for all of us.

Already overwhelmed by the bounty and kindness showered upon us, I had no idea yet of the magnitude of the gifts to come or the many blessings ahead that would be bestowed on us by the circle of kings who came together to help raise my son. I could never have predicted how life changing it would be. Their dependability, moral integrity, compassion, and sense of humor, mixed with a healthy competition, helped salve festering emotions, renew Max's bowed spirit, unleash his inner warrior, and define his trajectory for greatness. In addition to the many gifts, blessings, and lessons, some unexpected, bestowed along the way, we all gained so much more from the fellowship, unity, and shared life experiences with his mentors. I continue to be overwhelmed by the impact of their unwavering commitment to Max's lifelong mental and spiritual health and well-being.

Chapter 3

Between Men

The first year of Max's Black Mitzvah was a whirlwind. Max learned four lessons from his mentors in quick succession, and the changes in him were fast but good, really good. The lessons were quickly imparted and understood, because when men connect with other men, a set of rules is made clear right from the start.

First among them, Max learned that life is not always fair and that there are some things he has no control over. This does not mean that he is weak, but that the road to becoming a warrior is filled with challenges unique to his own personal self-development. He learned that finding the right playing field to suit his natural talent allows him to be who he is meant to be. He learned that there is no room for excuses on the path to greatness, and that if he chooses the right one and stays the course, even he can be president one day.

Max and I both learned that the comfortable, insular mother-son relationship of our first twelve years had radically changed. Becoming a man means trusting other men or discerning when not to, and recognizing a good one when you meet him. That goes for me too.

Lesson 1: There are some things a son will not tell his mother.

The first thing that happened, just months in, was a revelation that quickly bubbled up to the surface. Once Max was given the opportunity to talk to men he could trust, a long-kept secret, hidden in the shadow of shame, jumped into the spotlight.

I first learned that Max had been sexually molested after he had shared the information with his mentors. He had been keeping it under wraps for two years. Once the gateway was opened and the pent-up pressure relieved, he was able to confess to me the whole story. As I sat and listened in utter horror and disbelief, he described what had happened in vivid, nightmarish detail.

"Mom, I have to tell you something." Anytime he opens with those words, I know he is about to tell me something I need to give my undivided attention.

"I don't know how to tell you," he mumbled, his eyes downcast, his hands limp on his lap.

I could see that it was physically painful for him to get the words out.

"Just tell me," I said softly.

"I didn't want to tell you. She told me not to," he continued.

"Who didn't want you to tell me what?" I said.

He took a long pause and then let out a deep breath, followed by a long sigh.

"It happened two years ago," he said with a look on his face that expressed the misery of a thousand slaves. "I couldn't tell you. She said I would get in trouble and I believed her," he went on, crying now.

My heart was racing.

"Trouble? What kind of trouble?" I asked. It was like pulling a nail out of a wall with bare hands. Then his words slowly began to tumble out as he described what had happened.

"When I was at Wanda's house when you were on a business trip. We were upstairs watching TV in her bedroom," he said. Wanda was a friend who would often take care of Max when I was away.

"Who? Who was in the bedroom with you?" I asked sharply. But I knew I had to calm down or he might put the cork back in the bottle, never to be opened again. So I asked once more, this time gently rephrasing the question, "Who, sweetie? Who were you watching TV with?"

"Cassie and me," he said. Then he ripped off the Band-Aid. "Cassie pulled down my pants and got on top of me. I couldn't push her off."

My head exploded. Cassie is Wanda's niece and is not much older than Max. They were both about eleven years old when it happened, but she was bigger and stronger. He told me how she had pinned him down while she climbed on top. The fact that he is cerebral palsy dominant on the left side of his body prevented him from shoving her away and making clear the intense repulsion he felt.

"Where was Wanda while all this was happening?" I asked, unable to hide my anger.

"Downstairs," he answered.

The thought that this was going on while she was only a few steps away made me want to vomit. Still, to this day, whenever I think about it, which is often, it brings me to rage and tears and then, the worst, guilt. I questioned my judgment and was tormented by every possible answer. How could I have put my son in such an environment? What did I miss that would have told me that he would not be safe with her? I trusted her!

When I confronted Wanda, of course she denied that anything had happened. I wanted so badly to believe that Max had made it all up. But I knew he was telling the truth from the way he hung his head as the story tumbled out of his mouth. Tears rolled down my cheeks as he looked at me, still ashamed and scared.

Should I report it two years after it happened? Would it not be worse to have to undergo the expected barrage of lies and denials, reliving it in the public spectacle of a courtroom and, in this case surely, the media attention?

Max said he was afraid to tell me because she had sworn him to secrecy. He thought that maybe it was all his fault, as victims often do. He had been avoiding telling anyone for fear of some kind of retribution from her, or even me. Confused and scared, he had so many questions that had gone unanswered for too long. He so badly wanted to talk about it to someone so that he could unpack all his feelings. Had he done something wrong? What should he have done to stop it? He did not know how to process what had happened. Nor did I.

As painful as it was to know that Max had kept this from me, I completely understood why it was one of the first things he wanted to share with his mentors. And had it not been for them, who knows how long he might have kept it a secret, or whom he may have told that might not have been able to give him the kind of perspective and careful consideration that a crisis like this deserved. That information in the wrong hands could have led to a sordid outcome.

In this moment of crisis, which came so hard and fast, the mentors were there for me too. I myself needed their guidance through this gnarly forest of haunting thoughts and suspicions. Reeling from the shock of it all, I needed to pour out my own fear and anxiety about what had happened. I wanted to understand from a man's perspective how Max might be feeling about it and whether I needed to do something, and if so, what? Foremost on my mind was whether we should seek counseling. It had been two years, and he had said nothing, so what did that mean? Was he over it? Should I simply let time heal this wound?

I reached out to Uncle Chris because he has always been so easy to talk to about anything openly and honestly, and for as long as you needed, he'd listen.

"Did Max tell you what happened?" I asked him.

"Yes, he did," he said in a solemn voice. "It was difficult to understand exactly what happened since it was two years ago. I can only imagine that, by now, in his own mind, he has added a layer of self-protection when he thinks about it. So I'm not sure I know the full story. But the bottom line is that I'm glad that he told me and that he feels he can talk about it now. It may come up again later, and it may take small bits at a time, but we'll work through it. So I don't have an answer other than at some time in the future, you and he might want to think about counseling, maybe even for both of you. But you know that I'm always here for you and Max. All of us are here for you," he said.

Uncle Chris's words were like healing balm for my soul.

"I know you are, Chris. And now it's hard for me to imagine going through this without you. When I asked you to be his mentor, I could never have seen this coming, how much he really needed you, all of you, more than I could have ever known," I told him.

Then, suddenly overwhelmed by the magnitude of it all, I couldn't help letting out a mother's primal scream. "Oh my God! I can't believe this happened to my baby!"

It was a release as I cried into the phone. Uncle Chris was silent as he let me weep for a while. And then, he gave me a cyber hug.

"Hold on, sister. You are not alone," he said.

"I know. I know. I know. Thank God," I gurgled through the sobs in my throat.

After we hung up and my eyes dried, I sat in stillness until I came to resolve that all I could do for now was to love him and to be prepared. If Max needed counseling, we would cross that bridge when we got to it—together.

Max has never talked to me about the conversations he had with his mentors about what happened, and I never asked. I only know that on the other side of laying bare his personal trauma, like ripping the Band-Aid off a wound that needed fresh air to heal, Max received the courage and support that he needed to confront the truth. He finally found consolation and an immediate response from one of them that neither of us quite expected.

Uncle Jay thought it was time for Max to know how to use a condom. When he showed up at our home, having made a special trip to sit down with Max face-to-face, he made it clear there would be some man talk.

"What time is it?" he greeted Max at the door.

"It's my time," Max responded.

"That's right. Me and you, downstairs," Uncle Jay directed him.

Uncle Jay shut the door behind them. They were down there for a while, talking in low, muffled voices—too low for me to hear what they were saying.

When they both came back up, Max looked dazed, even slightly traumatized, repeating several times, "That was gross! I am never having sex!"

Uncle Jay assured him, "Yes, you will. When it's the right time with the right girl. I think you should wait for both, but if you're going to do something, protect yourself."

"No, I'm never having sex. Never!" Max retorted. He was adamant. Conversation over.

Before he opened the door to leave, Uncle Jay put his arm around Max's shoulder and said, "Everything is going to be okay, man. Just remember, call me if you need me. I'm here for you."

Uncle Jay left him with a supply of condoms, and we have never had to have that conversation since. To this day, there are no words to describe the weight that was lifted and how much that helped to heal Max's psychological burden, and mine. I am forever thankful that I did not have to have that conversation, which I knew I was not equipped to have. That's what men are for. That's what men do.

Lesson 2: The right playing field is key to identifying natural abilities.

For my and Max's sanity, we have periodic check-ins. I can tell by the look on his face, or the way he walks down the stairs, or how often the refrigerator door opens that it's time to ask, "What's up?"

We call it our "sacred space," and it requires that we both go completely offline from our computers and disconnect all our devices so that we can sit and simply talk face-to-face with no distractions.

Our favorite spot is in the living room, filled with streaming light from windows to the world outside. "Let's talk," I'll say, gesturing him to the sofa across from the one where I sit, with a backdrop of the lakefront as our backyard. There's enough room between us so that I can read his body language as he opens up. When he goes from sitting upright on the edge of his seat to relaxing into the sofa pillows, that signals we're done, problem solved—at least for now.

"How are you doing?" I might ask. Or he might begin, "Mom, I don't want to talk about it," which means he does and we are set for a long conversation.

It's usually one of four things: something hurts, he didn't do so well on an assignment or a test, he had an argument with a friend, or it's about a girl. But every now and then, something different emerges from beneath the surface; like a whale breaching the water, it's big and breathtaking.

One of those moments occurred when he was eleven years old. This time he needed to talk, it was two weeks before Max's scheduled surgery to lengthen his hamstrings, commonly performed for children with cerebral palsy. The goal of the surgery was to reduce the spasticity in the muscles behind his knees, which became tight as he grew and caused him have a crouched gait. Walking this way was fatiguing and caused chronic pain in his knees.

Just as we were settling down for a bedtime read of the next chapter of Harry Potter, and before I opened the book to where we left off the night before, Max stopped me. He needed to tell me how excited he was about his upcoming surgery and what it meant to him.

He was young and full of energy—aching to stretch beyond the boundaries of disability that our ableist society had imposed on him.

"I've always wanted to play basketball," he started.

I was stunned at his shocking revelation. I'd never even heard him mention the word before and, in our house, we never watched any sports on television, except when I watch my tennis like the fiend I am for the game.

"Now that my legs will be fixed, I can play basketball," he said.

Thinking about it, of course, he would want to be able to play a sport. Why wouldn't he? It seemed like all the other boys had a shirt with a number on it, a uniform that made them part of a team. Why not him?

"Now maybe I can get a girlfriend too," he said.

That did it. Listening to him talk about what having strong legs meant to him made me cry.

Before the guidance counselors at school would eventually reach the conclusion that it made absolutely no sense for him to take a PE class, Max was expected to sit in the bleachers and watch the other students learn to play a sport while he studied the rules of the game on a piece of paper. How fun is that? I had to intervene at nearly every grade level to insist that the school find a better way for him to spend his time than sitting on the sidelines and suffering the indignation of being excluded from play. This usually meant that Max would be sent to the library for tutoring or to do homework. I'm not sure Max has ever even had to enter a locker room to change into gym clothes. Like a trooper, he always made the best of the situation and never complained, even though I knew that it had to bother him to be the only one unable to run, jump, kick, and pass the ball to excited voices screaming, "Over here!" or scoring a "swish" for the team. Now this would all change so Max could join the team of flying arms and legs in constant motion racing up and down the gym floor or out in the field, or so we thought.

Upon examining the difficulty and pain Max experienced when he walked, the doctor had promised very matter-of-factly, "Oh, I can fix that." Max's eyes lit up as he sat on the edge of his chair, rapt in the vision of the future painted for him.

"He'll be climbing mountains," the doctor added for emphasis.

However, after the surgery and the following weeks of daily and intensive physical therapy, nothing changed. There was little if any difference at all. His legs were not stronger. His walk was not straighter. His knees still hurt. He would not be able to play basketball with his classmates.

So as it turned out, the doctor had made a patently false promise. We threatened a lawsuit and eventually had a significant portion of the cost of the surgery returned to us. However, that was little compensation for the devastating result it had on Max.

"I hate that doctor for making me believe that I could play basketball. I hate him for promising to take away the pain. I will never trust anyone again!" he said angrily.

He has never fully recovered from that experience. From that moment on, complete unmitigated trust had to be earned, even for his mentors.

Building trusting relationships with his "uncles" required time and patience. Planned annual visits with each mentor were critical for Max to develop a level of faith in men that he never had. He needed to overcome past disappointments and believe that they would be there with him to weather the tumultuous storms ahead.

Over the course of the six years of his Black Mitzvah, Max traveled to Dallas, New York, Chicago, Miami, and Hawaii to spend time one-on-one with each mentor, on their own time and dime, giving him an opportunity to see and experience them as men of honor and warriors in their own lives. Each visit provided Max with a window to the world of manhood and an open door with unlimited access to the wisdom and counsel of the tribe.

His first trip was to Dallas to spend Labor Day weekend with Uncle

Lawrence at his annual backyard barbecue with the boys. The full shebang includes a gathering of two generations of men, including his brothers, son, nephews, and cousins, plus a friend or two. It usually involves three days of grilling barbecue, trash talking, watching sports, and whatever else men do when they are "feeling themselves" with no ladies around. That was Max's first experience of a testosterone-filled weekend of male camaraderie, and he came back a little more nuanced and sure of himself than he was before he left.

What goes on in the men's circle stays within the circle, so I never know the details of weekends with Uncle Lawrence. When Max returned home from his first trip into the conclave of men, the only thing I had to go by was the new vernacular he'd picked up and the subtle changes in his attitude. When he came home and greeted me at the door with, "Yo, blood!" I heard my brother all over again. We both laughed and hugged. I missed both of them. Max also seemed to stand a little taller and be a bit more appreciative of Mom.

"Did you grow?" I asked him.

"Maybe a little," he said.

"I think you grew a lot," I told him.

I had to ask him to pick up his clothes and put the dishes in the sink less often. I even heard the words "Thank you, ma'am," more often.

There were some things that I did get direct feedback about. These were selective tidbits that each mentor would impart to me based on his own determination that it would be helpful for me to know and that we could all build on it together to help Max in some meaningful way.

Uncle Lawrence gave me one tidbit that was a blockbuster revelation adding a whole new dimension to how to maximize Max's potential.

"Max is quite the athlete," he said.

Wait. What? An athlete? Neither before or after his hamstring surgery had Max ever picked up, thrown, kicked, tossed, or hit a ball. It was just not his thing. He didn't run, jump, or swim. I could never have expected what he would say next.

"Max has one particular gift that defines who he is and why he will be successful," he told me. "Yeah, I saw it when we were all hanging out in the pool."

"In the pool?" I was totally blown away. This made absolutely no sense.

After two years of swim therapy when he was a toddler, where he learned to be comfortable in the water, Max had developed his tremendous fear of it after an incident at a birthday pool party with his preschool friends. While playing, one of the other kids pushed him into the deep end, and the shock of a forced entry made him forget everything he learned and he quickly went under. He took water in his nose and his mouth, and his body stiffened like a rock as he sank to the bottom. He had to be rescued. The parents of the little boy who pushed him into the pool called me to tell me what happened. I was visiting friends nearby at the time, so I was able to get there in a shot. I found him crying so hard, snot mixed with water from the pool was running out his nose. Though I held him hard to calm him and soothe his broken spirit, Max shivered for hours, and he never recovered from the trauma. It was one of the early blows to his self-confidence. To this day, if you can even get him in it, he is still the last one in the shallow end and first one out. It was a dangerous precedent that led to his reticence to dive into a new experience or a new challenge, and reinforced his trust issues.

In Uncle Lawrence's backyard, the pool is usually the center of activity on a hot summer weekend. While everyone else was diving in and out of the cool water, he observed that Max chose to stay perched in a chair under an umbrella beside the pool. Max projected himself into the banter to command attention from the sideline, dictating the play-by-play action.

"Hey, James, let me see you do a cannonball! Melvin, pull up your pants. Nobody wants to see that!" Max funned.

It was here that Max showed his role as a natural leader, large and in charge. Uncle Lawrence concluded that Max may not be a physical athlete, but that "he's a social athlete. He might be the LeBron James of the sport of conversation."

It was truly an aha moment.

Uncle Lawrence was absolutely right. Max has always been an extremely social being. For all his life, while other kids were taking swimming lessons, going to soccer camp, or shooting hoops, Max preferred being the center of attention from the comfort of a chair in an air-conditioned environment, chatting up someone, anyone, who would listen and engage. No one a stranger, saying whatever is on his mind, injecting his opinion in every conversation, and even taking over the floor to talk about what he wants to talk about may not always be a good thing, but it definitely is his strength. As my mom would put it, "He's no shrinking violet."

From that aha moment forward, we began to strategize about how to coach Max the social athlete into Max the social champion. Uncle Lawrence focused on the basics.

"How do you want to introduce yourself, young man? Show me. Are you going to shake my hand? What kind of grip is that?" he sparred with Max. "Your handshake should announce who you are. Who are you? . . . Who are you? . . . Who are you? . . . What's your name? . . . Look me in the eye," he demanded.

He tested Max to commit to his own resolve, teaching him he can stand toe to toe with any man. Once he got his intro down perfectly, Max began to transform into a first-class gentleman with the confidence that he could win respect by showing respect, and he could garner the envy of his peers and even grown-ups as MVP in the game of conversation with his natural-born talent, the gift of gab.

It was beautiful to watch him in action with his newfound confidence. He so impressed his sixth-grade teacher when they first met. She was dazzled by the social etiquette that Uncle Lawrence had ingrained in him.

"You're quite the gentleman! I hope you rub off on the rest of my students," she told him as she held his handshake. Because of his easy repartee, she thought he'd make a great lawyer. "Max is charming and he can be very persuasive. He is a natural-born salesman," she said.

He has proved his skill many times over. I'll never forget the time Max persuaded the random guy sitting next to us on an airplane to buy the movie *Ponyo* by Hayao Miyazaki for his daughter. From the moment he buckled his seatbelt, Max held him captive for the next hour with a conversation on his favorite topic.

"Do you like animation?" he asked of the unsuspecting gentleman beside him. Little did the poor man know that "I guess so" was an open door that he would not be able to shut, whether he wanted to or not.

"Do you have any kids?" Max probed, fishing with live bait.

"I have a stepdaughter. Why?" he asked.

"Has she ever seen the movie *Ponyo*? It's about a little girl. She would love it. What about *Howl's Moving Castle* and *Spirited Away*? Have you ever seen those movies? They are by Hayao Miyazaki. He makes excellent movies," Max continued, reeling him in.

The gentleman shook his head and replied, "No, never heard of him or those movies. Who is he?"

Oh boy. Max was in full form now. He had a lot of explaining to do to convince this stranger why he needed anime in his life and enjoyed every minute of it. By the time we arrived at our destination, Max was ready for the close. As his new friend was grabbing his luggage from the overhead bin, Max was able to get in his last plug.

"You'll love *Ponyo* too. You can watch it together," Max said as the man was inching his way forward in the aisle toward the plane's exit.

We all laughed, including the people who had been seated behind us, who could hear most of the conversation, especially when Max got to the "best parts" and forgot his quiet voice.

"You're quite the salesman," the man said. "I think I'll have to buy the movie."

I tried to apologize for my chatterbox. "I'm so sorry, sir."

"Oh no, I thoroughly enjoyed it," he said. "I'm happy to meet a young man filled with so much passion and so knowledgeable about something other than sports and video games."

We even kept in touch with the very nice stranger turned friend we met on that airplane long enough for him to report that he had indeed actually purchased *Ponyo* and that he and his daughter both loved it, just as Max had promised they would.

He may not be able to play basketball or swim with the dolphins, but Max discovered that he could excel at something else. He's got mad social skills!

By recognizing and celebrating his unique personhood, Max began to restore his confidence. Through his keen insight and encouragement, Uncle Lawrence helped Max develop the belief in himself that he needs to survive, thrive, and conquer. He can talk his way into and out of anything. He can win hearts and minds with mere words. Figuratively speaking, up until then, Max had been hanging on to the side of the pool and now he could finally let go and swim freely.

Most important, he also learned to truly trust another man, his Uncle Lawrence, in a way that he thought he couldn't anymore. Max trusted that Uncle Lawrence understood who he was and who he wanted to be. It meant everything to Max and allowed him to be accessible for learning hard life lessons, including those that come from tough love.

Lesson 3: Among men, no excuses are allowed.

Uncle Lawrence does not suffer lightweights. He and I and our siblings were raised by our father, a Navy veteran, an avid sportsman, and a compulsive organizer who believed in discipline. Our mother believed in discipline as well, which may be part of the reason she chose a soldier for a husband. When we were growing up, Dad's favorite pastime seemed to be issuing orders designed to instill in his children the importance of having a work ethic, saving money, and living within your means. We grew up to our father's version of Saturday-morning "Taps" at 7:00 a.m.—Beethoven's Fifth Symphony played really loud—to do chores. One week it might be painting the outside of our house. Another might consist of moving boxes of who knows what from the basement to the garage in the summer and then back from the garage to the basement at the end of the summer. Getting up at dawn to cut the grass with a push lawn mower was one of Uncle Lawrence's least favorite jobs. We didn't call it "mowing the lawn," because ours never quite reached the qualification of a "lawn." It was more like a patch of grass in various stages of trying to survive the neighborhood kids, ourselves included, who chased balls lost in play in the street in front of our yard. I felt sorry watching my brothers shoveling snow, sure to have that driveway clean before Daddy got home or there was going to be trouble.

Now, Max has rarely ever even seen snow, and his view of what work looks like is men outside with leaf blowers or riding mowers to take care of the landscaping. In other words, he's "soft," according to Uncle Lawrence. Well, Lawrence wasn't having any of that. So in addition to working on Max's social skills, Lawrence's next mission was clear.

"I'm going to make a man out of Max," he said.

"It's like boot camp!" Max complained when he came back from his first visit with Uncle Lawrence. Knowingly, I laughed out loud.

"I thought you had so much fun at the pool with the boys?" I said, feigning surprise. I know my brother and I know how our dad raised us.

"I did! But that was just the one day. He was hard on me the whole rest of the time," he complained.

Now, clearly Max is completely unequipped physically, much less emotionally, to handle an exercise such as painting the house or pushing a lawn mower. Just getting up before 10:00 a.m. on a non–school day is the equivalent to a form of physical labor. So, Uncle Lawrence's plan began with a 6:30 a.m. wake-up call to jump into action.

Max will never appreciate how lucky he has it, since the only thing on the agenda for most Saturday mornings for Uncle Lawrence is golf. But to Max, this was torture. To add to the audacity of it all, if there was going to be a breakfast, he had to make it himself.

"If you're hungry, you better grab a bowl of cereal. And you better eat it quick, because we're out of here in the next twenty minutes. You got your watch on, right? No excuses," he said sternly.

There was one warning, and if you didn't move on purpose, you were left on purpose.

Most would think that a beautiful day on a golf course would sound absolutely delicious. Max complained as if he were an innocent man being sent to prison. Uncle Lawrence was standing at the door when the minute hand on his watch ticked the top of the hour. Max did not have his shirt or shoes on when it was time to go.

No excuses allowed. He ordered Max to "get in the car right now."

By the tone of Uncle Lawrence's voice, Max recognized that he was pushing his red button that could spell consequences he was nowhere near ready to have to deal with. He grabbed his stuff, left the house barefoot, and finished getting dressed in the car as they hit the road. In the rush, he forgot his phone.

"Can we go back and get my phone?" he asked.

Uncle Lawrence cut back, "I can let you out now and you can walk back if you need it that bad, because you are out of your mind if you think I'm going to turn around and drive all the way back to the house because you can't get your act together. I told you what time we were leaving. You should have been ready. Now you know that when I say something, I mean it."

Max sat glum and defeated. Oh well, no phone.

Boot camp! Uncle Lawrence made getting Max into line look so easy. I wish I could be so firm. But he did arm me with an extremely effective threat when necessary: "Do I have to call Uncle Lawrence?" It works like magic.

There's something so powerful about the intense, innate dynamic between men. To witness it is nothing short of awesome.

I saw its effect again when Max returned home from his first one-on-one visit with Uncle Kevin, who lives in New York. Max got to spend a full week with the one person who could compete with his verbal energy. Uncle Kevin is a social athlete like Max, but with lots more practice.

Max gives a rapid-fire commentary of every moment and every feeling throughout the day, unfiltered and unabashed. As easy as it is for him to be charming and loving, he is as quick to complain that he is unhappy or uncomfortable, or not interested in what you want him to do. So he finally met his match when he spent time with someone who moves too fast doing what needs to get done, rather than dealing with "your issues."

Days start late and end late with Uncle Kevin. What happens in between is constant activity, hitting the streets, maneuvering through the bustle of people and the myriad encounters while conducting business with the hustle of an entrepreneur. One day, it's visiting an elementary school to read to students from one of the books in development in the children's series he is writing. Another day it's a photo shoot for a client. Then there were trips to Madame Tussauds wax museum, Shake Shack in Union Square, and to Century 21, just because you never know what deal you might find. In other words, just hang out the way New Yorkers do on any given day.

So when Max fired a missile in his direction, such as "I don't want to go," it was summarily deflected with "Okay, you can stay here all day, but I'm going and I'll be back whenever I get back, so you are on your own," while Uncle Kevin was putting on his fashionable motorcycle boots to head out the door.

So Max realized that not only would he rather go but also that he'd better hurry up and get a move on or he was getting left behind. He knew all the fun and excitement he would be missing, and if he did not have someone to engage with in nonstop verbal sparring, life would be very dull and boring. Uncle Kevin seems to enjoy the competitive banter between them as much as Max does. No matter what, Max's attempts to deal a blow land like feathers.

"Is that all you got?" Uncle Kevin checkmates him every time, and that throws Max off his game every time.

When I unpacked his bag after his return from New York, I noticed that he had not taken any of his medication prescribed for his ADHD. I immediately called Kevin. What he said turned out to be one of the most profound revelations that I had about prescription drugs and our expectations of our children, especially young black men.

I asked, "Did you know that Max did not take his medication? He is supposed to take his Vyvanse every day."

"What medication? What is Vyvanse?" he asked.

I was more taken aback than I was upset that he hadn't taken his medicine. I explained that the amphetamine was prescribed for his ADHD and that he needed it to reduce his anxiety, calm his nerves, and keep him focused and on task—his doctor's words.

"He didn't drive you crazy?" I asked with great surprise.

"No, not at all. I didn't notice anything. We didn't have any problems at all," he said in a voice that clearly communicated, "What are you talking about?"

I was astonished to learn that Max didn't need to be medicated and that he just needed to be active and mentally challenged. Rather than drugs, successive positive inputs and constant stimulation might be antidote to his hyperactivity. And Uncle Kevin was just the kind of person to provide just that.

"Max doesn't need any medication. He just needs to be busy," he said.

Max learned that he could trust that Uncle Kevin knew what he really needed and could count on him to give it to him, and make it fun—make him feel "normal."

Since that visit, Max no longer takes Vyvanse daily, but only when he feels he needs it, which is not often. He still forgets everything, but we both will take that any day over a pill that makes him feel "like a zombie" and stops the flow of his prolific works of art. Without medication, he can for draw for hours. I couldn't help thinking that it must also be better for his health. I'm convinced that a lifetime of drugs in his system would cause damage to his liver. I worried about this because the doctor asked for a test every time he had a checkup.

Max got rid of a crutch that he learned that he did not need. Free from the side effects of prescription medication, he was able to see more clearly, unleash his natural creativity, and add another rung to the ladder of belief in himself. Uncle Kev rocks!

Lesson 4: Greatness comes from the heart.

The first year of Max's Black Mitzvah was nearing its close and he was excited to end it with a visit to Uncle Chris. It serendipitously coincided with the ushering in of our first African American president. It was October, a month before the presidential election, so I was invited to join them in Chicago, since Uncle Chris and Ramona had made special plans in support of Barack Obama's historic run for office. Max was really looking forward to playing with their one-year-old son, Jeremy, his new "little brother." Nothing could have prepared us for what would happen on the second night of our visit.

We were invited to attend a fund-raiser held at the Union League Club of Chicago, a prominent social club. As usual, Max began complaining about having to wear a suit from the minute of the very mention that we were attending a semiformal event. He was locked into the mental agony of buttons and zippers during trips to the bathroom, and spending the evening in search of a place to sit down to rest his legs at every opportunity.

When we arrived at the club, thankfully we were waved to the front of the long line outside waiting to go through an airport-style security check; security could see that Max had a disability. Inside the grand ballroom, hundreds of people were already gathered, excited to hear then–presidential candidate and senator Barack Obama speak. With only a month to go before the election, his campaign was at a fever pitch of the promise of hope and change with health care reform, renewable-energy investment, financial regulations, infrastructure investment, tax reform, and STEM innovation. It was the future we all believed in, gave money to, and planned to cast our ballots for. The folks gathered in the room were full of optimism, with the wind at our backs.

The excitement was completely lost on Max. Uncomfortable in large crowds, he had already begun complaining that his legs hurt, and I could see him scouting for a place to sit away from the crush of the gregarious and animated audience waiting in anticipation of the man of the hour. The intensity of the energy in the room just made Max that more irritable by the second. More interested in spending time with his "little brother" than being "forced to behave" at an event, he found this to be just another one of those extremely intolerable situations. I was desperately scanning the room to find a place where he could sit and still have a view of Barack Obama when he went on stage. There had to be at least a thousand people in a room that had a capacity of eight hundred. It was not looking promising, and I knew this evening could quickly slip into misery for both of us. If he was in pain, compounded by his inability to see anything, there would be relentless complaining and guilt on my part for "dragging" him to this.

Then suddenly, Ramona appeared and swooped us up and out through a back way to an upper floor and into a huge, rich, dark wood-paneled room where she, Uncle Chris, and Jeremy were mingling in a ritzy party setting with comfortable, velvety upholstered chairs and sofas. Bingo! Now this was more Max's style. There was food and plenty of it: fancy hors d'oeuvres, desserts, and a selection of fine wines. Max made a beeline straight to the bountiful buffet, and all was right with the world again. We found Uncle Chris camped out in a quiet corner of the room, being the great dad and dutiful husband, while Ramona, the socialite, was buzzing about the room, filled with full-time volunteers and major contributors to the campaign. Max camped out with the boys while Ramona and I networked.

Unaware of the agenda for the evening for this more intimate affair, I asked another guest about the strip of red carpet lined with gold posts along the back side of the room. It was clearly there for a reason, and I wanted to be the first in line for whatever it was. I was over the moon to learn then that not only was Barack coming up there to meet us to thank us for our generous support before he went down to the packed grand ballroom to speak to the throng of supporters, but also that we were about to get a picture with him!

As the time came near for his appearance, people began gravitating to the back of the room to line up on the red carpet. Max could not wait on the line with me for our turn to meet Barack, since he could not stand for longer than a few minutes. I needed to think quickly to coordinate with minute detail this historic encounter. I instructed Max to wait with Uncle Chris, who was quietly sitting with Jeremy, who was squirming in his stroller on the other side of the room. We decided that when I was next in line, I would signal Max to rise to meet me where Barack stood waiting for us to join him for a photo. From where Max sat, was a straight line of not more than twelve feet from the target.

The handlers were wrangling purses, cameras, anything in your hand, to expedite the photo-taking process and keep the senator on schedule for the evening. On cue from staffers, each individual or couple was signaled to walk, shake hands, pose, snap, exit, and then you heard "Next!"

The line moved fairly quickly. Finally, it was our turn. As I walked toward Barack, I signaled to Max to meet me. Since the handlers and Barack were turned toward me, as I was next in line, they all saw my gesture and turned to see why. As Max approached, Barack paused to take in the full figure of the young man walking toward him. As he waited for Max to make his way, he signaled the handlers to pause the photo procession. And then he leaned in.

As he took Max's extended hand in his firm grip, he asked, "What's your name, young man?"

After Max told him his name, while still holding his hand, Max's very next words were, "I really admire you for being such a great father to Sasha and Malia."

I was just as taken aback as Barack was. It was visible to everyone within view of the two that something special had just happened when Barack shifted into a completely different manner from genuine politeness to genuine interest. In other words, he got real.

Barack and Max began a kind of tête-à-tête.

"How old are you?" he asked. Max told him and Barack responded,

"You know, you kind of look like me when I was fourteen. I had locs just like yours."

Max couldn't stop smiling, beaming up at him while I was trying to imagine Barack with locs. The two of them connected with light man-to-younger-man banter about school and family.

The last question Barack asked him was, "Tell me, young man. What kind of change would you like to see?"

Max paused for a second, brow furrowed, and then responded, "Someone like you as president. You're kind of cool."

Barack laughed and said, "Well, I'm working on that, and I appreciate your support."

At that moment, I took the opportunity to let Barack know that Max had brought something for him.

"Oh yeah? Where is it?" Barack said, signaling to the handlers to bring me my purse.

In it, I had put a copy of Open Road's *Hawaii with Kids* by Rachel Jackson Christmas, a dear friend. I had brought it just in case, because you never know. Max and I are contributing researchers to this island travel guide. Max provided input for reviews of the children's clubs and activities, so his name is mentioned in it. Earlier that day, I made sure that Max had autographed it for Barack. Max showed him the book and guided Barack to the page with his handwritten note that said, "Good luck! I hope you become president."

Barack grinned broadly and said, "Thank you, Max! I'm going to share it with Sasha and Malia. We'll use it next time we go to Hawaii." I felt like dropping a hula dance right then. I was never so glad that I had thought to grab a copy of the book, and get Max to sign it, and bring it with us, just in case, because you never know when you're going to meet the next president of the United States!

Barack thanked him for the book and they shook hands again. By now, the handlers were noticeably perplexed, as they stood by looking at their watches impatiently. It was time to pose, snap, exit, and "Next!"

I couldn't believe what had just happened. Though Max had a once-in-a-lifetime opportunity to meet the man who was about to become our next US president, the man whom he met took his time to talk to Max as if he was the most important person in a room filled with important people, showed interest in who he was, and saw him for what he was, a bright young man who could capture your heart in an instant with his own energy and pure, unadulterated honesty. In just his few minutes with Barack, he learned that part of greatness is that no matter your stature in life, treating people with respect and dignity makes you a real man. It was a moment we will cherish forever.

When Max returned to his seat next to Chris, his eyes still wide, he asked, "How did you do that?"

"Do what?" Uncle Chris asked.

"How do you know him?" Max asked.

"I know him because I have invested in his campaign, and I believe in his service to community. He's the kind of leader I think we need," Uncle Chris said. "That's why I'm investing in you. You could be president one day."

Max beamed.

Less than six weeks later, we were back in Chicago again to stay with Chris and Ramona to watch the election results in anticipation of the tremendous celebration the whole world seemed to be poised for. While Max was comfortably ensconced in the warmth and cozy comfort of their condo in a high-rise overlooking Bryant Park, he had a full view of the tops of dozens of booths of networks from around the world with streaming cameras and the thousands of people below that Chris, Ramona, and I had joined. As the election results were being broadcast live, I had the incredible opportunity to be standing just a few feet from the stage when the news came over the CNN live broadcast with Wolf Blitzer: "Barack Obama has been elected president." All at once, the shoulder-to-shoulder crowd of thousands leapt in the air with complete and utter joy. Tears streamed. Strangers hugged. The promise for a brighter future for America, for the world, for my son, for all our sons, seemed closer than ever before.

Though I knew it was impossible for him to spot me in the crowd, I waved up to Max to say, "We won!"

To experience what I felt on Election Night, I so wanted Max to come with me to the inauguration of our new president. However, the large crowds, the walking, the standing in long lines and waiting for hours in freezing temperatures were beyond even thinkable for him. He thought it a much better idea to stay home and keep warm and watch the highlights on television. Besides, Max had met the man, not yet president, and that was good enough for him. The magnitude of the historical precedent that he was being sworn in as the first black president was lost on him. From his perspective, he was surrounded by many fine, intelligent black men, any of whom he thought could be president.

"Why is it such a big deal that he's black?" Max insisted. "Of course, he should be president. He's a really nice person and he's smart. Uncle Chris said so. You go, Mom. I'll stay home and look for you on TV."

So, I went to Washington, DC, to attend the inaugural festivities and partied like it was 1999 for four consecutive days along with a record-breaking multitude of people from around the world who descended on DC to share a remarkable moment in history. Throughout, I never stopped thinking of Max and wished he could have been there with me to experience every moment. Determined to try to capture every moment so he could live each vicariously, I took tons of photos to share with him. He enjoyed hearing my animated account of all that happened as I took time to point out who was who in every picture, lingering on those that included Uncle Chris.

"Did you see President Obama? Did he ask about me?" he wanted to know.

The first year of his Black Mitzvah ended on a high note, and at the beginning of a new era of hope for young black men, especially for Max. His first year of mentoring was filled with many new revelations and personal growth for both of us.

The following years proved to be much more challenging. His confidence and self-esteem were shaken to the core, and his self-doubt became the bane of our existence for the next several years. Issues around learning differences, puberty, bullying, porn, and self-identity were ahead of us. We had work to do.

Chapter 4

The Secret Life of Max Zolo

One of my favorite movies is the 2013 version of *The Secret Life of Walter Mitty*, starring and directed by Ben Stiller. In it, Walter, a negative-asset manager at *Life* magazine, has worked for sixteen years in a room with only one co-worker, who is his only friend. He secretly pines for a female co-worker but lacks the self-confidence to approach her. Because he lives such a lonely life, he often daydreams of wild adventures of heroism, many of them starring the girl of his dreams. He "zones out," as his sister calls it. His odd behavior makes him an easy target of bullying by some of his co-workers. But the magazine's chief photographer sees Walter through a different lens. He relies solely on Walter to handle the original negatives he sends in from his work in the field in every part of the world because of Walter's dogged work ethic and integrity. He and Walter share fluency in a visual language that allows Walter to live out the adventures he only dreams of via these images. Each is the other's alter ego.

I love this movie because in the end, Walter emerges as the real-life hero of his dreams, gets the girl, and is featured on the final cover of the iconic *Life* magazine as "the quintessence of life."

Max is a lot like Walter. He's a warrior nerd, and his drawings reflect his dreams of his hero and alter ego, Max Zolo.

Lesson 5: There will always be bullies.

As a preteen, Max was slight. He had a pretty face with full red lips, light brown eyes, and eyelashes that women pay for. He preferred to let his hair loc because it was easy and he hates the daily hair-grooming process. It takes too many motor skills. His thick locs grew fast and hung down to his waist. Anyone and everyone who did not know him, without exception, thought he was a girl. If we were in a restaurant, when the waiter would ask our order, the question would be, "And what will she have?" On an airplane, "What would she like to drink?" And in a store, "Oh, the girls' department is that way." It happened so often that one day it occurred to me that this might not be cool. What might this be doing to his self-esteem? Thinking that maybe we should at least cut his hair shorter, I asked Max, "Does it bother you that everyone thinks you're a girl?" Without the slightest hesitation, Max responded emphatically, "No, I don't care what people think. I know who I am." At that moment, I could not have been more proud. I am certain that when I was his age, I was not nearly so self-secure. I thought I must be doing something right.

That self-assuredness began to crumble when my son was bullied at school. His voice lost its thunder. His eyes lost their gleam. He walked as if he were tethered to a long rope dragging a kite that had lost its wind.

The early signs of depression began to surface in seventh grade, when he was fourteen. It started with his heartbreaking report to me of being bullied by kids at school. As his words slowly climbed out of his throat from his sunken spirit, the blood drained from his face. Tears seeped out of his eyes and rolled to a point on his cheeks and arrested in place, as if becoming a part of his skin that would take years to shed.

Small for his age, Max also walked differently. The braces on his legs designed to correct his pronation caused him to scuff his feet in a manner that made his shoes squeak with every step. He walked on his toes in a way that made him look like he might pitch forward any minute. His left leg was the weakest, with a crouched knee. This exacerbated the whole issue, since it caused him to dip to his left with every other step, which made him to rock from side to side. Behind him he dragged his backpack on wheels that carried his whole world. It weighed a ton. It was stuffed with his favorite superhero manga (Japanese comic books and graphic novels), his sketchbook, pencils, markers, schoolwork, and books—his safety net of things that he could occupy himself with to avoid feeling lonely or the sting of rejection or the mean and insensitive barbs that the other kids would so freely zing. The assortment of snacks inside always included enough to share with a friend, if he could find one on any given day.

Often, he would come home angry. At first, he was reluctant to talk about it. When I'd ask, "What's wrong?" he would simply say, "I had a bad day." When I'd press for more, sometimes I could get him to talk while I would just listen. "You don't know how I feel," he would cry. "I hate my legs. I hate being different. You never had to go through school with no friends and everybody making fun of you. You were popular and smart. School is hard for me."

I would tell him over and over about how difficult it had been for me too and how insecure I'd been when I was his age. But I had to admit that I didn't really know what it was like to be him, to have to sit in the bleachers while the other students took gym class, to have to leave class a few minutes early to get a head start to reach the next classroom in time. He would often have to walk the hallways alone until the end-of-class bell unleashed the rush of students. He told me how they would nearly bowl him over without even an "excuse me" or an "I'm sorry." No, I cannot imagine what that is like. I cannot imagine never being picked to be on the team or never having a classmate of the opposite sex whisper, "I like you," and instead be the foil of an insult when other students would taunt a girl, "You like Max," as if that were the worst thing in the world.

Sometimes our talk would go for hours until we had explored every valley of despair and scaled every mountain of hope and we were both exhausted. I would always tell him, "You are stronger than they are. If they make fun of you, then they are the ones with the problem, not you." I would sit with him and listen for as long as it took, until I was certain that he felt better, until I got a smile out of him. I could not rest until I was sure that his internal battery was restored and reset for the next day.

There were moments of reprieve. Sometimes he would tell me about a new friend he had made. Someone who spoke to him kindly or gave him notes from the day's lesson or wrote down the day's homework assignment for him. I would come to learn that his singular criteria for who was a friend was someone who had stuck up for him on any particular day.

By ninth grade, we'd changed schools. But things got worse. Ironically, it was at a private Catholic school where the bullying was the worst. And this time it was not just the students but also a very mean-spirited teacher, who, I came to learn, thought that the best way to teach Max was to put him out in the hallway away from the other students. That's when I noticed that he started scratching himself in a way that left long, angry red marks on his arms. I began to check his arms when he came home from school each day. When the red marks appeared again, he finally broke down and released a vivid and heartbreaking account of the day's events.

"They called me 'cripple.' They said I don't belong in this school. No one will sit with me at lunch. I don't have any friends. They call me 'stupid.'"

He told me how some of the boys had made a dance mocking the way he walked. He tried to fight back, but going to school every day was like entering a boxing ring with no gloves. Max is deeply sensitive, so their punches not only sting, but they sink in, fester, and seep into his psyche. His mantra became "I don't like myself." "I'm lonely." "I don't care anymore." His anxiety became mine. I wondered, would he really seriously hurt himself?

And it wasn't just in school. It was also on the Internet, where he looked for friends. Careful to not invade his personal space, I skirted the perimeter with parental radar in an effort to monitor that situation. I know that social media is riddled with peril. I know that 33 percent of teenagers have been victims of cyberbullying, and the rate of suicide that goes with it.

Layer that with cyberporn, cyberdating, and cyberscams, and the fact is that our children are vulnerable to all kinds of Internet predators. It's hard for parents to monitor and protect our kids from these powerful influences that seep through the Internet into our private worlds, piercing the bubble of safety that we have created in our own homes. Parental controls are a stopgap, but not the fortress we need, since smart kids know how to get around them. And that smartphone is most likely smarter than you.

Those ubiquitous and insidious cyberscams got him more than once. They feed off vulnerable users in the online community, particularly young people who download lots of videos. When Max got a pop-up with the message that his computer had been infected with a virus, he responded to it and fell victim to one of those scam artists who ask for your credit card number to fix it. Fortunately, Max knew he needed to check with me, but did so only after he'd given it to them.

"Mom, my computer froze and I got a message to call a number, so I did. It's fixed now," he said.

"What? You called a number?" I knew it didn't sound right. "What happened?"

"I gave him my credit card. It was a hundred dollars. It's fixed now."

"WHAT! Never do that again. If anyone ever asks you for any personal information, never give it to them. Those people are scammers. They will steal money from your account," I explained to him.

After I read him the riot act about using the credit card before asking permission, Max said "I'm sorry" and "I won't do it again" enough times until I was satisfied that he wouldn't. Max felt defeated yet again, bullied by a cyberscammer. He felt a little better when I told him I was able to get the charge erased from the account.

Closing a credit card is easy, but cyberdating has been unholy torture for both of us. Throw out all the rules about courtship, boundaries, and protocol. Meeting girls on Facebook, on WhatsApp, or in some chat room, and dating through FaceTime and Messenger, left him vulnerable to an illusion of intimacy with no clue about what or who is real or fake.

The cyberworld required a new set of rules for safety and responsibility. Max and I had to learn these rules together. They include the following:

First, don't say anything to anyone online that you wouldn't say to them in person.

Second, don't post anything that you will be ashamed of later.

Third, decide what your personal brand or message is and then stay in that lane. That way you will attract the kind of people who connect with your message and avoid the trolls who are just looking to bait you for trouble. In other words, protect yourself, your family, and your community, offline and online, by behaving and treating others with dignity and respect, including yourself.

I knew he was desperate for friendship, to be accepted. Day after day, I'd spend evenings consoling, commiserating, giving pep talks, and reminding him of the people who love him and care about him. I made it a mission to look for and create events and activities that made him happy and that he could look forward to—all to ensure that I didn't lose him to sadness, lest he slip into total despair.

Then came the final straw. At school, Max scrawled, *I want to kill myself*, along with a picture of death, on his notebook paper.

There was an urgent message on my cell phone from the school psychologist. Panic set in. Did he really want to end his life? Within an hour, Max and I were sitting in her office listening to Max explain what he meant. I could not take my eyes off his face as he tried to assure us that he was just expressing his pain.

"I didn't mean it," he repeated over and over, his eyes pleading to be believed.

Just as he had learned that his words could win hearts and minds, he learned that his words could also lose them. Whether he meant it or not, his words caused alarm and fear. The school refused to allow him to come back until he saw a psychologist.

The first one we saw did not deem him suicidal, but depressed, and, he thought, justifiably so.

"I see nothing that I have not seen before with students his age who are being bullied," he reassured me. "It might help to talk about what you are feeling, and if you want I can recommend a few therapists," he said to both of us.

"I don't need to see a therapist," Max said. He was not interested in seeing more doctors. "I'm fine now," he insisted. The doctor handed me a couple of numbers just in case.

The headmaster didn't like that diagnosis and insisted that we see another specialist. So we sought a second evaluation from a Vanderbilt University PhD'd child psychologist who, after a consultation with Max, wrote a letter affirming that he didn't need therapy, but that the school had a serious bullying issue that it needed to address.

He was allowed to go back to school, but after a meeting with the vice principal a few weeks later, Max was unceremoniously kicked out of the school at the end of his first semester there. Ironically, this Catholic school had decided that it was easier not to deal with the issue at all than to address the problem of bullying.

When Max started midyear at his new school, the damage was already done. He was wary of his new schoolmates and had learned that he could not even trust his teachers. In an attempt to restore his self-confidence, I tried to summon his resolve to solve his own problems by probing him with rational questions.

"What is your red line? What, for you, is the breaking point of no return? Do you want revenge on them or an apology from them? What would make you feel better?" I asked.

His responses were irrational. "No one likes me. I don't know why you love me. I don't care anymore."

The image of his scrawled *I want to kill myself* was emblazoned in my mind and caused my words to choke in my throat as I tried to comfort him. "Your family loves you." I reminded him that his mentors were always there for him and how much Jeremy, his "little brother," adored him, which always seemed to cheer him up. However, the ongoing pep talks from me were not yielding long-lasting results. I couldn't help him find the solution he was looking for.

Things had gotten completely out of hand. I called the uncles—Lawrence, Chris, Kevin, and Jay—and told them what had been going on. I told them that Max had scrawled the words *I want to kill myself* on a piece of paper and that he was being bullied. They all agreed it was time for an intervention, and so for the first time, they came together to huddle for the game play.

The different approaches to handling a situation like this among his mentors emerged crystal clear and became a go-to indicator for years to come. Though none of them condoned fighting, they all recognized that Max needed a way to fight back, and each offered a unique perspective to help Max find his own.

Collectively, they strategized a plan of action to rescue Max from himself and lift him out of his feelings of despair, rejection, and loneliness. A succession of phone calls and long, heartfelt conversations ensued.

They confessed about their own confrontations with bullies, gave advice, and expressed lots of love. I was not privy to those private conversations, but Max shared some of the counsel he received in sound bites, and I could see changes in his behavior and attitude.

"Mom, Uncle Kevin told me to say, 'I'm going to pray for you' to someone who is mean to me. What's that going to do?" he asked with a helpless shrug.

Uncle Kevin had shared stories of his own school experiences of being bullied and having to fight, because he was smaller than most kids his age, something he and Max share in common.

"Is that what you did when you were bullied at school? Pray?" Max was skeptical.

"Not at first. In the beginning, I got in lots of fights and lost. So I got smart. I couldn't beat him, so I had to come up with something else. I thought of what my grandmother had taught me. I told them, 'I'm going to pray for you.' Sometimes it worked, sometimes it didn't. Maybe it changed somebody and maybe it didn't. But it helped me feel better about myself, and that was more important," Uncle Kevin told him.

Max didn't much care for that solution. His first reaction was to want to know how to fight, not pray.

"Why should I be nice to someone who is mean to me? Why pray to a God who let this happen to me in the first place?" That was a hard question to answer.

Uncle Kevin had a thoughtful response: "The power of prayer is for those for whom you pray. It is the power to let go of what you cannot control and to trust in the power of being who you are. You have the power to show others how strong your heart is, how courageous you are. That's a force that most cannot reckon with. And it may not shut them all down, but it will earn you respect. When they go low, you go high."

If nothing else, Max has a strong heart and the infinite power to forgive. He believes in the Golden Rule. So he tried it. Max reported that he didn't think it worked since the incidents still occurred, but it did seem to shut some of them down. He admitted that it made him feel a little better that at least he had a response. As Uncle Kevin advised, when they went low, he went high. He would be the better man. But he needed more ammunition.

Uncle Jay also steered him to the power of prayer and to seek refuge in the Bible when he was at his weakest. He referred him to Romans 5:3–5 (NIV):

> *Not only so, but we also glory in our sufferings, because we know that suffering produces perseverance; perseverance, character; and character, hope. And hope does not put us to shame, because God's love has been poured out into our hearts through the Holy Spirit, who has been given to us.*

Uncle Chris continued to remind Max of who he was and assure him that he was strong and that "the people who are saying ugly things are the weak ones."

But when the barrage of incoming attacks is to charge you as being weak because you are "crippled," it is hard to overcome the harsh words and mocking by peers whom you so want to be your friends. These were tough times and Max was looking for tough solutions, the kind in his world of superheroes who were misfits like himself—like the X-Men who fight the bad guys and win. In his heart, he was a warrior prince who could stomp out villains and rescue damsels in distress.

Uncle Chris teed up his love of anime and superheroes by encouraging Max to use his creativity to help salve his wounds, suggesting that he illustrate the scene where he is the hero in an altercation. That wisdom led to the creation of Max Zolo, his alter ego, who has become the central character in Max's stories that continue to help save his life to this day.

Max Zolo is a sword fighter who is not afraid to duel any foe in a fight to the death.

Then, it was Uncle Lawrence who gave him the answer he was looking for. He challenged him to "man up!"

"But Uncle Kevin told me to tell them that I'll pray for them," Max said in a voice that was more question than statement. "I don't think that works very well. I want to fight them, not pray for them," he said defiantly.

Uncle Lawrence agreed that Max needed a more direct approach, but first that required introspection.

"Well, first thing is you're going to have to get some thicker skin, man. You are going to be called many things in life. Are you going to let somebody else's words hurt you? You have to decide where you are going to draw the line. Then you have to stand behind it and decide what you are going to do if they step over it. So what are you going to do? Get in a fight because somebody said something you don't like? Now, if they put their hands on you, that's another matter," said Uncle Lawrence.

Max knew he was treading into serious territory now.

Sensing Max's insecurity, Uncle Lawrence added, "It's okay to be afraid. You need to have a little fear. A little fear gives you adrenaline and can help you do what you need to do. But don't get in a physical battle that you know you can't win. That's not smart. Sometimes you just have to let them know that you are braver than they think you are. Show them how brave you are. Look them in the eye and don't back down. If that doesn't work, if they hit you, hit 'em back as hard as you can and hope for the best. Then let me know how it works out. I'll be here for you."

Max needed that. He wanted more than stories and pep talks. He wanted a fight strategy, and his ace in the hole, his uncle, to back him up. More than that, he wanted relief. He wanted to be accepted and loved and treated with respect. Succumbing to the notion that he was somehow "less than," he was miserable. No matter how much tough love he'd been through, Max's skin was as thin as it was the day he was born, when it had to be taped inside his elbows and behind his knees to prevent it from tearing open. Now, just as then, he remained vulnerable and sensitive to the slightest abrasions. But now he had useful tools in his toolbox to deploy for whatever the situation demanded. All he needed was the skill to assess which to use when. That would come with time.

Relief from the agony of always feeling vulnerable and weak came in stages over time, and from varied and surprising sources.

Max travels with me everywhere, whether for business or leisure. It was during a business trip to New York that one such chance encounter provided him with some sorely needed inspiration. At a conference he attended with me, he had the opportunity to meet Allan Houston, a former basketball player with the New York Knicks. Mr. Houston was the keynote speaker at a luncheon being held that day. Ironically, he was there to speak about his Allan Houston Legacy Foundation, a nonprofit that produces a series of basketball camps to foster mentorship and bonding between fathers and sons.

For several minutes before the luncheon, while the grand ballroom was being prepared before the guests entered and Allan was to take the stage, Max had a chance to meet him and talk to him in a private, intimate exchange at the center of the empty ballroom.

The only other people in the room, besides Max and me, were the event director, Allan's manager, and the people handling staging and lighting. Max was focused only on finding a chair so he could rest his aching legs, and he chose the best seat with a view and immediately dropped into it, not once noticing anyone else in the room. The event director is a personal friend, so she walked Allan over to meet us.

When turning to greet Allan, Max looked up, his head tilting higher and higher to take in the full stretch of the professional basketball player's six-foot-six frame. *Whoa!* was the expression on his face. He extended his hand to meet Allan's in a handshake, apologizing at the same time, "I'm sorry I can't stand. My legs hurt. My name is Max."

What happened next brought me to tears.

The towering gentleman immediately responded, "Hi, I'm Allan. You know, Max, sometimes my legs hurt too." He then folded himself into a chair right next to Max with his legs stretched out and went on to tell him about his knee injury.

"Do people make fun of you?" Max asked.

I thought my heart would burst. "Man, if they do, that's their problem, not mine. I'm too busy doing what I have to do," he said.

He then shifted the conversation to draw Max out, asking him, "So, man, what do you like to do?"

"I'm an artist," Max responded confidently.

"Oh yeah? So what kind of artist are you?" asked Allan.

Max lit up. "A good one! I draw anime characters. Do you like anime?"

He completely forgot about the pain in his legs, lost in the excitement of sharing his passion. Allan was caught up as well, and they went back and forth on some of their favorite cartoons and TV shows. It wasn't until the handlers and event manager seemed to be getting nervous, not wanting to interrupt but needing to, since it was time to start the show, that the conversation cruised to an end.

They shook hands once more, and Allan told him, "Keep up the hard work, man. You're going to be great!" Max beamed.

"See, I told you, Mom. I'm going to be great!" There it was again. It was music to my ears to hear him claim it again.

At the end of an exceptional keynote speech about the importance of mentoring young men, Allan asked the audience if there were questions. Max's hand shot up in the air, and Allan picked him to be first up.

"Yeah, Max?"

But instead of a question, Max offered the quintessential testimonial that put the exclamation point on Allan's remarks.

"I just wanted to thank you for taking the time to talk to me earlier. It really meant a lot to me," said Max.

Allan responded, "The honor is all mine, man. Thank you for sharing a little bit about yourself with me. I learned something from you too."

The power and majesty of that moment permeated the room. There wasn't a dry eye in the house. Everyone was moved by the honesty and transparency of the impact that one simple, care-filled interaction between an adult and a young person can have. You could almost hear the pens clicking and checkbooks rustling opening. I'm certain Mr. Houston's foundation was generously rewarded as a result of his spontaneous act of generosity, his opening his heart and living his mission by providing a few words of encouragement to a young man who needed to hear them.

Moments like these—a good man with just the answer Max needed at just the right time—have made a difference in the trajectory of his life. And in between those moments, Max found refuge from his trauma of being bullied by re-creating himself as an anime hero, Max Zolo, the warrior.

Lesson 6: Porn and respect for women—it's complicated.

The Achilles' heel of any warrior is women. I learned that the hard way.

Porn is a $20 billion global industry. Given its multiple points of entry, it's only a matter of time before puberty awakens a boy's primal circuitry

and he discovers this world of unfiltered imagination. I had never prepared for or even thought about it until it happened. Who knew that it
would be right under my nose, on an office computer, while performing
an assignment that I had given him? So, in a nutshell, he was introduced
to porn because of me. That's right, me! I had no idea.

See, what happened was . . .

We had already been to Hawaii several times, Mexico, St. Thomas,
Puerto Rico, the Bahamas, and Turks and Caicos. What can I tell you?
I'm a sun worshipper, and my ideal vacation is defined by having a beach
close to the hotel. Max, on the other hand, with fully formed lifestyle and
leisure preferences, hates the sun and sand, and is NOT getting in anybody's ocean without Diver Dan. So this time I let him choose our annual
vacation destination.

At fourteen years old, Max had three great passions in life: anime,
manga, and sushi. So Japan it was. It seemed only logical that he should
research the places to visit and things to do on our trip to Tokyo and Kyoto.
So I gave him an assignment.

"I want you to help plan this trip so that we can be sure we do and
see the things you want. Use the Internet and look up attractions and
things to do while we're there," I instructed, knowing that he would enjoy
this kind of research.

I thought I was being a good mom, putting my son in charge of our
experience of a lifetime visiting the land of his dreams. Surely, I thought,
this will make it even more special than we could ever imagine. Well,
it became even more special before we even packed our bags. But I didn't
know it yet. What started as an innocent trip turned into a mine-ridden
jungle of beauty, mystery, and a complex arts and entertainment world
that I never knew existed.

First of all, Japan is exquisite, especially during cherry blossom season,
and we were going when they would be in full bloom. I had visions of the
grandeur seen in the movie *Memoirs of a Geisha*. As with so many other
women who love beautiful men, I have always had a crush on film star
Ken Watanabe, who is, in a word, "fwine." So my fantasy was fueled by
romanticism of an exotic world. It was everything I had imagined, and
some that I had never imagined.

Tokyo and Kyoto are very different from each other. Kyoto, the old capital of Japan, is slow and steeped in ancient culture, known for its peaceful gardens and classic Buddhist temples. We were able to easily move about on foot or ride the bus with other city dwellers. We learned to make origami with professionals at the Kyoto Prefectural International Center and toured Nanzen-ji Temple, a Zen paradise of lush green hills, where we first purified ourselves by cleansing our hands and mouth at the *temizuya* before entering the shrine. We encountered a traditional Japanese wedding and wrote a prayer for Max's body on a wooden prayer tablet called an *ema*.

At the foot of the temple is a marketplace for tourists, where we strolled, stopped to sample *daifuku* (*mochi* with sweet fillings), purchased art by a local artist, and met two geisha who giggled as they posed for a photo with Max in the middle. What Max most wanted was a kimono, a red one. The kimono is part of a tradition for "Coming of Age," a Japanese rite of passage for young men turning twenty years old. It didn't matter that Max was thirteen. He decided he wanted a kimono for his own rite of passage in the fashion of a samurai warrior.

In stark contrast to Kyoto, Tokyo is a growing metropolis with the energy of New York City. It was in this fast-paced city, where red-light districts and an open sex industry thrive, that it would later become apparent how an innocent assignment to research our travel itinerary on the Internet could turn into an introduction to the porn industry.

The highlight of our trip was the Tokyo International Anime Fair, the largest of its kind anywhere in the world, held annually at Tokyo Big Sight, also known as the Tokyo International Exhibition Center, the largest in the country. Unbeknownst to Max, I had purchased tickets to the event that serendipitously coincided with our trip. I had also invited a friend to join us. Takashi and I had worked together in New York and he had moved back home to Tokyo. He met us out in front of the site, and after a warm reunion, we joined the thousands of animators, artists, and fans flocking to their mecca to celebrate everything anime.

Here, all Max's heroes came to life: Naruto, Dragon Ball Z, Sailor Moon, live ninja, and all the other characters in the world of anime. To not be in cosplay—dressing up as your favorite character—meant that you stood out like a piece of fried chicken in a bento box.

Because of the expanse of the exhibition center, we needed a wheelchair for Max to cover nearly a mile of walking. He didn't want to miss any of it. There was no way he would last on his own legs for what I knew was going to be a very long day, judging by the fact that Max had lost all sense of time to a sheer adrenaline high.

For Max, this was bigger than Christmas! It was difficult to navigate amid the hundreds of booths and rows and rows of fantasy games, videos, action figures, plushies, and manga, with cosplay characters roaming among the slow-moving crowd. But with Takashi's help, we did. By the end of the day, Max was delirious with pure joy and exhaustion, and almost buried under his bags of goodies—all that he could manage and all that Takashi and I could hold. For the true *otaku* (anime fan), the biggest bucket on the list was filled! I, now and forever, officially hold the title of being the world's greatest mom.

Afterward, the three of us headed to dinner in the Tsukishima district, about three miles from Tokyo Big Sight. Takashi had chosen one of his favorite hibachi restaurants, where he taught Max how to make *okonomiyaki*, a Japanese pancake, on a grill right at our table. Our server brought bowls of raw ingredients of our choosing for the filling and Max chose shrimp and vegetables. It was as savory as it was fun to make. He also taught him a few more words in Japanese and about the culture. I observed that Max was not just having fun; he was receiving another lesson about the role of men, Japanese style. I noticed how Takashi spoke directly to him and intentionally engaged him in decision making and sought his opinions about the day. After dinner, we went to a popular Japanese dessert restaurant that features specialties made with sweet beans, rich plant sap, and flower nectar. Takashi turned to Max to make the selections for our table, which he was delighted to do. It was not lost on me that such deference was not just due to the fact that this day was for Max; it was an acknowledgment of his role as a man.

At the end of our time together, Takashi's last words to Max were, "You are a good man. It has been an honor to meet you. Remember, you must take care of your mother as she takes care of you. She is a good woman."

Respect between men, and especially of women. It was an important message that would need continual reinforcement, even more than I knew at that moment. My eyes watered as I hugged Takashi goodbye.

"*Sayonara*," Max said as we watched him walk away before we headed into the doors of the Tokyo Metro train to go back to our hotel.

The next day was more anime.

We made a visit to the Akihabara district, which Max had identified as a "MUST DO" stop in our itinerary. Mecca to anime enthusiasts around the world, the small district is filled with museums, cafés, and shops, and every building, sign, menu, and shop window is anime themed.

Here in the heart of Tokyo, Hello Kitty, Pokémon, and vibrant, colorful characters with doe eyes and exotic hair in a variety of colors are everywhere. From end to end of the district filled with multistory buildings, it's an endless sea of anime.

We entered one of the towering buildings. Each floor was crammed so tight with merchandise that only one person at a time could get through an aisle. The first and second floors catered to kids and included the familiar Pokémon characters like Pikachu and Mewtwo, *Yu-Gi-Oh!*'s Yugi, Kaiba, and Pegasus; and Digimon's Tai, Sora, Matt, and Tikei, which have become a part of the American anime craze. We discovered that, as we ascended to higher floors, the characters changed, as did the graphic images, and as did the customers.

Out of curiosity, we chose the sixth floor, thinking that we might find some of the slightly more mature anime that Max was into as a tween. When the elevator doors opened, the lights were low and the room was filled with the glow of video screens and game stations. We could see the tops of heads buried in dozens of game cubicles. The customers were predominantly male. It turns out that we had skipped right ahead into the adult section. Businessmen in suits relaxed with liquor and cigarettes, spending their lunch hour in an anime den.

It was easy to see that it was not a place for ladies. So I quickly pressed the down button, and we jumped back in the elevator, left the building, and called it a day.

We had seen enough.

Max and I thoroughly enjoyed our excursion in the Far East, but he had brought home with him something he enjoyed even more. It was something that I least expected and that I was equally unprepared for. I learned of it a couple of weeks after we returned home.

You cannot imagine the shock when a staff member came into my

office to tell me what he had discovered while performing tech maintenance on the office computer that Max had used to do his Japan research.
You could have peeled me off the ceiling when I saw for myself. The
desktop was covered with anime porn videos downloaded from the Internet. There were more than fifty of them! I clicked on them one at a time
and gasped every time. Each was more lewd than the next. There were
images of animated sex acts that I had never even seen before or could
have imagined. I was mortified. It's been years and I still can't unsee them.

Once that door opened, I couldn't close it. No matter how hard I tried
to shut it, slam it, lean on it, and put obstacles in front of it. I prayed on it,
cried about it, yelled about it, and lost sleep over it. Before that day, I knew
the Internet was a portal through which nefarious people and ideas could
prey on innocent young minds, but I had no idea how pervasive porn is in
society. That even an activity as innocent as doing research for a trip
abroad could be the gateway to unrelenting graphic images of hard-core
quadruple-X pornography. Call me oblivious, naive, or just plain stupid,
but frankly I had never seriously thought about porn as an issue up to this
point in raising my young man—until it snaked into our lives and its
poison crept into his every pore. Prior to this moment, I had thought that
Jessica Rabbit in *Who Framed Roger Rabbit* was over the top.

I remember that when we were young, my three older brothers would
hide *Playboy* magazines under their mattresses, and I used to think that my
brothers were "nasty." Now porn is so prevalent that the television show
To Catch a Predator, based on monitoring everyday chat room conversations
between minors and adults, is a long-running hit show.

Today we have to put parental controls on our televisions and computers. But that is effective only up to the age when our children can finally figure out how to undo our inputs. And while I'm busy being the
porn police, what about when he visits the homes of his friends, when
most of their time is spent doing what—watching television and playing
on computers. Does every other parent take the time to set up or even
care about parental controls? What about the computers in the business
center in the American Airlines Admirals Club? What about the computers in the library? It is too easy. Computers are everywhere and that
means access is everywhere. Then there was that time I got the hotel bill
when we checked out and the room charges showed purchases of adult

movies. Needless to say, I was not only embarrassed but completely livid. I would have never thought that he would risk buying porn at home, then came our cable bill. It even started to show up in his artwork. In his sketches, girls were voluptuous with huge breasts in seductive poses. It drove me nuts!

Every time I confronted Max about it, he pleaded, "I can't help it. I know it's wrong. I promise I won't do it again." And then he did it again. So now, not only was I worrying about the possible psychological damage, but it was costing me hundreds of dollars as well.

I thought about taking his computer away. But that wasn't feasible. He needed it for school. I thought about taking his television away. But because he's an only child and spent most of his days homebound, I questioned the sanity of that idea. Since he's limited by his inability to take part in sports and outdoor activities, then would I be his only source of entertainment? I had to admit that was definitely not feasible. Neither of us would survive that level of dependency. So I took away his video games for a while. That worked only a little . . . okay, maybe for one day. I was vexed. I was losing a battle that I could not win. Porn had taken over our lives. I couldn't control it, stop it, or stand it.

It was time to seek outside counsel. I called the mentors. "Okay, I need y'all to help me out here," I pleaded. "Max is addicted to porn. I've tried everything I know to do."

Apparently, I was overreacting. In fact, the mentors seemed to think it was slightly amusing. I was flabbergasted.

"So he's discovering himself. It's normal" was all I heard. That didn't make it any less shocking to me.

It seems men and porn have a relationship that transcends the female stomach for tolerance. If some experts say that men think about sex thirty-four times a day, it seemed that Max thought about it every waking minute. I swear, I'll never understand men, and that's exactly why I needed the mentors for this particular phase in our journey. They were there for Max as well as for my own sanity.

Uncle Kevin approached the "porn" conversation from a completely different angle. He took Max shopping. Before they left, he made clear to me that this was not shopping the way women shop.

"What does that mean?" I asked.

"Men only shop for a particular item, not as an activity, so it's not really shopping. It's about completing a mission." It was his way of letting me know that he was on a mission for Max.

"C'mon, Max. Let's go," said Uncle Kevin. "Let's get you hooked up with some cool kicks." Max was definitely down for that and threw on his coat to head out the door on his way to fresh new Nikes. I learned later what Kevin was really up to when Max came home with a second bag of fresh new boxers and briefs.

"Underwear?" I asked Kevin. "What's up with that?" I pictured Max's full drawer and thought, "Uh-oh, what did I miss?"

"It's important. A man needs his comfort," he explained.

The puzzled look on my face indicated I needed further explanation, so he went on. "I actually buy two kinds. It's a mix of comfort and keeping the package in place. If I am traveling or it's a regular day, I wear loose boxers. If I'm going out anywhere I wear more form-fitting ones to keep everything in place. Let's say the wind blows and you get aroused—you don't want any pervy imprint impression sticking out of your pants."

"Oh" was all I could say.

All the while Uncle Kevin was explaining to me the nuances of protecting his jewels, Max had a sheepish grin on his face. Impatient to end the uncomfortable conversation with his mother about a man's private parts, he interjected to change the subject.

"Look at my new shoes!"

"Yes, nice shoes!" My words dripped in insincerity. I was still absorbing the whole lesson I had just learned about my son. He's growing up! What else might I miss?

Thank goodness Uncle Kevin was looking out for a little brother. I bought a lot of briefs after that conversation.

From then on, their conversations with Max about porn were more about his level of consumption than whether it was acceptable. While I was freaking out, they assured him that he was normal. And me too.

"You need to relax," Uncle Kevin told me. "Men do porn. It's normal."

They explained to Max that there was a time and a place for it. They let him know how important it was that he did not let it interfere with his responsibility to take care of business. And they emphasized that women are to be respected and not to be treated as sex objects. However, they certainly did not think it was cool that he was spending money, especially his mom's money, on porn.

Having unplugged the hysteria and removed the Amber-alert level of what I thought was an emotional and psychological kidnapping, they reeled both of us back to earth by continuing a healthy, ongoing dialogue with him about the importance of responsible and respectful roles and relationships between men and women. They were calm, pragmatic, and sensible about it, while I was losing my mind in a futile attempt to cleanse the mind and soul of my innocent man-child. Apparently, he didn't need a mind cleanse, and I needed to get a reality check. I settled down and began to warm to the idea that I needed to accept that my son was a boy no longer.

His collective dads also advised me, "He needs to develop some other interests."

Uncle Chris suggested volunteer work. So we found some. Max served at a local community center delivering hot meals to seniors at least two days a week. He was so good at it that he earned the Volunteer of the Year Award. But it wasn't that easy. I would later learn that it was also the place where he could find a computer to surf Internet porn while he waited for the van driver. To this day, I am certain that everybody, or at least someone, knew that Max was the reason for the dirty browser history. It seemed that for every upside, there was a downside somewhere. Sigh. My head hurts every time I think about it.

Uncle Jay came by more often to pick Max up to go to his house to play video games in his big surround-sound game room. And on a couple of Saturdays, he came to see Max at his horseback-riding therapy program. The attention and refocusing on other activities he enjoyed, especially with a mentor, did help to lift the spell that left him lost in the world of porn.

Then, to add to my blood pressure uptick, at about this same time, Max began to think about girls romantically. *Oh, Lawdy! This is all I need,* I thought. The mentors remained proactive and engaged, realizing that they needed to be on alert. It was Uncle Jay who had showed up at the door armed with condoms after he'd learned about the incident with the sitter's niece, so I knew Max was carrying them in his wallet. Max didn't know that I was regularly sneaking a peek inside to count them.

Porn may be a slippery slope, but forming relationships with real girls is more like cliff jumping.

Max was consumed with the feeling of inadequacy and that he was not lovable since he didn't have a girlfriend, especially when there appeared to be so much coupling in the school hallways and in the after-school clubs. He joined an anime club that met in the library, which to him was fertile hunting ground. Any girl who shared his passion for anime is the girl for him! But the reality was that any girl who was nice to him, who stood up for him with a simple "leave him alone" hurled at a bully, or who promised "I'll sit with you" at lunch, even if it was just to be nice, Max would hang hope on the slight possibility that maybe, just maybe, he'd say, "she actually likes me." It seemed that every week he would tell me about a new "girlfriend."

"I made a new friend today. We sat together at lunch," he'd say, making it seem like it was a huge deal.

Of course, when I probed just a little, the truth was that she'd simply acknowledged his existence and thus he ceased to be invisible. Therefore, he felt validated as an acceptable person, or at least not as repulsive as the bullies made him feel about his physical disability.

"I'll never get a girlfriend," Max told me one day. My heart broke—again. The pain in his eyes riddled through the downward curve of his mouth, into his slumped shoulders, and seemed to deepen the crouch in his legs. "All they see is my disability."

But by the time he entered high school, I could see a change. "Girls" became one girl in particular.

We were all excited about Max's first date. He called each mentor to announce that he was going to see a movie with Margaret, the first girl he introduced to us as his girlfriend.

Uncle Kevin advised him, "Take it slow now, Max. Be a gentleman. Whatever you do, no matter how much you want to, don't touch her unless she makes the first move."

Uncle Jay dropped by the house the day before Max's date just to make sure he had enough money.

"Here, put this in your wallet. Make sure you get her whatever she wants," he told Max, slipping him a fifty-dollar bill.

"I can't believe you came all the way over just to give him some money. It was that important?" I asked, somewhat in awe that it was that big a deal.

"Well, I just wanted to be sure he was set up right. I want to make sure he makes the right impression," he said, winking at me. Then said to Max, "You got to make sure you don't come up short."

While Uncle Jay, the financial wealth expert, was making sure Max could treat her right, I found myself sneaking into Max's wallet to check if the condoms that Uncle Jay had given him were still there. I wondered if Max still had the same feelings about using them as he had when he first learned how to from Uncle Jay.

But I wasn't really very concerned about him having sex with Margaret. She was the kind of girl any mother would trust—a little overweight, self-conscious, somewhat motherly herself, protective. I could see why he liked her.

When he got back from his date, it seemed that he had aged a year. Women can do that—turn a boy into a man in an instant just by giving him her personal attention. He seemed to walk a little taller.

"Did you enjoy yourself?" I asked.

With a smile that said it all, he responded simply, "We had a good time."

I did not want to invade his privacy, but I really did want to know if he went in for the kiss. So had to ask, "Did you kiss her good night?"

"Oh, Mom!" and that's all he said. That's all he would give me. Darn!

Later that night I could hear his muffled voice on the phone with one of his uncles. A great sense of relief with a hint of joy washed over me. He was venturing into relationships with women and would not have to go it alone on a path that would be littered with broken promises and hurtful words mixed with bewildering smiles and "accidental" touches in hallways.

After his date high came the low just a couple of weeks later. "I need a break." There it was—the first heartbreak. Margaret, straightforward as she was, delivered the infamous "we need to talk" that left him completely lost and dumbfounded.

"What did I do?" he moaned. Then, just as girls often do, she suddenly decided that she liked him again.

Eventually and after many conversations with the uncles about the bewildering world of girls, Max was over it and moved on to doing what he loves most, drawing characters and writing stories. Margaret became a new character in the community he was building in his creative work and in real life—a community of people with flaws and feelings.

Then he met Lucy. Though Uncle Kevin had warned him to be careful of the "tricky" ones, Max fell for Lucy, any mother's worst fear when it comes to her son. Every story he told me about something she said or did caused my brow to furrow. Call it a mother's instinct, but I knew she was bad news. When Max told me they were going to the prom together, I wasn't thrilled, but he was so happy that he didn't have to go alone that I didn't protest too much.

"Is everyone going with a date?" I asked, to see if I could find a way out of this situation. "No, but I am," Max said proudly.

There was no out. Even though it was cool that his classmates were not taking dates, he was determined that he would have one. So when he was adamant that he was going with Lucy on his arm, all I could say with an insincere smile was, "That's great, Max. Let's get you a suit."

Usually, Max HATES to gussy up and recoils at the mere suggestion that he change a shirt that doesn't match his plaid shorts. Yeah, that's kinda my fault. Gap has a particular pant size that has always fit him perfectly, and the folks at Gap love plaid shorts. So maybe, not my fault. It's Gap's fault. They seem to think we all love plaid. I think they would make a fortune if they ventured into ethnic-influenced patterns. (If they do, it's in writing here. They owe me big-time.)

But this evening Max cleaned up real nice in his crisp black suit and tie. We had spent hours looking at pictures trying to decide between collar types: the spread, the forward point, the cutaway, the button-down, the club, and the tab. He decided on the button-down with the help of the Brooks Brothers salesman. They are very good at their job. He paid special attention to the fact that Max's pants had a difficult measure because of the way Max stands with his knees bent. It is extremely difficult to get that hem of the pant just right at the top of the shoe.

Uncle Kevin sent him a video of how to tie a tie, because I don't know how. After several phone calls for instruction and failed attempts to tie a tie with a mirror view, we gave up and went with a classic, simple bow tie. This turned out to be a really smart move, not only because it saved us an hour of frustration, but also because Max really loved the idea that he didn't actually have to button down his collar. That saved another fifteen minutes of time and an evening of tugging at his neck.

All tucked and tied, he made the perfect beau. He even agreed to pose for pictures, which he HATES even more than getting dressed up. Clothes have never been a good experience for Max, especially those with zippers and buttons. Everyday clothes for him are generally restrictive and uncomfortable. Putting them on is exhausting, and after all that work, in his eyes, the results are never worth the effort. Although he is extremely handsome, all he sees is his "broken" (his own word) body, and all he feels is the unwavering pain and fatigue of his legs. He refuses to use a wheelchair because he says he doesn't need one. Instead, every decision to get dressed and to go out, to change out of his favorite loungewear, and leave the comfort of his "boy" cave at home, is measured by how many steps he will have to take between point A and point B to stop and rest, and how long he must bear to wear them. For Max, walking is like sprinting is for the average person. Fabric that does not breathe means he doesn't much either. Being sweaty and constricted in a fancy suit is nothing short of torture. However, for prom night, pain aside, this was a moment that he would not miss.

I chauffeured him, corsage in hand, over to pick up his date at her home and took the celebratory tux-and-gown photos for all posterity, with the goal of capturing that perfect one commemorating the moment that goes in your scrapbook, that you'll turn the page to over and over and share with family and friends forever. You'll either love it or hate it, but hope that at least you'll be able to laugh about it one day. No matter what, Max looked fabulous!

I was so proud to see him carry himself so gallantly, which I had never seen him do before. As he approached her, he extended his hand to take hers in a warm embrace. I heard him tell her, "You look beautiful." She giggled and said, "Thank you." They both could not stop blushing and grinning at each other. I hopped out of the car to take pictures. The lighting was perfect. They stood side by side, their arms joined to form a perfect V between them. It was, dare I say it, the cutest awkward pose that I had ever seen in real life. It reminded me of a scene out of *The Andy Griffith Show* with Barney and Thelma Lou. Just as Uncle Lawrence had modeled for him, Max moved quickly to open the car door for her and held her arm to be sure she was safely inside. Once he got in to join her, it was off to the party center that had been just as elaborately dressed up as the guests coming there for the dance. Filled with pride, I watched him walk away into the early dusk, a handsome young prince escorting his princess, with his signature gait of a dip to the side. The sight took my breath away as I thought to myself, "He's not my little boy anymore." It was bittersweet.

But of course, with romance there is always drama. Turns out Lucy decided to go to the prom with Max to make another boy jealous. When that boy showed up, she left Max out in the cold. She knew she was wrong and told him not to tell his mother what happened. I was so angry I wanted to drive over to her house and rip that beautiful corsage that I had carefully chosen for Max to give her right off her dress. Max seemed to take it better than I expected he would. It's a good thing that Max so loves to dance, because that's what he did the whole night—without her! He showed off his moves until he sweated his tie and jacket off and was the hit of the party.

The mentors wanted to hear all about Max's prom night. I sent photos and Max called each of them to provide the captions and fill them in with the details.

Uncle Kevin laughed when he heard the story, as he always does about life's swerves and curves.

"The most important thing is you had a good time, man, and you didn't let her get you down. She may have disrespected you, but in the end, you showed her the respect that you deserve. You kept your cool, enjoyed your evening, and made sure she got home. That's all you could do. You're a good man. I'm proud of you," he said.

I told Max to think about it this way: "Of all the others she may have had to choose from, she chose you to make another boy jealous. You have something that made you the best choice to make someone else envious." That made him smile.

I also told him about my own prom, which was not without drama, as I'm sure is the case for many other prom nights. Because I was not allowed to see the guy I was secretly dating at the time, I went with a "nice guy" my mother approved of. The only difference is that I don't think that my prom date ever knew it—until now, if he's reading this book. Oops.

When I shared with Max what he perceived as a jaw-dropping

confession from his perfect, virtuous mom, he shook his head and said, "Girls are harsh." I'm not sure if I made things better or did more damage. To assuage his fears, I told him, "You'll meet lots of nice girls because you are a nice person. You'll know she's nice when you want to bring her home to meet your family. If she's the right girl, you'll know it because she'll fit right into your family and your community. Trust us, we'll let you know that's she's right for you."

According to Uncle Jay, God will too.

Love is divine providence.

"The first thing, to be honest, is that you have to be ready to receive your bride. If you aren't prepared, you'll mess it up. You have to be ready to see her when God sends her to you," Uncle Jay testified.

"How did you know she was the one?" Max asked.

"First, she was beautiful. I took the time to know her. She was able to accept my flaws and not just the best parts of me. She's also someone who doesn't open up to just anybody. I wish I could say it was love at first sight, but it was a process. We dated for three months and found we had a lot in common. I was dating other women at the time, but I saw that she was different and I wanted to know her better. So I had to get rid of the distractions and spend time to get to really know her. If you see what you want, you have to work for it, like everything in life. You have to be ready. What made me feel confident that she was the right one is that she accepts me for who I am. In life, people change, so it is also important that we embrace that change. We dated for two and a half years before we got married. The key thing is to take your time," he said.

"Besides accepting your flaws, what else do you love about her?" Max asked.

"She's creative, the opposite of me, so she brings a different perspective. She has great intuition, and that's important, because I can misjudge people sometimes. She's funny and we laugh all the time," he said.

"What were you looking for?" I chimed in, eager to hear the details for my own wonderment on the topic of what men look for in a woman.

"She wasn't out to be seen. She's a homebody. She wasn't trying to date me for what she thought I had. She's not a material person. She's most excited when buying furniture for the house to make our home comfortable. So while I'm out trying to make it happen, it's nice to come home to a nice environment that I can relax in," he said.

Max looked straight at me with a glint in his eye when he asked Uncle Jay, "What did your mother think of her?"

Uncle Jay chuckled. "My mom and her get along great. They spend more time together than we do." He chuckled again. "And you know, if you want to get to me, you have to get to my mother. However, my mom never voiced her opinion because of her own mistakes. She is an exceptional woman. She showed me what love is from the fact that she cooked every day and made sure everything was taken care of, that I was taken care of. That's very attractive to me in my own wife because of my mom's influence on me.

"Before I met my wife, I used to date women to be a power couple with multiple degrees between us. But I learned that doesn't really matter. It's not what makes a person. It took some time for me to understand that. I learned a lot from my first marriage. I had to experience the world with my own eyes, look inwardly, and think about my values and what over time I would have done differently.

"Most important, God is the leading cause in my life. When I made that change, the Lord sent me who He wanted me to have. The first institution that God made is not the church. It is marriage. It goes beyond the woman. It goes to God. The wisdom of the Bible is in Proverbs, Ecclesiastes, and King Solomon. Jacob worked for fourteen years to get Rachel and had to go through Leah, his first wife, to be ready for Rachel. I relate to that story," he said.

Max was visibly agitated and interrupted with his infinite wisdom of a teenager longing for that first real love. He declared in full righteousness, "When you get married, you should stay married. You should love each other no matter what."

Uncle Jay, slightly affronted, returned patiently, "Yes, you are right, Max. You should love each other no matter what. I'm not saying you shouldn't stay married. But relationships are difficult. It takes work every day. We disagree every day. We also know that we are committed to each other and that it is bigger than both of us. And I have been faithful since the day I met her."

After that remarkable love story, Max wanted to hear how each of his mentors met their mates and when they knew she was "the one." I was also curious, and so I was invited to listen to each of them tell his story. I knew I could learn something valuable about men and their view of women and relationships too.

Uncle Chris was eager to talk about his bride and provided a perspective about his relationship with Ramona that resembled what I most wanted in my next one.

Love is a partnership.

Uncle Chris began, "What hammered it home for me was when I took her to meet my stepfather. You see, I am not the obedient young son he had hoped for. I was serious about my convictions and my arguments. But he never respected them. Especially since he had seen so much damage in my previous two marriages. He just never backed me on any of it and just laid a lot of guilt stuff on me, as usual. She challenged him on that and held him accountable for what he was saying. She stood up for me and that really, really impressed me. She's got my back. That was a big moment. I recognized that she would be a good partner. So, my dad, he's scared of her now," he said, laughing. "Now he's more inclined to keep his opinions to himself. Nobody had ever been in my corner like that before. But of course, I kind of knew she was the one even before I took her home to meet my dad. In fact, I kind of knew it when I first met her."

"When did you first meet her?" Max asked.

"We met through a mutual friend who owns a hair salon. I was hanging out at the salon one day when that friend told me, 'I have a friend who wants to talk with you about the mental health system in Hawaii.' I had spent a good deal of my life on Maui. It's where I began my career as a community organizer. So she thought I might be able to help her friend. But she really was up to something else, I found out later."

"What friend did she want you to meet? Where was Auntie Ramona?" Max was confused.

"Her friend was Ramona. Ramona is a child psychologist, and at the time, she was fighting for the rights of underserved children, pioneering in the work on behalf of the juvenile mental health system in Chicago. She had traveled to Hawaii a couple of times on business to do some work on Maui, and when she arrived on the island, she was treated with "brown privilege," something she had never experienced before. When she was on line at a car rental place at the airport, the agent called her out of the line to come over to serve her first and proceeded to treat her with deference."

Uncle Chris recounted to us what Ramona had told him: "'She started asking me what other additional benefits I would like and didn't charge me extra for any of them. That has never happened to me before. Once you have that kind of experience, you want more.'"

He went on, "So, after that, she wanted to find out more about the mental health system in Hawaii, and find a way to make it better, and find a way to live there. So our mutual friend thought it was a good idea to introduce us."

"So what happened when you met her?" Max asked.

"Well, I was instantly struck by how attractive she was. But, aside from her being a beautiful woman, I was impressed by how brilliant she was, that she has a PhD in child psychology, and that she was focused on social responsibility. I am a community organizer. It was our shared values that brought us together. So I was moved when she spoke on my behalf to my dad, but before that, it was her social consciousness. Together, we're on a mission to create significant change in our community. We're a team. But she's the star of the show and I'm her sideman. In other words, I keep the lights on so she has the platform on which to shine," he explained. "I try to make it not about my ego."

"What does that mean?" Max asked him.

Uncle Chris put it in context with an example of what being a team player means to him. "You're too young to know of him, but one of the players I've always admired is Jerry Kramer. He used to be an offensive lineman with the Green Bay Packers. I'll never forget that game when he threw a block right at the end zone that won the game. I take as much pride in being the guy who throws the block rather than catching the ball and running the touchdown. I don't have to be the star."

Max was struck by this new revelation about a man who loomed large as a star in his eyes, and I marveled at Uncle Chris's humble spirit as he continued: "I've spent my life as a leader and an organizer. The ego part of me does rise up from time to time for not getting credit. Believe me, lying in the dust is not easy. My father used to say, 'You have to hold your fire until it's time to pull the trigger.' As a good partner to my wife, I had to learn how to be in the background, leading from behind."

"Wow! So she makes all the decisions?" asked Max with amazement.

"Well, no, that's not what I mean. We have discussed our roles and we are doing this on purpose. The world needs activists on the front lines and needs women to lead the way. Strong women who are on the front lines need a man to be a man to hold down the fort. So I hold down the fort. That's it," he finished.

Wow! Now, to be honest, for as long as I'd known him after all these years, I had not realized how truly lucky my dear friend Ramona really is.

"How can I find a man just like you?" I asked Chris.

"But you mean much taller and thinner, right?" he said, laughing.

"Nope, doesn't matter. Any man with a heart like yours is exactly what I'm looking for. As long as he believes in God and acts like it, I'm good," I said.

"You just be you. One day, if he's lucky enough, he'll find you," he said to me.

That made me feel good for a minute, but . . . well, you know, it will feel better when I do find THE ONE.

A warrior fit for his queen.

When Max asked Uncle Lawrence, "How did you know she was the right one for you?" referring to his wife of more than thirty years, his response was almost poetic.

"I felt rapt in her presence, and it lingered even when she was gone.

She was always with me then, and she still is, even when she's not around," he began.

"I knew two or even three years before I asked her to marry me that she was my life partner. I remember walking alone on my college campus on a bright, sunny day, and it just hit me all of a sudden that we were made for each other. I felt so good, so loved, and carefree, all at once. But I also knew I wasn't yet ready to ask her to be my wife."

"When did you know you were ready?" asked Max.

Uncle Lawrence paused to carefully think about his answer before he spoke, and then laid it on us.

"There are two significant moments when you know she is the one. The first may be the moment you discover that you are in love. The second is when you know you are ready to commit to that love. That could take one day, months, or sometimes years. For me, it took several years. Like a warrior who has chosen his mate, I felt there are certain demands and achievements to prove to yourself and to your mate that you are prepared to be a husband and potential father. I dare not ask a queen to be my bride unless I do everything required to be her king."

Max really liked that last part. I did too. "That's beautiful, Uncle Lawrence. A king and his queen," he mused out loud. I could hear Uncle Lawrence's smile through the phone.

"Well, first I had to become a king," Uncle Lawrence said. "When I became serious about my career and could provide the kind of support for my chosen queen that she deserved, that's when it started to come together for me. I had to go through the process to reach true warrior status, not just with her, but also with her family. It was important that her family would be proud. That's why it took five years. By the time we were ready to be married, I had a lot of juice with her family. We had friendship, kinship, love, and partnership. The whole village was supportive of us as a couple. That was important to me. I had proved my worth. It was a marriage that was talked about, encouraged, and celebrated. My brother gave our toast at our wedding. He said it best when he asked everyone to raise a glass to 'a couple who had first developed a great friendship,' and added that ours is 'a marriage that would not only survive but thrive and get better and stronger with age.' That meant the world to me. And it has.

Our marriage has gotten stronger, and I look forward to spending every day until the end together," he said.

Wow! Just wow! How many people have that?

I want to marry my best friend.

Uncle Kevin says he got married when he was too young. They lasted only a couple of years and had a daughter, to whom he remains devoted. More than twenty years later, when I asked him why he still hasn't found the right woman, he said, "I'm still looking for my best friend. I want more kids, so she has to be a good wife and mother, but first I want her to be my best friend.

"I was very young when I got married for the first time—too young. We were dating at seventeen, and I fell madly in love with her because she had a job! That was a big deal in my neighborhood. Most of the women I knew—in fact, most of the people I knew—were on welfare or public assistance. My friends were impressed with her. They would say, 'She's got a straight-up job? Wow!' We were married by the time we were twenty-one and had a child right away. We were forced to grow up quickly, and over the next few years we grew apart. When we were dating, we both had big dreams. But once we had a child, things changed, as they usually do. She chose to set aside her dreams, and I continued to pursue mine. At least, that's how I saw it. I would be out hustling as a photographer, and sometimes that meant I wasn't home by six o'clock. So we would argue about the long hours I would spend working while she stayed home to take care of our daughter, even though I believed I was doing it for all of us. Sometimes we would argue about why she wasn't going ahead to get her degree that she said she wanted. I would have supported her doing that, no matter what it would take. For her, that meant sacrificing raising our daughter. It got so we would just argue about the smallest things. I understood where she was coming from. But I also knew I couldn't change. I also knew that I deeply loved her. But I learned that love doesn't conquer everything."

Max could not hold his tongue at this point and burst in with, "Yes, it does! You just have to love each other enough, and then you can stay together no matter what."

With his typical style of humor in an awkward conversation, Uncle Kevin mused, "Personally, I think it should be against the law to get married before you're thirty. When you first meet someone, you meet their representative. By the time you're thirty you should have learned that."

I had to laugh because he's right.

Back to the point, he added with a touch of humility, "Seriously, it takes time to get to really know the real person and to develop a truly honest relationship. I'm still learning about myself as well. I have to be honest with myself before I can be honest with someone else."

His confession that "I have to be honest with myself" hit me right between heartbeats. Had I been honest with myself before I said yes when my husband popped the question, I would have definitely not. Had I been honest with myself, I would have had to acknowledge that I was vulnerable and in search of a rescue rather than a life partner and best friend, as Uncle Kevin had described. I wanted to be rescued from being single. I was tired of taking on the world on my own and wanted my hero to walk alongside me. Even on my wedding day, I knew it was more than just wedding jitters that were giving me cause for concern that I was making a mistake. I knew that there was so much missing information. I know of that out-of-body experience that many describe when you sort of watch yourself doing something and know that it's not really you. There I was, in front of family and friends, an actor in a beautiful scene, pretending, devoid of my own emotional and spiritual truth. But there was one reason for which it was meant to be. That reason is Max, who has led me to where I am today.

After listening to the testimonials of each of these four men, whom I admire, trust, and love most in the world, my confidence was restored that I will finally also know when I have found the right man. He is someone who has been preparing all his life to find me, his queen, his soul mate, his partner, and his best friend. After all, that one very special man, my warrior, will have to check in with my village for final approval.

Fortunately, Max will have the benefit of the love lessons learned from the brave men before him who have been trampled and who have triumphed, and who continue to face down the fear of the unknown in search of the holy grail, the right woman.

"Be patient. Love will come find you," I promised Max. "For now, just focus on honing your craft. Become the best at what you want to do. When you do that, you will stand out. You will be successful, and you will have your choice of any girl in the world. You will be turning them away. They will see your passion, your drive, and your special gift. There is nothing more attractive than a man who is confident about himself and his future. Nothing. Like Walter Mitty, in the end, you'll get the girl!"

Chapter 5

Warrior Rising

Over the next five years of Max's Black Mitzvah, from ages fourteen through eighteen, one-on-one visits with his mentors, phone check-ins, interventions, and the assurance of their support provided a life raft filled with the essentials he needed to survive adolescence. Max needed to learn to define for himself who he was and what he stood for. He needed to learn his purpose in service to community. He needed to learn that in order to love others, he first had to love himself.

Growing up with almond-brown skin, hazel eyes, and a different gait, Max would come to recognize that not everyone lives by the Golden Rule. He was difficult to define or put in a box, and so it seemed he, more than others, would need to demand to be allowed to do things lest he be underestimated or overlooked. The world was not ready for him. So he had to ready himself for an unempathetic world. The playing field is far from equal and rife with division. It can be confusing, scary, and painful. However, with love and encouragement, Max was able to find kindness, opportunity, and abundance as well.

In their teen years, young men are especially impressionable and vulnerable. Young men of color are at higher risk, as these years can also be lethal without the kind of investment it takes to ensure they have the fortitude to succeed in life.

Max needed to acquire stock in his self-worth to fully comprehend, believe in, and realize his full potential. And it was on this one particular issue that his mentors were the most focused and vigilant. It was not just important for Max—it was important for their own investment. Who Max will become is a manifestation of their efforts. Max is forever a member of their tribe. A tribe looks out for its own.

Each lesson took time, takes time. He had so much to learn.

Lesson 7: Only you can define who you are.

"Am I black?"

Max's question came out of the blue and hit me like a Tennessee tornado.

"Forgive me if I lose my chill, but what on earth do you mean!" I said a bit too aggressively.

The hurt look on his face made me change my tone and turn it into a sincere question that I really needed the answer to.

"Why are you asking me that?" I asked as sensitively as I could. I could see that he was feeling wounded and that if I wasn't careful I might just be throwing salt on it.

Because of his light complexion and thick, curly hair texture, he told me, other kids seemed to think he was "mixed," as they say in the South. One time, when he was in elementary school, he told me that some kids insisted that he was Puerto Rican because he couldn't be just black. So we had an opportunity then to talk about our proud heritage, which he seemed to embrace. This went on for a couple of years. From time to time, he would mention that someone asked about his ethnicity, and we would shrug it off as a silly question. However, I could sense that it really began to bother him. He lost a bit of his swagger, becoming sidetracked by others' preoccupation with his racial identity.

"Is your father white?" kind of knocked him for a loop.

Most of his friends knew who I was and so there was no question there. Despite his common sense, he was asked this often enough that he started to question himself until he finally asked me one day, "Is my father white?" This had gone far enough. It was time to end this plainly black-and-white issue (pun intended).

"No. Now you know your father is not white, just light. Baby, you know that, given our ancestry, black people come in many shades and yours is latte," I explained. "Don't be confused by other folks' confusion. You know who you are."

To be sure, one by one, we went through our circle of friends, all of whom come in a range of pigments and hues, personalities and belief systems, asking him what shade of beautiful is each. It is maddening that we live in the kind of society that would provoke a vulnerable young man trying to find his own place in the world to question his own heritage.

He was increasingly annoyed by the offensive questions and could not understand why it mattered what ethnicity he is, or how old he is, or whether he liked sports or not, or why he didn't eat meat. Who cares? He had already gone through years of strangers mistaking him for a girl because of his locs, which hung down to his waist.

"I don't care what they think. I know who I am!" he had always maintained.

But questioning his uniqueness, his identity, was becoming an issue that he wanted to make clear once and for all: "I am a black man!"

Truth be told, it was a strangely welcome distraction from the "disability" label that he had to bear every day and everywhere. He had long grown weary of being asked, "Why do you walk like that?" However, he was learning that as a black man, he would have to come to grips with yet another layer of disadvantage that he would have to overcome in his journey to become a righteous, respectful, and responsible man.

Like most every parent, it has been my mission to raise Max to be proud of himself, his family, and his heritage. Our home is filled with black art by Charles White, Elizabeth Catlett, Samella Lewis, Lois Mailou Jones, Romare Bearden, Jacob Lawrence, John Biggers, Twin, and many other iconic artists who vividly portray the beauty, strength, and endurance of people of color. A portrait of the two of us and Barack Obama with his hand on Max's shoulder is a centerpiece of pride in our living room. Just below it hangs one of Nelson Mandela's rare works, a lithograph called the *Struggle Series*. Photos with family and friends surround us with the warmth of beautiful moments reflecting our values and traditions in a celebration of weddings and graduations, family gatherings, and portraits of profiles in courage. Pictures of my mom and dad, Max's grandparents, are the first images you see displayed in honor on the table in the hall at the entrance to our home.

Books, in various stages of being read, are in every room, with titles such as *Because of Them We Can* by Eunique Jones Gibson; the award-winning trilogy *March* by John Lewis; *African Ark: The People and Ancient Cultures of Ethiopia and the Horn of Africa*, an extraordinary photo documentary by Angela Fisher, Carol Beckwith, and Graham Hancock; *The African Americans* by Henry Louis Gates Jr.; and *Dreams from My Father* by Barack Obama—just to name a few of the hundreds of black literature books in our library.

Every birthday and every Christmas, Max gets a new special book from me. He developed a passion for reading inside the fantastical universe of the Harry Potter books. (Thank you, J. K. Rowling, for giving him a love for the power of the wonderful, magical world of great storytelling.) He voraciously consumed coming-of-age books, including the Maximum Ride series by the prolific author James Patterson, and later Paulo Coelho's *The Alchemist*. One year, I gave him Hill Harper's *Letters to a Young Brother*, which he has read and reread several times. The last book I gave him was *The Black Count* by Tom Reiss. It is the story of the real Count of Monte Cristo, General Thomas-Alexandre Dumas, the highest-ranking man of African descent ever in a European army. I knew Max would like the cover jacket featuring the handsome, dark swashbuckling hero brandishing a sword astride a rearing stallion. His personal library also includes the catalogs of works by two of his favorite artists, Kehinde Wiley and Jean-Michel Basquiat. And because he loves the storytelling anime art of Hayao Miyazaki, he has *The Art of Howl's Moving Castle* and *The Art of Ponyo*, his two favorite animated films. I don't care whether he reads them now or later; I thought it important to surround him with knowledge and access to diverse existential thought, creative expression, and ideas.

When he was six years old, he led the Martin Luther King Jr. Day parade with the mayor and his wife. When he was eight years old, he took African drumming lessons with a group of men who wore locs like his own, as did some of the young girls learning African dance to the pounding rhythm, which made their locs swing in sync with their swaying hips and feet.

When he was eight years old, we began loc'ing together. It is something that I had wanted to do for myself for a very long time. I have a lot of hair, and it became too much to care for with my limited time between taking care of Max and running a business. I needed a solution, I needed freedom, and I was finally ready. I was ready to begin my hair transformation to embrace my own self-identity. And Max was ready too.

As with those who have gone before me, I learned that loc'ing is an emotional and spiritual journey. As a woman who has built a successful career and business in the corporate world, I had to reach the point when I had complete confidence to go fully natural. At the time we began loc'ing, it was long before natural hairstyles were as popular as they are today, with braids, flat twists, puffs, finger coils, mohawks, and faux hawks.

But for Max it was easy. He appreciated that it eliminated the challenge of daily grooming. For five years, Max wore his locs at different lengths, from waist long to a short cut with a fade at the back inspired by the little boy who played Simba in *The Lion King* on Broadway.

As anyone with locs knows, maintenance involves long hours at the hair salon, which is a sacred and safe space for our community. In any black hair salon, the conversation is bound to get real, as sister girlfriends and menfolk are known for gut-busting honesty. Around midday, the delivery of home-cooked soul food from some lucky local caterer or neighborhood restaurant means a break for a meal with a proper blessing for the locticians, patrons, and folks just hangin'. The salon is the hub of time and family management steeped in black values and tradition.

These black-owned and -operated establishments are among the few places where Max has felt entirely comfortable and able to be himself and express his views openly and without judgment with people who look like him. These touchstones in our community are where we would receive gentle schooling from men and women who, just like him, were trying to make a way for themselves in the world. The mother whose daughter would show up to the salon with two kids to pick up twenty dollars to run to the grocery store, the sister who came to deliver the car she'd borrowed because now her boyfriend could run her back home, the doctor who had to attend a dinner in her honor the next evening, the young man going for a job interview the following day, the college student whose hair had grown too long and who was tired of his mom complaining how "you need to look like you belong to somebody"—we all are in this thing together.

I was relaxing on the sofa with my feet up, my head buried in the Sunday *New York Times* Style section when Max interrupted me, "Mom, I think I want to cut off my locs." His pronouncement from out of the blue caused me to pause mid-sentence from the New Age perspective on self-empowerment I was reading, to perhaps get another take on the subject firsthand from my own son. I shut the paper so I could peer at him over my reading glasses. "What?" I asked, as I sat up and put my feet on the floor to give him my full attention. This was no small matter. After five years of growth, maintenance, and the fact that our story was literally woven into every coil of his hair, it seemed to me that this decision to cut his locs required deep reflection. This was akin to a spiritual transformation. "Yeah, I think I'm ready for a change," he said. I let his statement hang in the air while I drew a deep long breath and then finally asked, "From what?" I was relieved when he said, "I want my hair like Uncle Lawrence." My heart smiled. Then he added, as if to explain, "Did you know he and I are the same?" "In what way?" I asked. I was glad I was already sitting down when he responded, "He has a learning difference like me. He uses Touch Math too." I had never even heard of Touch Math before his second-grade teacher taught Max this tool to master basic math skills using tactile sensory. I was flabbergasted to only now be learning that my brother, who earned his masters in mechanical engineering, needed multisensory learning tools. "He's cool," Max said with an ocean of admiration. "Logan cool or Morpheus cool?" I asked him, referencing his favorite superheroes from the X-Men and *The Matrix*. "Hmmm, that's a hard one," he said. After careful consideration, "Morpheus cool," he decided. Then with wisdom beyond his years, he said in his warrior voice, "Mom, cutting my locs will never sever our cosmic connection, not even the mightiest sword could do that. You know that, right?" No words could express what only a hug could. At fourteen years old, he wanted to identify with one of the men he had come to trust most, and whom he clearly related to in a way that I could never have imagined. It was something only the two of them could understand. I could not have been more proud of both of them at that moment. Excelsior!

Though jubilant at the thought that Max saw himself in a black man who had overcome adversity to rise as a superstar, his news was bitter-sweet. I felt a wave of melancholy rise up in me with the realization that he was transitioning from being my momma's boy into his own man. After years of our loc'ing together, he had chosen to unlock his own self-identity.

When he decided it was time for him to choose his own look, with it came a change from the hair salon to the barbershop. From the moment he walked in the door, his eyes began scanning the walls of photos of men of every hue and color of black and brown, with perfectly sculpted heads and goatees, brimming with unique looks ready for the choosing to suit your own style and personality. There were some that looked just like him, with a light-skinned complexion, dark and thick textured hair, hazel eyes, and full lips. His eyes wide, he walked around the shop stopping at each wall to gaze at the eight-by-ten photos lined in neat rows.

"Ooh, I like that one with the temple fade. Oh, no, that one. What about a faux-hawk fade? Mom, what do you think? How about that one?" He was acting like the proverbial kid in a candy store.

"As long as you don't get your initials carved in your head, I'm fine with whatever you choose," I told him.

"Oh, Mom! That's just what I wanted," he joked.

He finally settled on his new look, and when he heard "Next," he hopped in the chair, ready to be transformed into the new Fresh Max, transitioning from his Marley locs to his Will Smith *Fresh Prince of Bel-Air* fade cut. Whether locs or an afro, wearing and caring for your hair with pride requires full commitment and self-confidence. The only difference is the swiftness of the arrival to your end goal. Afro to locs, one year. Locs to afro, ten minutes. Either way, you have to be sure.

"Are you sure you want to cut off your locs, man? Looks like they've got some history," Mr. Nick said to him.

"Yes, I'm sure," Max said without hesitation as he sat straight up in the chair, anticipating his transformation.

I wasn't as sure. "How about we just trim them again?" I asked Max.

"Nope. I want a clean, fresh start. Let's do it!" he said looking directly at Mr. Nick through the mirror, mano a mano.

"All right. Let's do it," Mr. Nick said.

As he made the first snip, I winced a little, sad to see his beautiful curly locs drop to the floor in a pile of memories. But for Max, it was time to make new ones. Since it was hard for me to watch as Mr. Nick's scissors whizzed around his head, I thought it best to leave the shop before they saw me cry. But before I did, I stooped to collect one of his locs from the growing mound and placed it carefully in my purse, then asked Mr. Nick, "What time will he be ready for me to pick him up?"

"Give me about half an hour," he said.

Max just looked at me and smiled, as if to say, *I'll be all right, Mom.* It's what he wanted, and I knew I had to let go. It was his decision. He was becoming his own man. With a seat at the center of the big man's conversation, where grooming and touch-ups are about more than just hair, Max was sure, and he got the vote of confidence he needed from the other men in the shop.

"Mr. Nick is going to hook you up," I heard one of the other men waiting for his turn say to Max.

"Yeah, I got you, little man," Mr. Nick said.

I had lingered long enough and finally turned to leave and said to both Max and Mr. Nick, "Mr. Nick, I don't know if I'm ready for this. I'm leaving him in your hands."

It was my best attempt to sound like a mother understanding that it was time to let her son make his own decisions. Mr. Nick gave me a knowing look to assure me that he, too, recognized the full import of this moment for Max.

Within the next hour, I got a text from Max. It read, **You can come pick me up now, but you might not recognize me.** He added a smiley face.

I was nervous and maybe just a little excited, not just about his hair but about his first men-only experience in the barbershop. I arrived just as Mr. Nick was completing his final touches to Max's new do. I barely recognized Max. With his head cleared of his mop of hair, his hazel eyes stood out in a way that I had not seen in a very long time. I thought he looked so handsome and I told him so.

"Wow, I forgot how beautiful your eyes are," I said to him.

Max blushed openly. When Mr. Nick finished to his own satisfaction and began whisking the hairs off Max's neck and shoulders, he spun him around in the chair to look at his new do.

"So, what do you think?" he asked Max.

A look of surprise crossed Max's face, and then that adorable grin broke out. He slowly ran his hand over his hair and after a pause, said, "Nice!"

Max turned back around to show off his fresh cut to the other men waiting for their turn in the chair. Heads nodded approval, and one chimed in, "Looking good, little brother." Max beamed.

We cannot control everything that our children see, hear, or think that will impact their self-image. But it is important to fill that bank of self-esteem with as much currency as we can to draw down on when they need it most. That question, "Am I black?" was a call to action that still shakes me to my core and has caused me to consistently and carefully answer that question responsibly. What does being black mean? And if I didn't define it, then I knew others would in ways that could scar him for life.

By the time Max entered middle school, things changed.

The school he was attending was a haven for the elite, and nearly all white. When he'd first entered the second grade in that same school, I wanted to be sure that he had a strong sense of identity. I knew he would need it. I have always tried to instill in him the fact that no one is better than him and that the only difference is access to resources, and we made sure he would have that access. I knew he would also learn that even with the same access, he would still have to work harder. But he would have the advantage of building bridges to a community of people with resources and of helping to dispel myths about people of color among some who have never had the opportunity of knowing a strong, loving, intelligent African American male.

Fifth grade at the same school, which had begun to give him such a strong academic foundation, began to eat away at his spiritual foundation, something that we had spent the first twelve years of life working at every day. The hours spent on physical, occupational, and speech therapy to overcome those challenges that he could with sheer determination, and to prove to himself that he could do anything, were being undermined by the unhealthy messages being communicated to my son, who was one of only two black students in his class. For the first time ever, Max began to complain about school.

When he was suspended for using a curse word, I decided it was time to have a "come to Jesus" moment with the school warden. She reminded me of Sister Irene at my elementary school, who carried a ruler under her habit, ready to whip it out to rap knuckles when she thought one of us stepped out of line. We called her "the terrorist."

I'll never forget the warden's steely face as she made it crystal clear that, no matter what the truth was, she was going to suspend Max.

"You know we have to do this," she said.

"No, I don't know that you do," I countered. "Did you hear him say it?" I demanded to know.

"No, but another student heard him," she said.

"Nobody else? Just the one student?" To this she nodded. "So you believe him and not Max?" She didn't respond. "So based on hearsay, you're suspending my son?"

"We have a zero-tolerance policy for profanity," she responded.

"There are obscenities written all over the walls in the girls' bathroom, so are you suspending them too?" I demanded. "If it is such a crime here, then you must be suspending students left and right. I'm curious, what's the penalty for writing it on the walls? Expulsion?" I said, meeting her cold, hard gaze with my own.

"Our policy about profanity is clear." Her explanation sounded like an unsubstantiated indictment. I fumed, biting back a few curse words of my own.

"You may want to reevaluate your zero-tolerance policy. It is clearly not working and it is clearly applicable at your discretion," I said, and she knew what I meant. Though she got my drift, she seemed to have no problem being caught in it. She was firm in her conviction that Max had to go. So we did at the end of the school year.

It made me feel a little better to know that her tenure at the school didn't last another year. But at the time, she made it abundantly clear that this school was not the ideal environment to help him to continue to develop the kind of self-esteem he needed, especially given its importance for an African American boy becoming a young man and his unique challenges. I had to make another big decision—this time based on dignity, respect, and human value. Learning should be joyful. Educators should be careful. Parents should be mindful. It was time to move to a school with more diversity, one more inclusive of differences, one that would allow him to define and celebrate his uniqueness and to share his many gifts.

Lesson 8: Social cues are critical.

For sixth grade, we transferred to a public middle school. With it, came a new set of challenges.

Max was immediately and acutely aware of the different behaviors and attitudes of his peers inside his new school. It wasn't just how the boys treated the girls. Sometimes it was about how the boys treated one another. During the years when they're honing their armor and earning their brand, machismo dripped with the mastery of the language of the streets.

The first time I heard him use the n-word was in the form of a question framed in a statement.

"Mom, some of the boys at school like to use the n-word."

I knew he was looking for a way to process this and was waiting for my reaction. I looked at it as a gauntlet throw-down.

"Oh no, we will not use that word!" I said, followed quickly by, "Did you say it?"

"Some of the kids at school, the black kids, they say it. They call each other that," he said defensively.

"Did you use it too?" I asked again, sensing he was evading the answer.

"No," he lied, in that voice that tells you it is a lie.

"Why is it so wrong?" he asked me.

"Because it has a history of racism. It was and still is used as an expression of hate and degradation. Some of us say it can also be a term of endearment between black people, but that's not what I feel whenever I hear that word. It makes me angry because it represents the deep disrespect for black people. I don't need to be reminded of that every day in our own community, and certainly not in my house. Now, that may sound old-school to you. I know your friends think it's cool. Well, I may be old-school, and as long as you are living in my house, you will be old-schooled." Period.

But I wasn't through yet. "Understanding now where that word comes from, would you call your Uncle Lawrence the n-word? What about Uncle

Jay or Uncle Kevin?" I asked him. And then I went down the line, calling out nearly every man in our community that we call family.

After I exhausted the long list of names, I then ended with himself.

"Would you call yourself the n-word?"

Max vigorously shook his head.

"That means that anyone who deserves respect does not deserve to be called the n-word. Would you agree?"

He nodded.

"Would you agree that everyone deserves respect, even when it's hard to give?"

He wasn't ready to agree so quickly. "Even if they don't respect you?" Max asked.

"At the end of the day, Max, if you give respect, it says more about you than it does about the other person. And if you give respect, you get respect. Always remember that."

That was pretty much the end of the n-word, at least in our house.

But we still had to deal with the b-word. He was especially sensitive to how other black boys treat and talk about girls. He hated when they called them the b-word. The irony is that though he didn't like it and would get upset and offended when other boys did, he suggested that some of the girls seemed to act in a way that encouraged it.

"What do you mean?" I asked him. "Do you think black girls, or any girl, want to be called the b-word? Do you think they deserve that?"

He seemed conflicted when he responded, "I don't know. They seem to like the boys who are kind of rough, you know, like they are from the hood or something."

Unfortunately, I understood too well what he meant.

Best-selling author and sociology professor Dr. Michael Eric Dyson talks about the complicated dynamic in his book *Why I Love Black Women*. In his beautiful poetic prose, he writes about how some "black men complain that many black women prefer the hard-core, thugged-out brother, the bad boy, the player." He illuminates the issue by referencing an essay penned by Jonathan Farley for *Essence* magazine in which the Harvard- and Oxford-educated suitor recounts a conversation he had with a young lady he was in love with. In the essay, Farley recalls that "she outlined the difference between men like me and the men black women preferred, between mere African-Americans and 'niggaz': African-Americans are safe, respectable, upwardly mobile and professional black men. Niggaz are strong, streetwise, hard black men." I heartily disagree with the woman Farley loves, and I'd like to reiterate that I hate the n-word and would never use it to refer to any man, let alone someone I love. Period.

I assured Max that, in no uncertain terms, beautiful, smart, respectful black women who prefer a man who can offer respect, protection, and financial security largely outnumber available black men, and that he would meet one who deserves him. Unfortunately, statistics bear this out, given the high rates of incarceration and unemployment for men of color.

"Stay true to who you are, focus on doing the best you can, and always show respect for women, as you always have, and you will find the kind of girl you are looking for," I assured him. "She will not be a 'b,' or act like one. She'll appreciate you and value you for the kind and generous person that you are."

That said, over time I could also sense his development of a certain disdain for people who used that language. He began to self-identify that "street-talking" people are not his tribe. He expressed embarrassment when other young black men, his peers, while hanging out in the cafeteria or after school, used language that he recognized as denigrating, and he was completely uncomfortable with it. He would often bemoan and disparage those who seemed to be the reason "why they hate us so much." He would often complain about how black people behave. When he announced to me, "I don't want to be black," I didn't know whether I wanted to scream or cry.

"What are you saying! Why don't you want to be black?" I had to hold back a rush of emotions while silently sending apologies to the ancestors.

"Because black people are always killing each other. And they make rap music that I don't understand. It's filled with cursing, violence, and disrespecting women," he said with disgust.

"But you are black and you don't do those things. What black people do you know that are violent and kill people? Let me answer that for you. You don't! What about your mentors? Are they bad people? So is it fair to say that all black people are bad? And what about white people who are violent and disrespect women? Are they bad?"

I could sense that he understood the double standard that society had taught him, but that was not the point. He just so much wanted to connect with and love his brothers and sisters of color, and some of his peers were making it difficult.

I reminded him that our president, Barack Obama, was a black man. I reminded him of how much he admired Barack because he was a great father and how much Barack loved and respected his wife, Michelle. He thought about that for a while before he responded.

"Yeah, but what can he do for black people?"

That's a deep question and deserved a thoughtful answer. So I asked him, "What would you like him to do?"

"Black people need jobs," he said.

This from my fifteen-year-old! He was already thinking about his own future. He also recognized that he may be at a disadvantage because of the color of his skin.

I broke it down as best I could in a way that he could understand.

"A president can't create jobs. He can only champion job creation and provide leadership to foster a healthy economy that can support job growth. Businesses provide jobs. If the owner of a company where you would like to work doesn't give you a job, that's not the president's fault, nor can the president take credit for you getting the job. If you apply for a job and don't get it, then you have to ask two questions: One, are you qualified for that job? And two, if so, then why didn't you get it? The second question is complicated and out of your control. Lots of people want that job. You will always have competition, and often the odds may be stacked against you for whatever reason. That goes for anybody, whether you are black or white or Asian or any race, religion, or gender. But whether you are qualified or not is something you can control. You have to work to be the best at whatever you want to do. That's all you can do. No one is going to give you a job just because you want one. You have to be prepared. You get hired if you can do the job, and you will keep it if you can add value."

To add some context that he could relate to, I explained how I recruit and train employees in my own business, which he has been trained to think of as "our" business. He knows every employee personally and has even been in the room during an interview. One day he can be a job creator, and so he needed to think about what kind of people he would want to work for him.

"We own a business, and I have to hire people I can depend on, who show up every day ready to work and want to do a good job. I get hundreds of résumés. It's not just about a string of achievements. It's about effort and commitment. Some résumés may stand out over others because they show leadership, like yours will. It's what you're good at. But I'm not always looking for a leader. Sometimes I'm looking for someone who is consistent, knows what they're good at, and follows through on whatever they start. You have to decide what you will bring to the table. And then bring it with all you've got. Are you willing to do that?" I asked him.

He understood every word. But that still did not get to the core of his issue with some of the black people he interacts with every day at school. It wasn't really about black people not getting jobs. It was about respect. He was immersed in a culture of divisiveness and disrespect pervasive in our society in and outside of school. He was angry and needed somebody to blame. Most of all, he wanted to fix it. He started with his best friend.

Max loves Andre like a brother. After our talk about the n-word, he was so conflicted and bothered that Andre would refer to him as "my little nigga" that he brought him home to address the issue head-on. He wanted it to stop. He asked me to mediate a conversation with both of them like the one I'd had with him about the n-word. He didn't know how to confront the issue without offending his friend and felt that bringing him into our sacred space to discuss it would show him how much he cared about him and about how important it was for him to know how he felt.

Andre had always been respectful to me, and so I was looking forward to the opportunity to show him that I respected him as well. I would be honest and forthright with him, treating him just like I treat my own son. We invited Andre to our quiet space reserved for my and Max's serious conversations. The three of us sat face-to-face for an open, honest dialogue. I turned to Max first.

"Did you let Andre know why you don't like it when calls you his 'little nigga'?" I asked him.

Max was looking directly at him when he nodded yes. He was leaving the talking to me.

"If he is your friend, that should stop right now," I said as I pivoted to Andre and said, "Right, Andre?"

"Sure, man. Cool. It's just how I talk. I didn't mean nothin' by it. That's cool," he said to Max, avoiding my eye contact. I knew he felt awkward, perhaps a little embarrassed. It was understandable, so I trod forward carefully.

I paused a moment, waiting until Andre summoned the courage to look at me. Then I asked him pointedly, "Do you understand how some might be offended by that word?"

He hung his head a little and then apologized.

"If you are feeling the least bit uncomfortable right now, then perhaps you should take a minute to think about that," I told him.

He apologized again. "I'm sorry, ma'am. I won't say it around Max anymore."

I caught his note of defiance. He let me know that nobody's momma is going to tell him he can't choose to talk the way he wants to. But I knew that I had struck a chord he had never heard before and that it made an imprint. So that was that.

But it wasn't, at least not for Max. We had fixed one small problem, but there was still a much bigger one. He still did not yet feel comfortable in his own skin color, a psychosis that stems from a history of slavery and systemic racism that has stagnated deep in the heart of our communities. It was time for a proud black history immersion, and so I pulled out the big gun, Alex Haley's *Roots*. It seemed the ideal place to start what would become an ongoing dialogue about who we are, where we come from, and why we deserve to be treated with dignity and respect, especially by one another.

After watching the series, he was angry. He also now fully understood why I took such offense at the n-word.

"Kunta Kinte is awesome!" he exclaimed. "I would have been like him. I would never accept being a slave. I would have killed those bastards."

It was a natural, vociferous response for a young black man endowed with his hard-fought civil rights written into the Constitution decades before he was born. For anyone born after the time of slavery, the level of human suffering and indignity is completely unfathomable.

"Yes, you are just like Kunta Kinte! A warrior!" I told him.

He raised his arms in a muscle pose to demonstrate his sheer awesomeness.

We continued our conversation about our black history as well as our future and his role in it.

"Just think, Max, after the end of slavery, black people were still being lynched and killed, even as so-called free people. It took another hundred years for black people to have rights. That's what the civil rights movement is all about. People died for our dignity, respect, protection, and justice. That's why we celebrate Martin Luther King Jr., Robert F. Kennedy, Rosa Parks, and many others who fought hard and sacrificed their lives so that you have the opportunities you have to be free to live your dream to be the world's greatest writer, director, and producer of anime film. So with your success comes a debt of gratitude to the men and women who paved the way. Never forget that. You are borne by heroes so that you can be the one you want to be."

It was Uncle Lawrence who perhaps best grounded him in an important truth about what it means to be a black man in our society. A highly accomplished man recognized by friends, family, and the community for his integrity, intelligence, and mad athletic skills, he is yet a victim of the everyday injustices and the struggles of black life in America. Climbing the ranks in corporate America, he learned all too well of the barriers to reaching your full potential. He had himself faced the barrier of the corporate glass ceiling, where the politics of leadership are steeped in the American tradition of advancing the ideals of the "good ole boys." He felt compelled to leave the company that he had helped grow to find a new opportunity that would allow him the freedom to be in charge of his own success and free from the indignity of being sidelined while others less competent were allowed to advance.

"The most important thing to any man is his dignity. Men die for it. Having it is worth dying for and will be the life of you. Not, 'will be the death,'" he told Max.

"Dignity is in your heart muscle. It is where your passion lives. So they go hand in hand. Follow your passion and do it with dignity. Whatever your challenge, whether an injustice you may suffer or critical acclaim you may earn, always keep your dignity."

"Do you know what it means to be dignified?" he asked, as if he wanted to be sure Max was listening.

He was.

"I'm sure you are going to call me out if I don't give the right answer, and I know you're going to tell me, so let's not take away my dignity," Max replied.

Uncle Lawrence chuckled at his clever comeback and gave him a high five.

"It means carrying yourself in a manner worthy of respect. Hold your chin up. Speak up for yourself. Speak up for your truth," he told him. Then with arms akimbo, chest arched, chin up and to the side, he added, "The men of our tribe do it with style."

Max grinned at his "mannetism."

"Don't do that anymore," Max chided him. "That didn't look dignified. You look goofy." After such a serious conversation, it was fun to end it with a good laugh.

Lesson 9: Young men need heroes— the right ones.

When it comes to assessing their self-worth, young people can be easily influenced by outside forces, one of the strongest being the media. Movies, television, video games, and beyond are rife with stories that seem to tell them how to feel about themselves. Uncle Lawrence has always been particularly passionate on this issue.

Max is an action film aficionado with an affinity for fight choreography and cool weaponry. So naturally, hanging out with Uncle Lawrence typically involves going to the movies or watching videos. The selection process is complex. If it ain't sci-fi or sports, this usually leads to a stressful debate about what "we are going to watch," since every option has to go through the "black experience" test to check for how many black people, what are their roles, and how we are generally portrayed in the show. Let it be known, it is "universally held that *The Matrix* tops the list," according to Max and Uncle Lawrence. The two of them agree that hands down, Morpheus, played by Laurence Fishburne, stands alone as the most BADASS of all time. It's a high bar, but when all options being considered fail to meet the basics of being non-offensive, there is always an episode of *Star Trek*, Uncle Lawrence's favorite because it's sci-fi AND includes a diverse cast of characters in intelligent and leadership roles.

So when *Avatar* came out, we were all excited, greatly anticipating th
newest sci-fi technical wonder. Max and I went to see it on opening da
in a big-screen theater. When it was over, we both gushed about ho
much we loved the film. We loved it so much we bought the DVD. H
couldn't wait to share it with Uncle Lawrence. We all watched it togethe

When it was over, Uncle Lawrence looked at Max, clearly perturbe
and declared, "This movie is racist."

Max was shocked, and, I must admit, I was similarly taken aback.

"What do you mean it's racist?" I asked.

"The hero in the movie is a white man who saves the tribe and wii
the love of a black woman," he said with clear, utter disgust.

"Wow!" Max fell silent, crestfallen.

I countered, "Yes, but he had to become one of the tribe to find tru
and ultimately turned against his own people when he recognized th
they were evil."

We argued back and forth and the discussion about the hero of *Avat*
evolved into one about how often black people are portrayed as gangster
hookers, perpetrators, convicts, slaves, or otherwise subservient to whi
people as sidekicks and janitors.

Clearly agitated, Max blurted out, "Why do they hate us so much?

After that question hung in the air for a minute, the discussion shifte
to a conversation about the reality of racism. How do you answer tha
question that is tormenting a young black man who has an entire futui
ahead of him? I could, as Martin Luther King Jr., speaking of his ow
young daughter, phrased it in his "Letter from a Birmingham Jail," "se
ominous clouds of inferiority beginning to form in [his] mental sky, an
see [him] beginning to distort [his] personality by developing an uncon
scious bitterness toward white people."

Acutely sensitive to how media undermine the value of the contribu
tions of black people through negative images that are pervasive throughou
every media platform, Uncle Lawrence is vigilant and protective when i
comes to Max.

"Capitalism is efficient, effective, and hard at work. The media in
dustry knows what makes money and that television shapes opinions
They can thoroughly and comprehensively influence the masses," he
schooled Max.

"I refuse to watch another show with a negative image of a person of color as perps, drug addicts, and prostitutes," he said. "The hero in *Avatar* could have been a brother and would have been just as good, if not better," he put on a point on it.

He is especially critical of films produced by African Americans that perpetuate these stereotypes and pointed to *Boondocks*, created by Aaron McGruder for Adult Swim. Max was excited to introduce him to this show because it had black characters, one of only two animated television series for adults that did so at the time. The other was *Black Dynamite*, created by three African American men: Michael Jai White, Scott Sanders, and Byron Minns.

After just two minutes of watching an episode of *Boondocks* with Uncle Lawrence, Max knew it was a mistake. The story began with two black males behind bars, taking a shower and speaking at the lowest denominator of conversation.

"I've had enough," Uncle Lawrence proclaimed and changed the channel.

No explanation necessary. Max completely got it.

In its defense, *Boondocks* is a satire that is tough on racism. But at first glance, the images are provocatively misleading. It's the kind of show that if you're going to watch, you have to watch it all to understand it. And for a young man, the mix between message and images may require some tutorial guidance.

In an industry in which people of color are woefully underrepresented, it is ironic that the most popular hit shows, such as *NCIS* and *Locked Up*, are filled with negative stereotypes of the people who are watching. Unwittingly, viewers are drinking the Kool-Aid and, at the same time, see too few images of black people as successful and powerful.

It brought to mind something that I had read by Dr. Darnell Hunt, a professor of sociology and the director of the Ralph J. Bunche Center for African American Studies at UCLA. As he told in an article in the *Los Angeles Times*, "Presenting stories that have minorities in stock, static roles instead of dynamic ones, painting a picture in which white men are still privileged to lead and others are followers or tangential to the main narrative—it reinforces the idea that there's a racial pecking order in the broader society. People may tend to internalize those images, and treat

[minorities] accordingly, maybe even vote against them because they're harboring this perception."

Uncle Lawrence shared with Max a few of his heroes.

"Too often we only have athletes to look up to as our heroes, but Muhammad Ali was more than that. He was articulate, strong, and embodied the full measure of a man. He stood up for his values and held his head up high with pride and dignity no matter what they did to him. They took away his career. Took away his income. He never backed down. Never. He fought back. In the end, he won the respect of people all over the world. I respect him more than any other athlete. I respect him for being a real man. That's why he's the Greatest."

He asked Max, "Do you know who invented the gas mask? Garrett Morgan, a black man. Do you know who did the first blood transfusions? Charles Drew, a black man. Do you know who pioneered laser eye surgery? Patricia Bath, a black woman. If they are not teaching you this in school, then you need to take it upon yourself to do your own research. If you don't see these images on television and in film, then you have to look for them in books. You gotta read, young man. Spend a little less time playing video games and pick up a book, or use the Internet. You have access to a world of information. All you have to do is click a button to learn your history."

Uncle Lawrence went deeper.

"Come here. Let me show you something."

He pulled up his sleeve and showed him his scarification, the Kappa fraternal brand, resembling an African tribal mark. Max's expression said it all.

"Woooowwwww," he exhaled in an extended breath of awe. "Did you join a gang?" was Max's first question.

Not quite prepared for that one, Uncle Lawrence responded calmly, "No. I joined a prestigious fraternity. You know what this stands for? It represents a rite of passage into a special brotherhood. Brothers supporting brothers to become leaders. It's the Kappa brand."

"Am I ready now?" Max asked. "Am I ready to be a Kappa man?"

"Are you? Let me tell you about what it means to be a Kappa man."

Uncle Lawrence went on to explain the history of the Kappa Alpha Psi Fraternity and what it's meant to the men in our family.

"It was founded over a hundred years ago by ten black men and today represents achievers in every field of human endeavor. I pledged when I was in college, as did my father, your grandfather, when he was in college. Our family is filled with Kappa men and that will always be a part of your legacy. This brand means that I will always be here to support you, because you are part of my tribe."

Understanding who he is and the pride he felt in himself and the men around him whom he admired and respected most in the world made that ominous question "Why do they hate us so much?" even more confounding. It didn't make sense. What his mentors showed him and taught him didn't align with the worldview.

Lesson 10: Keep your head up, your nose clean, and your eyes on the prize.

Besides the barrage of negative images in film and television, the evening news compounds and underscores these messages with a litany of stories that emphasize the plight of black America rather than the stories of triumph, of communities coming together to uplift their own. Police shootings, gang violence, and societal unrest reported by white talking heads who represent the authority for world order is confusing and, even worse, effective. Naturally, it caused Max to become uncomfortable in his own skin and to question whether he might be forced to make the decision to be the victim, the hero, or the survivor in an altercation. It seemed inevitable that at some point he would have a police encounter, and not in a good way.

Arrested by his own unrest, he confided in Uncle Kevin, whom he saw as a man of the streets, having grown up in Brooklyn, New York.

"I'm not going down like that," Max told him.

"Like what?"

"Police are always shooting at black people."

Uncle Kevin usually has a joke at the ready, but not this time. He knew exactly what Max meant and knew that he needed to respond with a seriousness and intensity that Max would recognize as gospel from the unwritten handbook on living while black. A simple misunderstanding or benign movement could be a death knell for black men. Max needed to hear and heed Kevin's every word like his life depended on it, because it did.

"Well, first of all, use your common sense and try to avoid getting yourself in a situation with the police. But if you do find yourself in a situation, whatever you do, remember to always keep your cool. Even when you know you have done nothing wrong and you feel you are being treated with disrespect, just remember that you want to stay safe and stay alive. That's more important than being right and dead or in jail. Keep your hands in sight. Be polite no matter what they say, even if it is offensive. Don't argue. Always say, 'Yes, sir.'"

Of course, Max questioned why he had to be polite and say, "Yes, sir," if the officer had no right to pull him over in the first place. But Uncle Kevin was firm with him.

"You want to stay alive? You want to stay out of jail? Then listen to what I'm saying. Don't give them any reason to hold you or claim that you resisted. To them, because you are a black man you are suspect. But, knowing who you are is also knowing who you are not. You are not a criminal. Don't give them a reason to make you one. It's not fair, but there are a lot of things in life that are not fair. You have to learn to pick your battles wisely. Right as you may be, racism is blind to righteousness. But you, Max, have the eyes of an eagle and the heart of a tiger. So you need to channel your inner Batman and use your intellect to outsmart them. It may feel like it's swallowing your pride, but it's not. You have nothing to be ashamed of. W. E. B. Du Bois said, "Make yourself do unpleasant things so as to gain the upper hand of your soul." Sometimes it's hard to take the high road. But you'll find that that lane is wide open.

Uncle Kevin's effort to add a spoonful of sugar did not help the medicine go down.

Max's brow stayed furrowed and every now and then he would attempt to protest with his body language. He tightened his hands into fists of fury. Sensing the fight brewing inside Max, Kevin added, "Not all cops are bad. But you just never know if you got the wrong one. So you have to be extra careful out there so that you don't find yourself in a situation that you could have avoided if you had just stayed calm."

Uncle Kevin had told him what to do, but Max remained conflicted about the fact that it was not fair that he should live under a threat that was unjustifiable.

His faith, trust in humanity, and boyhood invincibility twisted into

"What the heck is going on? What's wrong with people? And where is God in all of this?"

He continued to look for answers. He needed justification. Uncle Lawrence gave him something more, the strength of self-pride.

"Know who you are and never forget that. No matter what, remember, we've got your back," said Uncle Lawrence. "You are my nephew. You have a proud legacy of righteousness, durability, resourcefulness, entrepreneurship, and achievement. No one can take that away.

"Keep your head, and hold it high. You can't live your life in fear. Live it with purpose and respect for yourself and for others. My father, your grandfather, showed me that if you are not living with purpose, then you are going backward, not forward. My mother, your grandmother, taught me to respect my role as a man. Your grandparents raised me to be the man I am today. The blood that runs through your veins makes you exceptional. We will not let you not succeed at whatever you choose to do. We got your back. You can count on it."

But could Max count on himself to rise to the occasion when he needed to? He was so fearful of becoming another tragic statistic, of falling short of his dreams. He wanted so badly to be the hero of his own story filled with so many villains in the forms of prejudice and bias to thwart.

"You can be anything you want to be," Uncle Kevin told him. "But you must be fearless. Those are your own words. Remember you wrote that in your essay on what it means to be a man. It was the best line in it. Believe it. I do."

Uncle Kevin himself is the poster child for "where you come from does not determine where you go." He grew up between the mean streets of Bed-Stuy in Brooklyn and the down-home country life of Norfolk, Virginia. He was raised by his maternal grandmother, who brought him up the old-fashioned way: "Respect your elders or I'll make you regret you didn't." But she did more than teach him respect. She instilled in him a love of God and a reverence for women as the home where the heart lives. With her unconditional love, he knew that no matter what he had done the day before, the next day breakfast would be on the table. She made him memorize Psalm 23.

The Lord is my shepherd; I shall not want. He maketh me to lie
down in green pastures: he leadeth me beside the still waters. He

restoreth my soul: he leadeth me in the paths of righteousness for his
name's sake.

Through scripture, she raised him to believe that no matter what you're going through, God is looking out for you, and he always remembered, "Whatever I do, I have to answer to the Lord." He credits her wisdom, strength, and bosom of grace for giving him the foundation to forge his way forward against all odds.

"'One monkey don't stop no show,' she used to say to me. I learned from her that in life, whatever the environment or the situation, you have to decide how you're going to deal with it. That philosophy also follows in how I run my business. No one is indispensable. In life and in business, you have to decide what role you are going to play. Both will go on with or without you either way," he said.

"Growing up in my own neighborhood, I never thought much about my blackness," Uncle Kevin continued. "There was discrimination around light-skinned versus dark-skinned people, but I was somewhere in the middle, so I never got targeted. It wasn't that I didn't see it, but I didn't feel it in the way that made me think of it as an obstacle. My awakening occurred when I became interested in the stock market. I wondered why I couldn't get the *New York Times* or the *Wall Street Journal* in my neighborhood. It dawned on me the lack of business information made available to my people. All I ever saw were rappers and celebrities, never businesspeople. My first girlfriend had a job and that was a big deal. It was probably part of the reason I married her, though it didn't last. My dreams were bigger than just working for someone for the rest of my life and my ambition grew beyond the relationship. I realized that had I grown up in the white world, it would be different. Access to information, resources, and role models makes a difference. That's when I knew I needed to promote positive images of African Americans doing positive things. Even though I knew nothing about the magazine business, I started one to tell stories about successful black businesspeople."

Today, Kevin's personal success story as an entrepreneur who holds no degrees but who holds several patents is one for the history books. He defied typical stigmas and statistics for blacks in failing schools and marginalized communities to become a bootstrapping self-made millionaire.

He has a vision of the kind of life that he wants and he is still going after it, leveraging every tool in his kit and using every available resource. For Kevin, anything is possible.

Upon Max's graduation from high school, amid all the cards, texts, and phone calls wishing him congratulations, it was Uncle Kevin who talked to him about the importance of having a vision for his future.

"Now, what are you going to do next? What are you going to do with that diploma?"

Max told him of his plans to pursue a career in animation.

"That's great, Max. I look forward to seeing your name in the credits one day. Dream big. No one can stop you from realizing your dream. Only you can do that. Anything is possible, young man, when you decide nothing is going to stop you. Once you decide who you want to be and are willing to do what it takes to get there, anything is possible."

Uncle Lawrence, Uncle Chris, and his wife, Ramona, and their son, Jeremy, all flew in to attend his graduation. As the students left the stage to go find their families waiting with triumphant cheers and hugs, Max floated on the wave of beaming smiles in our direction. We fawned over him with high fives, hugs, and flashes of photos with this one and then that one.

Uncle Chris grabbed him in a firm handshake and pulled him close to tell him, "Congratulations, Max. We are all so proud of you. What you have accomplished no one can take from you. An education is the most important thing that will allow you to define your own path and control your future. No one can hold you back with a good education, and you have worked hard to earn it. You should be proud. I know we are."

Uncle Kevin echoed our pride and joy, but inserted his rising expectations.

"It is not a time to rest on your laurels. What is next for you is mastery of your education. When you are confident and clear on what your mission is, it will enable you to take more risks so that you can step outside the box and into your own uniqueness. Whatever you choose to do, become the best at it. It is mastery that creates true freedom," he said.

"I want to change the world," Max told him.

"How are you going to do that?" Uncle Kevin asked.

As he often does, Max complained about how the world is unfair and how people don't care about the planet and the people who live on it. He talked of his love-hate relationship with technology, because as much as it advances and improves convenience and access, anonymity creates loneliness and insulates us from personal relationships.

"I wish people talked to one another rather than just talk on Facebook and Twitter. People are lazy and just say mean things to each other. It's stupid!"

"So what are you going to do about it?" Uncle Kevin asked. "Don't complain. Be the change you want to see. Tell a better story."

I've repeated it to him dozens of times, until the day he shot back, "I'm going to be the hero I want to be." Touché.

He's going to be great!

Lesson 11: Pursuing your passion is a test of will and discipline.

Since the day he held his first coloring pencil, Max knew what he wanted to do for the rest of his life. He wanted to tell his own stories with images of his own heroes.

His early works were of two people with stick legs on stick bodies with circles on top for the heads, standing side by side with their stick hands touching. One was always taller than the other. "This is you and this is me," he would tell me every time. The background was usually a house made with four strokes, each side and the vaulted roof. It was always a sunny day and at least one tree was in the yard.

Everywhere we went, whether to Blockbuster to rent a movie, to the grocery store, or to the airport, Max's backpack was filled with original signed art to distribute to "new friends" we met along the way. Once he captured your attention with his charm, he would wrap it with a bow with a gift of his art. It worked every time. Smiles all around. In places we frequented, his artwork began to accumulate on display for all to see. There were many times when we would be out and about and someone would say, "Hey, you're the kid with the artwork, right?" It was an actual thing.

Art was always his favorite class in school, but his annual summer arts programs at a professional design school made him leap out of bed each day. By his fifth summer program, I began to realize that his obsession had turned into a career path. What I had thought of as a form of therapy to relieve his ADHD-related anxiety was much more than that. It was the way he openly expressed himself and connected with people to help them see his authenticity rather than his disability. It was his true calling.

On the last day of class in his eighth-grade summer arts program at Nashville's Watkins College of Art, Design & Film, there was an art show of student projects for parents. Max was giddy with excitement and told me several times how hard he was working on his presentation. So we invited Uncle Kevin to join us for the special event. Max thought his mentor, a fellow artist, might appreciate his work.

"Would you like to come to my first art show?" Max asked him.

"I wouldn't want to miss it," Uncle Kevin told him. He flew in from New York just to be there for Max's "opening."

When we arrived at the school, we were met by Ms. Woodard, the art teacher. "I'm so pleased to finally meet you. Max has really been looking forward to this day, and I have really enjoyed working with him," she said.

Uncle Kevin was as proud as a dad, which everyone there thought he was. So he played the role to the hilt. "Nice work, son," he said. Max smiled so wide it made his ears wiggle and his eyes twinkle, or it could have been the mist in mine.

A brief refreshment of tea cakes and lemonade with some of the other parents was interrupted by Max, who asked with impatience, "Are you ready?" He was excited to show us what he had worked so hard on. He took us both by hand and guided us through the narrow rows of art on display to his own station, carefully staged for our private viewing. As we got closer, we could hear Celtic music playing on his portable CD player to set the mood. It was similar to the theme music of his favorite movies. Because of his love of anime, it had become part of the soundtrack of his life. When we came to a stop, his work stood on an easel draped for the big reveal. No matter what he was about to show us, I was already dazzled by his attention to detail for his presentation.

"Are you ready?" he asked again, with more drama this time.

We both nodded yes. Then with a "Voilà!" he pulled back the cover to unveil his masterpiece, an eighteen-by-twenty-inch self-portrait of an artist. It was an abstract in chalk, wallpapered in his favorite color, red, with strokes that made it appear as if he were standing in front of a brick wall. He was wearing a black turtleneck with blue-green pants, and his arms came out the sides of his body like wings spread to fly. A cap of brown hair, piercing light brown eyes behind wire-frame glasses, and full red lips, it was unmistakably Max. It was his first real work of art, and it was brilliant!

His teacher had come over to stand nearby so she could watch our faces. She was grinning the entire time. "It has just been a delight to work with him on his piece. It's one of my favorites. But what has been most impressive is how much effort he has put into making this day so special for you," she said to me.

"It shows," said Uncle Kevin. "Man, I could not be more proud of you today. You've got talent!"

Max beamed and hugged us both so hard that we all nearly fell over. We hung out for a while, enjoying his music selections and chatting with a few classmates he'd grabbed to create a spontaneous intimate art salon featuring his special guests, Mom and Uncle Kevin. That was the summer when I learned what he had known all along. He will earn his keep as an artist and a socialite. It is what he was born to do.

"You're ready for the big time," Uncle Kevin told him before leaving to go back to New York.

Feeling validated, Max decided it was game on. Between ninth and tenth grade, he applied and was accepted at the UCLA School of Performing Arts summer program in animation arts for high school students. It was a one-week program, so it would be his first experience away on his own and his first immersion in a college-level arts program taught by an active Hollywood producer who was one of the leading media arts professors at the critically acclaimed school.

Just as he had done many times before when he visited his mentors in different cities, Max flew out to Los Angeles by himself. He knew the routine. After I helped him get his wheelchair at the ticket counter, we waited for the passenger assistant, wiling away the time saying our goodbyes.

"Do you have your ID ready?" I asked him for the tenth time.

"Yes, Mom. It's right here," he repeated.

"Remember to tip your passenger assistant," I said.

"Why do I have to do that? I want to save my money," he fussed.

"Because it's the right thing to do," I said.

"But don't they already get paid for doing their job? I have a disability. Why do I have to tip?" He asked a good question.

"Well, yes, they do, but it's like when you go to a restaurant and tip the server," I said.

"I don't agree with tipping when they're just doing their job. I wouldn't charge for helping people who need it. I don't have much money," he said.

"You make a good point. But I suspect they don't make much money, and perhaps they should be paid more for what they do. But we don't have control over that, so for now, just give what you can, even if it's just a dollar. They will appreciate it," I told him. Begrudgingly, he agreed.

"Now, when you get on the plane, don't talk too much. Keep your business to yourself. Can you do that?" I cautioned.

"Yes, Mom. I know," he said, a little annoyed with having been told that so many times.

"I love you."

"I love you too."

When the assistant arrived, we hugged and kissed and said goodbye one more time, and then he quickly slipped into his chatterbox mode as he was whisked away to his gate.

A dear friend met him at the airport and safely delivered him to campus. At the end of each day, Max called me to report in on his activities, and every recount sounded better than the previous day's. Things went swimmingly. Except for losing his money somewhere in the middle of the week, there was no catastrophe, no drama. Phew!

At the end of the week, parents are invited to a creative revue of the student projects, ranging from dance and acting to film and video. I was not going to miss Max's first stage presentation to a Hollywood audience, so I bought an airline ticket. What made it even sweeter is that I planned to surprise him.

The auditorium was packed with families who'd come from near and far to celebrate the accomplishments of the students. It was difficult to sit patiently through them all while waiting for Max's turn to present, which, of course, was last. Each member of his team had created their own 2-D animated video project, a series of individual drawings that, when fed into a video projector, create an animated short. When Max came out to take a bow for his video short "Bouncing Ball," I was up first so that he could see me right away in the crowd that stood to give him a rousing round of applause. He nearly leapt off the stage with joy when he spotted me, and the audience enjoyed his reaction too, as if they were in on the surprise, which made them applaud even louder. I was as excited as he was.

Afterward, parents met their students and the faculty and staff at a reception right outside the performance hall. I could see a man making a beeline straight toward me. I didn't know him, so I looked around to see if he was approaching someone else. But no, he was coming directly to me.

"Are you Max's mom?" he asked as he stuck his hand out to shake mine.

"Why, yes," I said a little skeptically.

"I'm the head of the program here," he said.

I wasn't sure what to expect next. I was kind of used to getting feedback about Max that was not always exactly what you want to hear.

"Max is a wonderful student!" he exclaimed. "We absolutely loved having him with us. He worked great with the other students and he is a great team leader. He would be great for our next class. In fact, we would like to offer to extend his stay for another week."

I was flabbergasted.

"I thought it was closed," I said, confused.

I had already tried registering him when we signed up for the first week. I mentioned that to the program director, and he came back with, "It is, but we will be happy to make a special place for him."

What!!! I could not believe my ears!

"Max, did you hear that!" I was so excited and overwhelmed I nearly cried. So, imagine my crash when Max flat out said, "No, I don't want to. I want to go home." Just like that. In my mind, I'm thinking, *Are you crazy?!*

"Why? They thought you were terrific! You didn't enjoy it?"

By this time, the co-director had joined the effort to enlist Max into staying for another week. Despite the incredible praise being sprayed all over him, he was persistent with the "NO." I couldn't understand it. Nor could they. The pleading with him went on even as she joined us on our walk to the car to drive back to the airport. As we stood there in the parking lot, Max finally explained why not. He said that he did not like the way the supervisor assigned to his dorm treated him. And though the co-director insisted that she could assign someone new to him, he could not be convinced.

So as she shut his car door for him, and gestured for him to roll down the window to ask him one more time, Max gave his final, "No. I don't want to. I just want to go home."

We both sighed, shrugged, and gave up on the cause. He would come to regret his decision to not participate in that second session at UCLA's summer arts program given what happened the following summer.

By the end of the next school year, he was a bit more excited and ready to commit to the two-week summer program at the prestigious Ringling College of Art and Design. After going through a rigorous application process that included a site tour, an orientation for parents and students, and an interview, he received his official acceptance letter, a big deal worthy of celebration! And celebrate we did! Sushi, all he could eat, at his favorite restaurant in town!

He couldn't wait to tell his mentors, especially Uncle Kevin.

"Congratulations, man. That's an excellent school. You belong there," he told Max.

Unfortunately, it didn't go at all as well as his previous experience at UCLA. Nowhere near.

The summer program at Ringling is much deeper and intensive, learning from legends in the field at one of the finest art schools in the country. The program includes more accountability, stringent rules and expectations, and strict guidelines. We had spent the weeks before we left checking off every item on the clearly detailed list. Pillow and pillowcase. Check. Light blanket. Check. Laundry bag. Check. Small clamp-on desk lamp. Check. Alarm clock. Check. Wastebasket. Check. Closed-toe shoes. Check. Earbuds. Check . . . Rules read. Check.

Given the magnitude of the occasion, I invited my mom to fly down to join us for the ride to take him to school. So the three of us piled into the car, packed with two weeks of dorm-living supplies, to head to Sarasota, Florida. We hit the road for the five-hundred-mile ride to the opportunity of a lifetime.

When we arrived, we had a meal of his favorite food, sushi, for our last night together until I would return two weeks later to pick up a newly minted professional artist in training with a game plan and a foothold in the community that he so much wanted to be a part of. The next morning, we headed over to the school, delivered all his stuff to his dorm room, got the tour, and met his roommate. Once settled in, Max began to get antsy, eager for me and his grandmother to leave so that he could do his own thing. So after several hugs and kisses, my mom and I left our young man on campus and began the long drive home. Mission accomplished. Or so I thought.

Two days later, when my phone rang and I saw the Florida area code and heard an unfamiliar voice asking, "Is this Max's mother?" I knew it was serious.

"Yes?" I said, with my heart in my throat.

"I've got Max here," he said. His voice sounded ominous. He continued, "We've got a problem, and unless we can find a solution right now, I'm afraid he will not be able to stay with us."

Max had misplaced his meds. He had called me and I had a prescription called in to a nearby pharmacy for him. Apparently, Max had asked one of the student assistants to go pick up his medication rather than the appropriate authority.

As it turned out, that wasn't the only problem. There were layers. Max seemed to think that the explicit rules for behavior in class and in the dorm didn't apply to him. So the rule that you are not to use earphones to listen to music while in class didn't involve him, because, he insisted, "I have to have music."

To be fair, that is not entirely untrue. In fact, throughout his years in high school, he was allowed to listen to music because it calms him, helps him concentrate, and reduces his anxiety. However, it is neither the norm nor an excusable exception at Ringling. That was made very clear. Max knew it and had agreed to it when he signed up, but thought he could just charm them into letting him get away with it. It didn't work. Then to further complicate his situation, he befriended a troubled student who overshared, much like himself. She apparently was going through a dark period of her life, and so she and Max got into a conversation about suicide that was overheard by another student. That student was so alarmed he reported it to the dorm rep. So, by then, he had crossed nearly every line to be crossed and landed in the hot seat and on probation in just his first two days.

I don't remember much of that conversation with the program director other than the sinking feeling in my stomach. After my pleading, with promises and assurances, that Max would behave, he put Max on the phone.

"Hello," he said in a voice so low I could barely hear him.

"What are you thinking!?" I squeezed out through grinding teeth and drawn lips. "What is going on with you? Do you want to stay or not?" I asked.

I reminded him of his unshakable refusal to stay a second week at UCLA when he'd had the chance. "I'm sorry. I'll behave. I want to stay," he pleaded. Max said everything he could to convince me and the authorities that he would shape up and get his act together from that moment forward.

Two days later, the phone rang again. This time all I heard was, "You'll have to come pick him up as soon as you can. When can we expect you?"

It was crystal clear that I needed to get in the car and head back to get him immediately. It had been just four days and he was out of the program. There was no negotiating at this point. The decision had been made. So I got in my car and headed straight to the campus, where they had him in isolation from most of the other students, who were witnessing what could happen to them if they didn't toe the line. As I drove, I had several hours to think about all the ways I was going to just kill him—no video games for the rest of the year, no allowance for three months, or, worse, no more summer art classes ever. I was just through!

Meanwhile, they never told Max that he had been kicked out of the program. They knew there would likely be fireworks. They had kept him occupied in the rec room while I went to pack up his dorm room and load the car. I was to call them to let them know when I was done before I came to collect him. I knew this was not going to be pretty. When he saw me enter the room where he was hanging out with a couple of other students, including the young lady who had gotten him in the crosshairs on the first day, he was shocked and had a total meltdown.

"Nooooooooooo!" he exploded. "Noooooooo, I don't want to go!" He was blindsided, angry, betrayed, heartbroken, and belligerent all at the same time. "Noooooooo!" He yelled over and over, with futile promises of "I'll do better! Please, I'll do better!" and charges that "It's not fair!"

It was one of the worst days of my life too. When we finally got into the car, Max was sobbing uncontrollably. I was silent for a long time.

When he could finally speak, he blasted me with, "Why did you do this? Why didn't you let me stay? How could you do this to me? How could you take this from me?"

"It was not up to me," I explained to him. "It was up to them. Actually, it was up to you. You knew the rules. We went over them thoroughly before you got there.

"Why would I have spent all that time and money to buy all those new clothes and supplies, drive you hundreds of miles to school, only to snatch you out of it? Why would I do that?"

Turning the focus back on his own accountability, I asked, "Why did they make you leave? What did you do?"

There was a long pause. Of course, at first he insisted that he had done nothing wrong and attempted to justify every bad decision he made.

"They wouldn't listen to me. They wouldn't let me explain. They misunderstood everything."

"They . . . they . . . they . . ." was all I heard. But it was a very long ride home, and by the time we were closing in on the final stretch, he had grown completely sullen and silent. I could see that he had started to accept that it was his own fault that he had not followed the rules that he himself had agreed to.

It was a hard and painful lesson, one that is still a bitter pill to this day. It was the first time he had paid such a high price for his own actions; the door shut on a gilded gateway to the promise of success. He was devastated.

Max fell into a depression that lasted for weeks. He refused to talk to any of his mentors because he was too embarrassed, ashamed, and hurt. He was mad at the world and mad at himself. While he sulked in a deep funk, he could barely look me in the face and spent days on end in his room doing little else other than watching videos. When he did pick up a pencil and draw, his work was lifeless, and some of it was even dark with angry, violent images. I left him alone because I thought his pain was punishment enough, and honestly, I didn't know what else to do. But after this had gone on for too long, I felt that he needed to snap out of it and re-focus his energy to move forward.

It was our rule that only he would contact his mentors when he needed to and on his own terms. It was on a very rare occasion that I would reach out to them without his knowledge. This was one of those times.

I called to let each of them know what had happened. Since Max was still raw with the emotions of humiliation and self-doubt—he had big-time failed—the mentors all thought it best to give Max some time to reach out and initiate the call to talk about it. Max never did. So one by one, each called him to check in.

When forced to tell his mentors what had happened, he returned the call from Uncle Kevin last because he thought that conversation would be the hardest. After all, it was Uncle Kevin who had told him that he be-longed at the school. He thought he had let him down. I had to push him a few times. "Tell him. He'll understand." He did and Uncle Kevin was perfect.

"Yes, I told you that you belong there. But maybe I was wrong. I'm not wrong often," Uncle Kevin said, chuckling to lighten the gravity of Max's mood. "But I can admit it when I am." He conveyed to Max that accountability also requires humility, and he followed with wisdom and encouragement. "Maybe you don't belong there now. But that's okay. Maybe you just weren't ready. With talent you must also be disciplined, and you need to work on that. You have to play by the rules, especially from teachers who are there to give you what you need to succeed. So you messed up. But now you need to pick yourself up off the floor and move on. I've made some pretty big mistakes in my life too. But look at me now. I'm the better for it. So you made a mistake. I'll bet you won't make that same one again. You'll be better for it too."

Max really needed to hear that.

His mentors gave him permission to admit that he had let himself down. I was not privy to what was said between them. I only know that over time he began to forgive himself and the dark cloud surrounding his spirit seemed to lift. He finally arrived at closure by admitting it to me.

"Mom, I need to talk to you," he said to me in that tone that let me know that I needed to listen with care and compassion.

So we moved to our quiet space in the room filled with sunlight streaming in through the windows to discuss what had been weighing so heavily on his heart. I sat directly facing him and waited patiently for him to begin. I could see it was hard for him. After a long sigh, his first words were defiant.

"You should have told me that you were coming. I would not have liked it, but you should have told me. You weren't on my side. You took their side. You should have fought for me. You let me down."

Oh, here he goes, I thought.

"Oh no, you don't. You are not going to blame me, young man."

Sensing that this was a tough one for him to bear on his shoulders alone, I shifted into a more sympathetic voice.

"I did fight for you. My fight is always for you. But you have to do your part too. This is a partnership between us. We're a team. I can only do what I can do. I can't save you from you. Only you can do that," I said.

"I'm sorry, Max. I'm so sorry that it all happened the way it did. I wish we had the whole thing to do over again. I know you do too. But don't be so hard on yourself. It may be hard to face your failures, but they help you grow," I added as gently as I could. I shared with him one of my favorite inspirations from Maya Angelou: "Do the best you can until you know better. Then when you know better, do better."

He lifted his head, slowly got up to hug me, and said, "Thank you, Mommy. I love you. I'm sorry. I'll do better."

He entered his senior year in high school with a personal commitment to prove to himself that he had learned a valuable lesson from his experience of being kicked out of art school. It was the last thing he or I would have ever expected, given his love of the subject. So he was eager to start anew. But it was his new art teacher who truly motivated him, and not in the way one would expect. After his shocking pronouncement that Max should give up his dream to be an animation artist, it became Max's mission to prove the teacher wrong.

I learned of the teacher's devastating blow when I got a frantic call from Max while I was at dinner with friends during a business trip. He was hysterical and crying really hard. In a panic, I nearly yelled through the phone, "What's wrong?!" The thought of being miles away while he might be in serious trouble scared the life out of me.

Through uncontrollable sobs, he told me that his art teacher had told him, "Animation is not a real career. Your passion for anime is a waste of time. At best, you might be a graphic artist."

That was probably the most heartless untruth that anyone could have ever said to Max—especially coming from an art teacher! How do you explain the success of Disney and Pixar films? Had he ever watched the thousands of credits roll after a film? Had he ever watched the Oscars? There are no words to describe the rise of anger I felt at that moment. How dare he dash my son's dreams to the ground! Who was he but some washed-up middle-aged man whose own ambitions had been diminished and who perhaps had dreams of his own that either he had given up on or failed at. How dare you pile your failures onto my son?

After I calmed myself down, with a controlled voice I told Max to call Uncle Chris. He would know how to handle this. I was too angry.

"Call me back after you talk to him and let me know that you're all right," I told him.

"Don't you ever let another man tell you what you cannot do," Uncle Chris told him. "Only you can determine what you can or cannot do. You are your own man. Don't you ever forget that. Forget what he said to you. He may be jealous of your passion for what you do because he's all burnt out. Pray for him. But don't listen to him."

By the time Max called me back, his sobs had turned to sniffles. He had regained his sense of self and affirmed, "Yeah, what does he know? I'll show him." Attaboy!

We had a parent-teacher meeting shortly after that incident. The art teacher showed up, and before I could even open my mouth, he began defending himself. Apparently, Max had told him what Uncle Chris had said in response to the teacher's dream-killing counsel. When the teacher finished stumbling through some lame explanation about what he'd meant, I let him know my truth in front of Max and his counselor.

"I know my son, and I believe him and I believe in him. I don't know you. What I do know is that your job is to encourage students to do the best they can and to inspire them to dream. You did just the opposite, so you are not doing your job."

After I'd done my job, Max held his head up and with a look of total defiance told him, "I will be an animation artist. Even if you don't believe it, I do!"

After the meeting, I told Max, "That day when you are receiving an Oscar for Best Animated Feature, be sure to let the audience know his name, the one who said you couldn't do it. And don't forget to thank your mother."

Max brightened up and beamed a smile with a dreamy look, as if he were imagining the very day.

"Can I thank you now?" he said.

"Yes, I'd love to hear your acceptance speech," I said, happy to see his confidence return.

"I want to thank all of my mentors, and most of all, I want to thank my mom for always being there for me and supporting my dream," he said, holding an air mic in one hand and his pretend Oscar in the other. I did the royal wave to imagined onlookers, and we both laughed. He was all healed, at least for now.

Fortunately, soon after being demoralized by one teacher, he found a new one who did just the opposite. He began spending the next few summers taking private in-studio art lessons from Mr. Jared, a local university art professor who recognized his passion and potential and nurtured it.

Mr. Jared's studio was a kind of local mecca for multigenerational artists and conversation, always filled with music and lively banter. Typically, Max would study alongside a couple of other students at various stages in their skills development. To add to the spontaneous spirit of community, without notice or fanfare, a friend might drop by with food and beverages for anyone and everyone to enjoy, or in might walk an art patron interested in buying a piece of art. More often than not, the studio was filled with men of all ages and all walks of life, so art lessons would quickly and easily turn into hours of deep conversation about life and times, like the kind carried on at a barbershop.

While Max was mastering drawing figures in 3-D, he also benefited from multidimensional life lessons. Max matured just as his work did under the tutelage of another man who took him seriously and respected his commitment to the work it takes to become a thriving artist.

"You have to put in the hours, young man. You and I are a lot alike. It wasn't easy for me either," Mr. Jared said to Max, who was so hungry for acceptance for who he was. Max ate it up.

"You, Mr. Jared? But you are a great artist. It seems so easy for you."
Max was awed by Mr. Jared's creative genius on display on the walls and
easels all over the studio.

"It took me years. You just keep at it. Keep practicing. You'll get
better and better," he encouraged Max.

"I will? You'll help me?" Max seemed to be asking for more than art
instruction.

"Yeah, man. Meet me here on Saturdays. We'll work on it together,"
Mr. Jared said as he put both of his hands on Max's shoulders.

It was the support Max so desperately wanted and needed. With
Max's open embrace, Mr. Jared nurtured Max's natural talents into bold
strokes of self-expression on the canvas called Max.

Confidence restored. Check. Passion refueled. Check.

Inspired, Max started his own art studio at home. His team of co-
creators was made up of friends he had collected by design. Unpreten-
tious, loyal, earnest, and a little nerdy, his cohorts had one common
interest: anime. Their conversations, activities, and even political views
were filtered through the lens of the anime world of fantasy, heroes, and
the creators who produce them. Hayao Miyazaki, the Japanese film director, producer, screenwriter, animator, author, and manga artist, is
their god. Cartoon creators such as Craig McCracken and Butch
Hartman represent their dreams of having the ultimate career. When together, they spend most of their time discussing story lines, weaving tales
about superheroes, conquering demons, and exploring new worlds filled
with techno drama.

The mentors, in turn, benefited from Max's infectious passion and
fascinating interactions with his motley crew and became enlightened
about the phenomenon of anime fandom. It was not at all easy to convince
the mentors, especially Uncle Lawrence, to support and encourage his enthusiasm to pursue a career in anime. It took years for Uncle Lawrence
to finally accept that a plushie is a valuable collectible and not just a doll!
After all, he has his own collection of *Star Wars* memorabilia, including a
talking R2-D2 that I had given him for Christmas and that he displays
proudly in his office.

With full disclosure to the mentors, without fear of judgment, Max
coordinates a group trek to an annual three-day anime convention. On

the big day, like clockwork, cars arrive in the driveway as the crew assembles their carpool to hit the road to Oz, where the anime world comes to life. With Max at the nexus, rules are set, schedules and meeting points are determined, and the shopping lists for new anime-collection acquisitions are finalized.

Witnessing the months of preparation for the three-day marathon, I think their enthusiasm comparable to the fever pitch of the cultural phenomenon Burning Man. As it comes together every year, I admire and respect Max's community organizing skills, which he has honed out of a sheer passion and commitment to his fellow *otaku*. He has become masterful at establishing consensus and inclusion, recognizing strengths and teamwork, and, most important, sharing.

I have also watched him recruit, train, and manage a team of creative collaborators driven by his own vision to realize his mission to tell better stories. Their collective talent infused with Max's relentless inspiration is now put to work on his own productions.

Lesson 12: Look in the mirror and love what you see.

Self-identity and independence are challenges all kids face. The only difference is the flavor of the issues, like chocolate versus butter pecan. For Max, it was his physicality. His physical health was so directly tied to his emotional health, and Max needed to grow into his own swagger. He had to learn to play to his strengths, the parts of himself that would allow him to express his own style.

Self-love is not something you can teach, but you can model it, the way his mentors did. They are men who carry themselves with dignity, pride, and respect in a way that communicates to the world that they value their own self-worth. The ways they treat others and live their lives show the world that they love themselves.

As a mother, I have tried to role-model the same focus on the importance of a daily regimen of personal grooming, diet, exercise, and meditation.

"You have to take care of yourself inside in order to be beautiful outside," I would tell him.

Okay, so that's my belief system. Getting Max to believe it is something else entirely.

Every day starts with "Good morning. Did you sleep well?" and ends with "Good night, sweet dreams." In between are constant reminders to make each day a good one so rest comes easy and the next day he starts fresh and renewed. Every good day followed by another good day leads to a good life. At least that's the idea.

Sounds good, but here's what a good day actually goes like:

"Tuck your shirt in, or if you're going to wear it out, at least make it neat . . . Zip up your pants . . . Can't you at least try to fix your hair? . . . Pull your pants up . . . What, you are not going to put a coat on? . . . Did you brush your teeth, because it doesn't look like it . . . What's that hanging out of your backpack? You're going to lose those headphones . . . Got your wallet and your key, because I'm not coming home if you get locked out . . . Now go look in the mirror . . . What do you see? Are you good with it? . . ." is how we typically spend the last five minutes before we can leave the house.

Some stick, some don't, but I believe that the constant reminders of proper presentation to the world help him build awareness of his own self-image. I want him to learn that how you present throughout the day, inside and outside, influences how people respond to you.

"If you look good, you feel good, and when you show it, others will respond well to you," I would tell him.

Looking good may make you feel good, but there were two specific things that mattered most to Uncle Lawrence and that he demanded of Max: to speak clearly and to show good manners. Max learned them quickly in "boot camp."

"Don't talk with your mouth full . . . Wipe your mouth before you talk . . . That napkin belongs on your lap . . . Elbows off the table . . . I didn't hear 'yes, sir' . . . Respect your mother, and go do what she just said . . . Nobody is going to hire you looking like that . . . Speak up. I can't hear you when you mumble . . . Think before you speak . . . Look at me when I'm speaking to you . . . Did you make up your bed? . . . Why are your shoes in the middle of the floor? My wife is not your maid . . ." is how a typical day sounds with Uncle Lawrence.

"To speak clearly you have to stand up straight and make eye contact. That's important if you want me to take you seriously," he set in stone.

Eye contact with others is important, but I understood that, for Max, it was even more important that he be able to look himself in the eye. It took a while for me to realize how important it was to ask Max to look in the mirror. I always do it naturally before I leave the house. I never thought to ask him to do the same. I was just so happy that he got both shoes on the right feet, that by the time he looked fine to me, we were out the door.

Then one day when he looked particularly crazy and unkempt, it occurred to me that if he learned to do a personal assessment of what he looked like before he walked out the door, he might start to care about it. He had never stopped to look in the mirror to assess himself, to see what I saw. I was deeply saddened when I discovered why.

I asked him to look in the mirror, and what I saw was how much he hated looking at himself. After a hasty glance, he straightened his glasses a little and then shrugged and said unenthusiastically, "Let's go."

Wow, that was not at all what I expected. What did he see that made him react that way? So I asked him. His answer broke my heart again.

"I hate my body."

There was absolutely nothing I could do to change how he felt about his body. That he would have to resolve on his own. The boy in the mirror would need to come to love the man in the mirror he was to become.

Gordon Parks, the critically acclaimed African American photographer, wrote in his autobiography of his own personal struggle with self-love:

> No doubt it was wisdom that taught me that my most dangerous enemy could be myself. One morning, with shaving razor in hand, I had stared into the mirror and asked myself some rather bothersome questions. With hard eyes I stared back at myself and reeled off some disturbing facts, along with some advice: "You're approaching manhood and you dislike yourself. That's why you're interrogating me. *(Well, make up your mind to do something about it.)* You're so thin-skinned that the

softest criticism rubs you raw. *(Accept criticism, man. It can't hurt, and it could be helpful.)* Envy of others' success hangs around your neck like a rope. *(That's stupid. Use their success to give you inspiration.)* You squander too much time on trivial things, always hurrying to nowhere, and in a rush to get there. *(Take your time, man. Think things out first, then go.)* You avoid questions about yourself that you find hard to answer. *(Figure things out. You just don't have the right answers. So admit to it.)* You talk rapid-fire just to be heard, and without having anything worthwhile to say. *(That's downright ego. Listen more. Keep your big mouth shut and keep your ears open. Your insecurity's showing.)* Well, enough for now. There's plenty left on the list for tomorrow. *(One last thing: Until you're sure of yourself, you won't be sure of anything. Think it over. See you tomorrow morning.)*

Max was definitely living a Gordon Parks moment that lingered far longer and with more complex questions because he has additional challenges that most don't have to overcome. It was clear that he needed a special assist in the form of an intervention from the mentors. When it came down to something as specific as his body, they would know as one man to another the tender psyche of the ideal physique. I confided in them that Max needed to develop a healthier perspective about what he saw when he looked in the mirror.

The mentors automatically knew exactly what he needed. "You just need to put some muscles on those bones," Uncle Lawrence told him.

Max was already used to therapeutic exercises, but Uncle Lawrence meant something different. He was appealing to Max's sense of vanity rather than his disability.

"Can you do a push-up?" Uncle Lawrence asked him.

"Sure I can," Max responded.

"Well, try starting out with ten a day, and then add more reps as you get stronger. That will build up your arms and chest," Uncle Lawrence told him.

The next couple of years of annual visits to his mentors mandated gym time. In between, they provided plenty of encouragement. "How's your workout going? Are you keeping it regular?" Max was obliged to show his pecs and abs when using FaceTime. It was working slowly but surely.

When Max finally found a regular workout buddy to go to the gym with, there was a dramatic change in his attitude. His slim upper body grew buff as he developed his new "guns," and his back broadened into the coveted V shape that can stop a clock. He began to like to look in the mirror and admire himself. He wanted to wear only those shirts that showed off his muscles, and I bought a dozen of them, so happy to see him strut his stuff.

Once he gained a bit more respect for his physique, he seemed interested in adding his own style to it. Uncle Chris wears classic Hawaiian aloha shirts and has a closet full of them. He gave Max one, and with it came Max's first brush with his own style.

"Here, try this on," Uncle Chris said, giving him a black one with a white-and-yellow floral print. It fit him perfectly. That was it! Max loved the loose fit, and the colorful Hawaiian print perfectly suited his artistic side and outgoing personality. Max is a touch flamboyant. Uncle Lawrence gave him a handsome fedora for his birthday. His finishing swash of suavity has grown into his own gentleman's collection of fedoras, panamas, and even a leather safari hat. So Max's signature look is now a Hawaiian shirt, boat shoes, and a stylish head topper. When his hair gets so long that the bush won't fit under his hat, he's au naturel with his aloha fro.

The first time he heard a woman say to him, "I like your style," it was as if a thousand white herons were released into the sky. Like the sacred bird that is rarely seen, the corner of his mouth turned up as his head tilted to the side and his eyes twinkled. Suddenly, the switch flipped and looking "fresh" made a difference. He would never ever admit it, but she woke him up into being a new man, and he began to dress for the ladies.

His Hawaiian style is dress-up for Thanksgiving dinner, visiting the elders and Mom's friends, dinner at a restaurant with Mom, or a movie date. He also has a second look: a warrior tee, his favorite red Bucketfeet shoes, and his casual white fedora with a red band, compliments of Emirates as sponsor of the US Open. His self-identity was the first stage of self-love. He began to understand who he was and who he wanted to be. He was a sophisticate and a warrior, but a warrior first.

"Fashion serves a very important function for success," Uncle Jay said, looking dapper as usual in his custom-fitted, tailor-made suit. If success has a smell, Uncle Jay reeked of it, with his impeccably manicured style.

"When you look good, you feel good, and you might also earn more money because you do," he told Max.

Uncle Jay is living proof. As a financial professional and self-made millionaire, he exemplifies the fact that, according to *Forbes* and the *Wall Street Journal*, the bibles for business professionals, the better you dress, the more you achieve. When you are dressed well, you think more "big picture" and are inclined to make bigger decisions. When you are dressed well, you are perceived as a leader.

"My photography skill was equivalent to my college degree, so I dressed like a photographer," said Uncle Kevin. "I started my professional career wearing a suit with cowboy boots. My first fashion mentor was the photographer I worked for. He always wore cowboy boots, and I always thought he looked kinda cool. So I did too, until I developed my own style. I always wanted to be different, to somehow incorporate my own style into conformity. I wanted to stand out, but not in a way that how I dress or wear my hair would be a distraction."

"Why can't I just wear anything I want?" Max asked.

"Well, you can, but you gotta think about who you are dressing for. I always have a strategy, and I put thought into who I am meeting with and the impression I want to make. And that's how I decide on my style—one day, one meeting at a time."

Fashion tips from the mentors were helpful, but we all knew that it's much easier working on the outside than the inside.

I could tell how Max felt about himself each day simply by what he chose to put on to start his day. A nice clean shirt and fitted pants meant he was confident about his plans. A shirt strewn on the floor days ago, picked up off the floor, and thrown on meant he was not feeling well. Clothes can do only so much. It's not the hat, it's what is under it. It's not the warrior tee, but the soul inside of it.

Lesson 13: Self-love includes your relationship with food.

"What you put inside your body is more important than what you put on your body," I remind Max often.

Slow food, no fast food, is the rule in our house, and is why Max never had a McDonald's hamburger until the one time he tried it while hanging out with his friends, who were in utter disbelief that it was his first. He hasn't had another since.

In his younger years, when I had charge of his every meal, it was easy to be sure that he ate well, with a mostly natural and organic diet of fresh fruits and vegetables, juices, whole grains, seafood, and water. Every day, Max could count on a stovetop-cooked breakfast of oatmeal, pancakes, or waffles to start each morning; a fresh-cut sandwich with sides of tomatoes and cheese for lunch; and a warm dinner of comfort food with dessert to open the digestive system and set the stage for sweet dreams. His favorites are pancakes, pasta, sushi, and chocolate chip cookies. (Yeah, that sushi habit is expensive.)

"You better get a good job so you can afford to eat the way you like to!" he has heard me say more than a few times.

By now his preference for the quality and flavor of healthy, home-cooked food over processed food is ingrained. He totally appreciates that self-love simmers on the stove in the kitchen. Mom's stovetop-cooked macaroni and cheese with salmon, made with my secret sauce, is all about love. A batch of home-baked original-recipe molasses cookies warm out of the oven is all about love. His love for slow food over fast food is one of the things that I am most proud of because I know that it directly impacts his physical and mental health as well as his quality of life.

If he has heard it from me once, he has heard it a thousand times. I preach and teach every day to anyone who will listen that the impact of fast food on our self-love is extremely detrimental and far-reaching.

"What do you see when you drive through an urban neighborhood? Within a quarter-mile radius, there are rows of storefront signs with 'dollar deals' at McDonald's, Kentucky Fried Chicken, Subway, Pizza Hut, Wendy's, Captain D's, Mrs. Winners, White Castle, Popeyes, Arby's, Taco Bell, Jack in the Box, and what did I miss? These fast-food belts are indefensibly exploitative of low-wage earners, many of them single parents with mouths to feed. Cheap and convenient can become very expensive and debilitating when poor food options in food deserts present as a key factor in a major health tragedy in communities of color. It is no wonder that there is a disproportionate rate of heart disease, diabetes, and high blood pressure. It is not unlike tobacco and alcohol companies that market so aggressively to people of color, who suffer most from the lack of self-love. I believe that, as with tobacco and alcohol, there ought to be tighter regulation of the fast-food industry, starting with the number of franchises allowed in any one neighborhood. It is particularly insidious, since the industry knows the statistics but has prioritized profit over healthy communities and paying living wages. Yeah, I said it!"

"There she goes again," Max will say, rolling his eyes.

"Food is the most personal thing there is—it's what we put into our bodies three times a day—and yet we're so disconnected from it," say Nikhil Arora and Alejandro Velez, the founders of Back to the Roots, a food brand with a mission to "undo food" and reconnect families to the tradition of growing and preparing healthy, simple food the way our grandparents did. They gave Max his first mushroom kit to grow his own right in our own kitchen.

Max instantly took to the concept of urban gardening (he grows roses now too). Learning to cook was the next step. Self-love is cooking for yourself, and learning how to cook is an exercise in patience, science, and creativity that also prepares you to cook for others. Max loves cookies, so we started there. Learning how to bake Mom's molasses cookies was his first request. They are fun and easy to make together while learning to use the oven. Once he learned to use the oven, then we moved to the stovetop, beginning with making scrambled eggs with cheese, his second favorite breakfast only to pancakes. Now he loves to cook and takes great pride in it. When his friends come over, one of his first questions is, "Are you hungry? Would you like something to eat?" He loves to prepare meals for all his friends. I'm pretty certain that's why the house is so frequently filled with them. Aside from the food bill, some woman is going to be very lucky.

As his mother, I recognized that it was important for Max to learn the relationship of food not only to his body but to his soul, and to the nourishment of our relationships with one another. For the mentors, the concept was much simpler. Men love to eat! It wasn't difficult to convince them of the value of the lesson of eating well for the Black Mitzvah celebration. So it was their idea that one of the central activities of his Black Mitzvah opening weekend would be the Real Men Cook day where the stakes were high among the men to show off their kitchen skills when preparing their favorite foods. It was then that I realized that there are lots of men who really do love to cook. Makes sense, and I want one!

The Back to the Roots brand of home gardening kits showed Max how he can grow his own food, and expanded his intimate relationship with food beyond Mom's cooking and made it cool. The mentors made it manly.

Uncle Chris was the first one to teach Max some epicurean skills when he showed him how to make guacamole during the Real Men Cook day of his Black Mitzvah celebration. Max learned the recipe so well that he has developed his own special twist to make it his own. When Uncle Chris learned that Max's favorite breakfast is eggs with cheese, he told Max, "Well, if that's what you like to eat, then you need to learn to make that." Then he handed Max a pan and a spatula.

Uncle Kevin is the mentor who seems to most enjoy cooking, mainly because he is a single man who had to learn to do it for himself. He swoons when he talks about how his grandmother, who raised him, always had a meal on the table for him no matter what, and he learned to take pride in his own delectable creations. Uncle Chris is known for his guacamole, while Uncle Kevin is the one inclined to take on more complex dishes that require a bit of culinary skill. Off the cuff, Uncle Kevin can make magic with brussels sprouts roasted in olive oil with sweet garlic, ginger, and a dash of chili sauce, and he can make a smoothie with kale actually taste good. In a New York bachelor pad with an efficiency kitchen, Max learned to cook a full meal on a double burner or blend one in a Vitamix. And no one has self-love like Uncle Kevin. He has created a personal brand that spells success, confidence, empowerment, and pride in a dish well prepared.

When Max came back from his first visit with Uncle Kevin, the breakfast he made for us the next day was French toast cooked in a pan! Self-love with fringe benefits! Thank you, Uncle Kevin!

Uncle Jay does not cook and doesn't like to, but loves a home-cooked meal.

"I know food is important, and I know that I don't cook very well. But

I do not eat red meat or pork, because my family has a tendency for hypertension and high blood pressure. They are all heavy, and so I know that I need to be careful, and I know that I need to exercise every day. So when I chose my wife, part of the reason is that she is such a good cook. And that she cooks what I love to eat. The first thing my wife ever made for me is a chicken dish with blue cheese sauce. She had never made it before but knew that I love blue cheese. It's my favorite dish for that one reason."

He describes what it meant to him to know that, no matter what, his mother would always have breakfast waiting for him at the table, and he knew he would have a meal ready for him every evening, assuring him that someone cared about him. She planted the seed for self-love because he ingested his mother's love through every delicious morsel of food.

Uncle Lawrence gets nutritional love through honey-coated stickies on the refrigerator door: *Take your vitamin. Don't forget to drink a glass of water. Leftovers in the container are good for one more day.* We often kid Uncle Lawrence that he is under the complete control of his wife because he is so spoiled, and he knows it is true. After having earned the right to take her as his bride, his self-love allows him to enjoy all the love she has to offer.

By age seventeen, Max was learning that when style, fitness, and a healthy diet reflect the man in the mirror, it's easier to love yourself. Good manners and proper comportment will earn you respect. And when a man's relationship with himself is well tended, it will lead to independence, success, and the love of a good woman.

Lesson 14: You have a responsibility to community.

The purpose of Max's Black Mitzvah was to build a community of intent around Max's growth and development. Living responsibly *in* community is distinctly different. Sharing and giving back are central values, and Max had much to learn.

Your family is your first experience of living in a community, even if it starts with a community of two, a single parent and a child. There is a unique dynamic that can swing wildly from functional to dysfunctional in the second it takes to make a decision to eat that last slice of chocolate cake in the box in the refrigerator that you know is not yours.

Our extended family of aunts, uncles, cousins, and grandparents is our community by blood, and our family of friends is our support community by choice. All together, these people have wrapped us in an unconditional love that has created our belief system in humanity and our value system for community.

However, living responsibly in community with one another, whether by choice or by circumstance, takes training and mindfulness. Max is naturally a giver and gives often, with one caveat: it has to be what he wants to give. He is a giver but not a sharer. There is a vast difference. Giving is an act of generosity that can be conditional or unconditional. It can be sincere or insincere. It can be material and transactional or benevolent and completely free. Giving is a moment that is easy to forget, especially if it requires very little of you to do it. But sharing is an intimate interaction that brings out the best in humanity. Sharing is a virtue.

You never forget a shared experience with a sibling or a friend—like chewing a Twizzler from both ends until your mouths meet in the middle to fight for the last bite. Since Max has grown up as a single child in a single-parent household run by a doting mom, most days I'd ask him, "What do you feel like eating?" And then that's what we'd have. "What movie do you feel like seeing?" And that's usually where we'd find ourselves. Besides his annual birthday bash and occasional playdates and sleepovers, Max rarely had the opportunity to learn to share. No negotiation. No compromise. Spoiled rotten.

There was little that he asked for that he could not have all to himself, especially Mom. And unless there was a really good reason to say no, it was usually easier to acquiesce to his wants and demands. Add an ice-cream-scoop-size dollop of mother-son love, and I was wrapped around his finger. So yeah, it's my fault too.

Learning to share takes discipline until it is routine, until it becomes natural. I knew a good place to start.

It was Uncle Chris who had suggested volunteer work to help him develop outside interests. I thought Max would enjoy it because he would get to meet so many new people, and young people like himself.

When Max was fourteen, he did enjoy his work at the community center delivering hot meals to senior citizens. He got to ride in an air-conditioned van all day and chat it up with the driver. At each home where they stopped, a knock on the door would be met by a very grateful senior who loved having a smiling young person bring food and visit for a few minutes. Some insisted on giving him a dollar or a few coins. It was right up his alley. It was effortless work and he was always rewarded. At the end of the summer, several of the seniors had written letters thanking him, and that earned him recognition as the Volunteer of the Year. Even he was surprised to be honored in such a way, since, in his mind, this was the easiest job in the world. That summer, he learned how to provide care for others. However, I wasn't confident that this care expanded to the kind of generosity of spirit to give up a seat for those same seniors to whom he delivered hot meals, at least not without being urged to do so. We still had a lot of work to do. He was generous, but only after he'd had enough for himself. He was quick to ask of others, but he would not ask much of himself. If he wanted something, he was inclined to just take it without so much as a thought. That's not living in community.

Whenever I would check him for being selfish, he would pout and sulk. He could be made to feel bad, but he would quickly turn giving into a manipulation of the situation and require acknowledgment of his supposed act of comity. He was good at it.

Uncle Chris was the first to start calling him on it.

"I see you, Max. I get you because I was just like you," he said. "I am an only child and my mom would do anything for me. You know your mom will do anything for you and you abuse that. I did it too. But I learned that it's not going to serve you well as you get older."

In fact, Max had become a master manipulator of not just Mom, but of his therapists, teachers, friends, family, anyone who would soften because of his disability layered with his impish charm. With a mischievous smile and that irresistible twinkle in his eye that would sparkle through those long eyelashes, he would test to see what he could get away with and otherwise wear you down with his insistence on getting his way.

At school, he would demand special treatment outside the rules and seek extraordinary accommodations beyond those afforded him because of his disability, such as insisting that he had to be able to listen to music while in class or he couldn't focus because of his ADHD; or insisting that he had to have snacks in class "for energy." There was always a certain degree of truth in his case, but most of it was BS, and we both knew it.

However, there was a thin line, which he masterfully tiptoed, and inevitably pushed to the edge to achieve his personal goal. It was a problem, and I often had to answer for it in parent-teacher conferences and with friends and family whose patience was tested.

Later in the same year that he had received the Volunteer of the Year Award for his work at the community center, his selfishness reared its ugly head.

We were invited to spend Thanksgiving weekend in Minneapolis with Uncle Chris and Ramona's family friends. They lived in a big, beautiful house—big enough that we all had our own individual guest rooms. It was the first time I experienced heated bathroom floors! Art and photos everywhere reflected the warmth of memories and ancestors. The bed in my own room was swathed in layers of lush comforters and fluffy pillows. It was so beautiful that I looked forward to settling in when it was time for the house to go to sleep. The hosts had generously prepared primo accommodations for Max on his own floor with immediate access to the entertainment room with the big screen and gaming system, and his own bathroom—the dream bachelor's pad. What more could you ask for? All we had to do was be good guests and get invited back.

The house rules included that you make your bed, we eat together, and everyone shares in meal preparation and cleanup. Max refused to do any of it. When asked to help, if he did it at all, it was not without complaint and with the least amount of effort. No amount of my pulling him aside to threaten, cajole, or admonish him helped very much. Then he did the completely unforgivable. He had been given privileged access to the controls of the television, and then, claiming it was inadvertent, he preempted the programmed recording of our host family's favorite show so that he could watch his show.

To add insult to injury, in an embarrassing show of disrespect, he asked the man of the house, "What's your name again?" after we had been there for two days! Suffice it to say, we have not been invited back. I don't blame them, and I'm still ashamed.

When Uncle Chris confronted him about his selfish behavior, Max became very agitated, especially when Uncle Chris referenced his tactics targeted at his own mom.

"Max, you are a guest here because I invited you. Remember that.

How you behave reflects on me and your mother. You may be able to manipulate her with your apologies, because she loves you. But that's not enough for me. You need to straighten up and either be a part of this family, which includes the responsibilities of pitching in and being respectful, or we can't invite you to be a part of Thanksgiving with us again."

Max, in perfect form, went straight into his default mode by rerouting the subject. "I am not trying to manipulate my mother!" he protested. "I love her. Why would I do that?"

"Because it's what you do. I see you. You need to work on that," said Uncle Chris.

It was clear that Max was embarrassed. Also thin-skinned, he conflated Uncle Chris's gentle wisdom with criticism, which Max never takes well. Any and every word that he perceives as a negative takedown of his character is met with anger instead of as a cause to pause and reflect on what is meant to be counsel and guidance for his own good.

The day finally came when Uncle Chris put his foot down. He'd had enough. I'll never forget that day. We were visiting Uncle Chris and Ramona and their now-toddler Jeremy at their vacation home in Hawaii. We had just arrived from the airport and immediately got busy moving luggage into rooms and getting situated and comfortable for our weeklong stay.

As usual, the first thing Max did was go to the refrigerator to see what's in it. Meanwhile, everyone else was still preoccupied with some small activity, such as plugging in chargers, unfolding sheets and arranging pillows on beds, opening windows, and pulling out toys. When everyone was finally settled and ready to dig into our communal living experience, Ramona opened the refrigerator door and began searching for something.

"I know it was here," I heard her murmur.

Then more loudly I heard her follow with, "Did you eat ALL of the blueberries, Max?"

Uh-oh.

That's when Uncle Chris emerged on the scene in the kitchen. He repeated the question in the sternest voice I had heard him use ever. "Max!" There was a long pause for emphasis to be sure he had Max's attention.

"Did you actually eat ALL of the blueberries?"

At this point, Max was caught, cornered, guilty as charged, and totally feeling like he might be put on a plane back home right then and there. Uncle Chris was hot under the collar, but remained cool. Gotta give it to him. I know if I had done something like that, my father would have clocked me.

Then with measured calm, he asked, "Max, you didn't think anybody else would want some blueberries?"

Uncle Chris was about to take it to him. Max looked like if he could cough up those blueberries right that minute, he would.

"I guess so. But I didn't think—"

Before he could finish his sentence, Uncle Chris finished it for him.

"You didn't think. That might be the problem. You didn't think about the rest of us. Don't you think that is selfish? Now what if we can't find any more blueberries at the store? What if Jeremy wanted some blueberries? He's your little brother and you take food out of his mouth?"

To make it worse, by this time, Jeremy, only two years old, got in on it.

"I want blueberries!" he said, pouting.

Max hung his head and must have pleaded "I'm sorry" a dozen times. But Uncle Chris dragged that moment out and beat it like it was a shag rug on the clothesline. We had only been one hour into our communal holiday and it was already off to a rocky start. Once Uncle Chris felt he had made this point very clearly and was satisfied that Max was thoroughly schooled, we finally moved on. It was going to be a very long, hangdog week if we didn't change the mood quickly.

Ramona and I had stood by quietly listening the whole time, letting Uncle Chris handle it. When he finished his verbal whupping, Ramona put the period on the subject with, "Okay, so let's see what we can all share together."

Relief filled the air, and we began planning our activities for fun in the aloha sun and shifted the focus on where I could get my two favorite Hawaiian dishes, *lomi* salmon and *saimin* soup.

The next day we drove up the Maui coast to the North Shore. It's a long, slow, curvaceous, and scenic drive through lush forest and waterfalls, some so close that, if you are up for it, you can stop, get out of the car, and dive into the small pools. The five of us were all packed in with our towels, cameras, and snacks for the excursion.

True to form, Max didn't take long to start rummaging through the food. Everyone in the car heard him pop open the container of fresh-cut mango slices. The smell filled the inside of the car and made my mouth water. Now usually, Max would have inhaled every single slice before you could even have time to consider whether you wanted to enjoy a slice now or save it for later. But this time, Max, for the first time I ever witnessed, asked each individual person in the car, "Would you like a piece of mango?" before he even took one bite.

Ramona, acknowledging his newfound sense of self-restraint and community, politely responded, "No, not right now. But I'd like some later."

Jeremy hungrily took a slice, and Uncle Chris said, "No, I'll have some later. And thanks for asking."

Then Max told everyone, "I just ate two pieces. I'll save the rest for everyone else."

It blew me away. I had spent nearly seventeen years trying to teach Max to share, and it took Uncle Chris only thirty minutes of a "man check" in one day to get him to ask before scarfing down the first and last bite of food.

Max has been sharing ever since. To this day, he will ask me, "Mom, would you care for the last piece?" or "Is it okay if I eat this?" It is clear that there is something about the bass in a man's voice that has a completely different resonance than a woman's.

I was committed to work much harder to find ways for Max to learn to share and to give back, especially when he had been blessed with so much. With the help of Uncle Lawrence, I found a way.

During the time he spent away while visiting his mentors, I would be able to take time for myself to rest, rejuvenate, and refocus, something that single parents do not often get to do. Those moments are precious, and how we choose to use that time is critical. Sometimes I would use it to take a quick trip on my own to visit a friend or to sit by the ocean. Other times I would just stay at home and properly clean the house and enjoy having my favorite meal while listening to my favorite music, or enjoy just sitting still and taking in the view of Old Hickory Lake from my window in the welcome silence.

It was during one of the stay-at-home occasions that I came up with the idea for a lesson for Max about learning to share. It was inspired by Uncle Lawrence during one of his visits to our home to spend time with Max.

"Max, what are you doing with all these toys? There are enough in here for four or five kids. You are too old for most of these. You need to do something about this. What are you going to do?" he said in a voice that conveyed his annoyance as he stood with his six-foot-five frame filling the entrance to Max's boy cave.

For this no-nonsense man who demands efficiency and precision reasoning, Max had no defense for the clearly irrational clutter in a room filled with years of stuff that he had refused to get rid of.

So while he was away and I was in my cleaning mode, I started in on his room and amassed a knee-high pile of toys and books that he hadn't touched in years. I knew that once he saw the pile of riches he had hoarded over the years, suddenly he would think that he had to keep every one of them because they were his and his alone. Purging to make room for the growth that Uncle Lawrence laid the groundwork for was not going to be easy.

I had to have a plan. I made the decision that when he got back home, we were going to sort through the pile to determine what to keep, what to trash, and what to give away. It was almost Christmas, Max's favorite holiday. There would be more incoming, so this would be a good time to pounce. To capitalize on the spirit of the season of giving, I went to the Salvation Army to pick three letters to Santa from the Angel Tree to fulfill dreams of children who might not otherwise get a gift under the tree.

When Max saw the pile, his first reaction was as I expected.

"What are you doing with all my stuff!" he protested.

"That's up to you," I quickly responded.

I was ready for the resistance. I reminded him what Uncle Lawrence had said about him being too old for most of his toys.

"Maybe there are some children who might want some of these," I said.

That seemed to work. Defused and repurposed, Max reluctantly gave in to help reduce the pile to just a few of the items that he could not part with.

One item in particular stood out. It was his two-wheeled Rocket scooter. He had received it as a gift from his physical therapist, who thought that it might help improve his balance and help his gait. It was barely used and looked like it was fresh out the box, still-shiny wheels with no scuff marks. After one or two attempts to ride it, he found that it was too hard and lost motivation. Though he could never master it, he loved the idea of it. It came to represent his aspiration for freedom and something he could do just like the other kids whizzing on Rollerblades and skateboards through the neighborhood. He would sometimes touch the handles, as if he longed to take it for a ride, and tell me, "Mom, I'm going to try it again this weekend." But he never would. It was time to let it go, and he had to make the hard decision to give it away to fulfill another kid's dream.

After some discussion, he decided to give the gift to someone who actually could enjoy it, as a way to give back to the community. So we tied a bow on it and delivered it to the Salvation Army Angel Tree addressed to the little boy who'd asked specifically for a Rocket scooter for Christmas.

He was proud to report back to his mentors that he had gotten rid of a bunch of toys that he had outgrown or no longer wanted.

"So what did you do with the scooter?" Uncle Lawrence asked. He knew how difficult it would be for Max to let it go.

Max told him that he had given it to a little boy who wanted it.

"Man, I'm really proud of you. That was special. I know that was a hard decision. You did a good thing there," he told him.

It was just the kind of therapy he needed. Those words provided the kind of balance that improved his gait as he walked a little taller with self-pride. He seemed to turn the page from lingering childhood instincts to embrace a new phase of maturity.

After that, giving to the Salvation Army Angel Tree became an annual tradition. Once the tree goes up, Max will say, "Mom, are you going to go pick up the letters from the Salvation Army? Let's make somebody happy this Christmas."

Those seeds of giving and sharing planted by his mentors took root and began to grow like honeysuckle. Max opened his heart and began to attract a healthy and supportive community of friends who dug in and would not let go.

With affirmation from men who have instilled in him the value of a mission of giving, service, and sharing with others, he has built his own creative community and has learned what it means to be of service to it. The impact of Max's compassion, empathy, and love attracts and retains the friendships that sustain him.

With a new grasp of giving, sharing, and community organizing, Max, with help from Uncle Chris, expanded his community service beyond his immediate friends and family to think about his role in the broader community. Uncle Chris has taught Max civic responsibility, the importance of supporting and voting for candidates who promote local interests for the common good, and the importance of investing his money in local businesses.

Since he has come of age, Max votes in every election, but only because he has to because Mom and Uncle Chris insist. He vows that he hates politics, but he loves to spend money. We can work with that.

"We can exercise power through our vote with our ballots and with our dollars," Uncle Chris explained to him.

Uncle Jay has taught him the value of financial investment, and Uncle Chris has taught him where to invest it for the best social impact. So we all work with Max together to spend his money wisely and to "shop his values."

Uncle Chris spelled it out plainly for him.

"If one of your core values is respect for others, then only buy from businesses who respect others, who don't discriminate, who pay fair wages, and who don't use slave labor. If you value the environment, then only buy from businesses that do it no harm. If you value the health and well-being of people, then only buy from businesses who sell healthy goods. Fortunately, we live in an economy where you have choices. Make responsible ones that are best for the community, and we all benefit."

With a new mission and purpose, Max spends less time on porn (thank God!) and more time using the Internet to research the brands and products that he spends his money on. He's even got his friends doing the same now. He's helping to build a conscious and responsible community, and I could not be more proud.

He is learning that community starts with self. You have to know who you are in order to have the impact that you want to have and to be the hero you want to be. For Max, there is still much more to learn, and he is growing more open, challenging convention, and seeking answers.

Chapter 6

The Circle Widens

There is a South African philosophy known as *ubuntu*, which means "I am because we are." It underscores my personal relationship with God that informs me that our purpose in life is to be here for one another.

Award-winning writer and culturalist Milisuthando Bongela taught me an extension of the *ubuntu* philosophy—the concept to *khapha* Max, which means to accompany him as a way of support, in a way that brings him comfort that he is not alone.

Raising Max to be a global citizen has meant drawing upon our privileged access to professionals and leaders and their families, of every race, class, religion, ability, and sexual preference, to *khapha* him to remove barriers to Max's ability to move about the world comfortably in his own brown body.

By design, I created his Black Mitzvah to be a cross-cultural experience to provide exposure, opportunity, and connectivity to the spirit of *abantu* (humanity).

Our lives were so enriched by the wisdom from Max's Black Mitzvah mentors that I began mining for others. Some were unintentional, their paths simply crossing ours at an intersection that changed a course or a direction or added a significant contribution to his life mission.

Among his inner circle of our trusted friends and mentors is the owner of a race-car-driver training school in Tampa, Florida. It was on a professional racetrack where Max had his first experience behind the wheel. Beyond the thrill of it all, it was the ideal way to learn to drive, since the number one lesson in driving a race car is safety. Max learned to do figure eights like a fiend to master the art of going into and coming out of a turn, and he had the experience of a lifetime while doing it.

It was his tenth-grade creative-writing teacher who recognized his talent as a visual storyteller. Max hated writing on a computer, since it was too difficult for his fingers to access the keys on a keyboard because of his lack of fine motor skills. The frustration interfered with his ability to freely express his ideas. So Mr. Dean assigned him to storyboard his essays rather than just typing words into a computer. Storyboarding gave him the room to draw and put on paper what he could visualize in his mind's eye.

It was a neighbor turned mentor who went on long walks with Max to walk his dog and get in some exercise and some man talk who taught him the Cherokee "Tale of Two Wolves."

"Which wolf are you going to feed?" he taught Max to ask himself whenever he was battling his inner demons. I've relied on that pearl of wisdom often, not only to remind Max that he is in control of his reactions to his own emotions, but also to remind myself at times.

He never made the distinction or cared that these three men—a racing instructor, a creative writing teacher, and a friendly neighbor—were white. With them, it never mattered. He trusted that they had his best interests at heart. They don't hate black people. They demonstrated that they care about him.

Close friends, his doctor, a basketball player turned business mogul, and professionals in the industry that he has chosen to chart his career have all helped to adorn the golden fleece of courage and character worn by my gentle warrior. Together they have created what functions as an external neural network that, as with gold, the more Max uses, the more vibrant he becomes.

Uncle James

Still riding high on the breathtaking election of our first black president the month prior, we floated merrily through the holiday season and spent Christmas with our friends in New Jersey, Auntie Cheryl and Uncle James. We love to visit Cheryl and James because she is the consummate homemaker and he the pleasant and pliant homemaker-ee. She makes everyone feel like a special guest in her artfully curated kitchen, equipped with smart appliances and perfectly matched silverware and stoneware, where we spend most of our time catching up on life while she is doing skillful food prep for the next meal.

One of her specialties and Max's favorite is muffuletta with olive relish that even Bobby Flay would aspire to. Besides being top chef at home, she also happens to be a professional in the prime of her civics career. And so from current affairs to an update on what's new with her "nephew," we enjoyed catch-up conversations between bits and bites.

"How's Max doing?" Cheryl always wanted to know first.

"Oh, he's fine. He's a lot of work, though. It's hard to find 'me' time anymore and my waist is beginning to show it."

"Me too. I'm in a size twelve now, girl. I know, I've got to get back to the gym too."

"How's work?" was a more comfortable topic.

"I love the new girl on my team. She's got some great ideas. I just have to try to keep everybody else from getting in her way. You know how folks can get when they fear for their jobs."

"Yeah, I hate the whole hiring process. I much prefer keeping the talent I have to spending so much time training new people."

"I know that's right," Cheryl said with a verbal high five.

We trailed off into so many different areas, covering ground about our families, work, and a lot about our aging parents.

"Girl, I might have to move my mom into our home, and she's not having any of it."

"Yeah, I don't blame her. My mom is the same. Think about it. Would you want to move away from all your friends, the house you've lived in for so many years, and become a burden on your kids? It's something I'm thinking about now. I don't want to leave a decision like that up to Max."

While we talked, completing each other's thoughts and leaving little room for air, Cheryl cooked. Eventually, the smell of food lured the men into the kitchen like flies.

"Ready for your muffuletta, Max?"

Heaven on warmed bread is the way to Max's heart.

"Uncle James, you are so lucky. You get this every day?"

"Pretty much. You've got to marry well," he said with a twinkle in his eyes. "I knew what I was doing when I picked a woman who can cook. She takes good care of me. Better than I could my own self. That's the key, Max. You've got to marry well," he said grinning proudly.

When James is not on the golf course or the tennis court, he's an advocate in superior court. And when he is relaxing at home, he's reading the paper at the kitchen table with his ball cap on and pretending like he's not listening to your conversation. But every now and then he can't help himself and pipes up with an amusing quip or a harrumph that lets you know he's heard every word. He's a great listener who has worked in and around the justice system for nearly forty years. That he spent days in the courtroom "with suspects and criminals" was fascinating to Max.

Before learning otherwise from Uncle James, Max thought criminals were mostly black and brown people who were chased by cops, cuffed, and thrown to the ground, or needed to be killed. He had learned that from social media, television, and movies. If you Google "images of black men in the news," the first picture you might see is of a black man handcuffed behind his back. The memes mostly reflect negative or cartoonish characterizations of black men as suspects, violent or ignorant buffoons. It is no wonder that Max's perception of criminal justice begged for an explanation of why this was so. The black men he knew were righteous, respectful, and responsible. I didn't realize how much he had internalized this until I overheard a conversation he had with Uncle James. He had an opportunity to learn something important that many do not get: insight from inside the justice system.

"Are all criminals black people?" asked Max.

Uncle James is known for his distinctive chuckles. He does it before, during, and after nearly every response. He has a full-throated chuckle that conveys that he finds something genuinely funny and a rippling chuckle that says something more like you've got it all wrong. With the latter, he responded, "Oh no, no, no. They come in all stripes and colors. I never know one day to the next who's coming in. I've seen it all."

"How does it feel to send someone to jail?"

Max wanted to know how one who has the power to take away from another something as fundamental as the right to freedom can justify that.

"Well, it doesn't feel good. So if I can help it, we try other options. However, my job is to protect the community. And some people need to be off the streets. Others just need some time away to think about their mistake with the hope that they will make better decisions in the future," he answered.

"With that said, I do have compassion for the young men and women who have to stand before an imperfect system and who, I recognize, have not had the best of circumstances before they wind up there," he continued. "It doesn't matter what color they are. I hate that life is not always fair. But it is not up to me to judge who is guilty and who is not. That's for the jury to decide. I do try to take all the facts and the circumstances into consideration in every case. I try to give them the fairness that life doesn't always give them."

Max has always been quick to litigate in a situation where he thought someone was being taken advantage of or hurt by someone else, having often been a victim himself. Uncle James helped give him perspective on the kind of challenges people face that may make them be mean to one another. He learned to not always be so quick to judge others and that sometimes kindness is better than punishment or revenge. It was similar to advice he had received from Uncle Kevin, who told him to pray for his bullies. It all started to make sense. Sometimes it is important to give someone another chance. It makes you a better person too.

James easily recognized that Max was teachable and became an "uncle" who gave special time to mentor him whenever we visited. Max enjoyed much of it in the passenger seat of Uncle James's Mercedes-Benz as they cruised around town running errands, taking the long routes. The success of a distinguished gentleman was not lost on Max. Quoting Uncle James became a regular go-to reference as the best answer to a question or an opinion that was worthy of the highest respect.

"I don't know about that," Uncle James likes to say when he disagrees with you or you say something that needs substantiation. So when I told

Max, "You could have gotten a B in science if you had turned in your homework on time," I got, "I don't know about that. Uncle James said a B is great if you tried your best."

"Did you?"

"Well, maybe not my best, but at least I tried."

"And you think that's what Uncle James meant?"

"Well, I don't know about that."

"Uh-huh. Well, I do," I said with the one-eyebrow uplift that let him know that I would not tolerate his nonsense.

Sometimes "being Uncle James" almost got him in trouble.

"If you picked up your clothes, I wouldn't have to fuss at you," I once scolded him.

"Oh, I don't know about that. If it wasn't my clothes, it would be something else," he responded.

"Oh no, you didn't!"

He doesn't realize that he almost got a shoe thrown at him for that one.

On a much more constructive note, since spending one-on-one time with Uncle James, Max has begun to assess other people with nuance and make better decisions about when to walk away and when to intervene. He is more forgiving, choosing his battles more carefully. Like Uncle James, he became a better judge of character and, in turn, developed his own.

Uncle Moe

Moe joined the mentoring circle a year after Max's Black Mitzvah began. It happened when we met up with my dear old friend and his partner when we vacationed on Martha's Vineyard the summer after Max turned fourteen. It was love at first meeting.

Of all his mentors, Uncle Moe most treats him like a peer, allowing Max to be himself and to be taken seriously by a very successful man who is an international finance expert, a world-class diversity trainer, and fluent in at least three languages, but who still enjoys life like a little kid—which is likely the secret to his success. Moe quickly became fluent in Max, and when they are together, they are just boys, and they laugh a lot. He quickly earned status as the fun uncle.

The relationship began when Max went stag to the "Teen Party" on the Vineyard. The island community is small and feels exclusive, though it is absolutely not. Anybody can visit. However, the journey and the cost to vacation there tend to squeeze in only the elite. This particular summer was special, and I especially wanted to be there. It was the summer of Obama, and the smell of his recent presidential win wafted in the island breeze off the Atlantic Ocean.

During our first day out for a bit of a walk around Oak Bluffs, we ran into a dear friend who gave Max a very special invitation into the community's inner circle. Since we were not frequent visitors, we didn't know many of the people on the island, and so I didn't know what to expect for Max when he decided that, if he did nothing else for the entire week, he was going to his first teen party with his peers and no grown-ups, the social event of the year.

I was excited for him too. But I also had concerns about whether he would fit in and be accepted for who he is. With his unusual walk and crooked arm, would he once again be rejected by members of the opposite sex or made fun of by the other boys?

One of his mentors, who will not be named to protect his dignity, gives a hilarious recount of the first time he asked a girl to dance.

"I was so nervous that I lost my voice. When the words finally cracked out of my throat after a very awkward silence, and with her friends staring at me like I was toad, I said, like a complete nerd, 'You don't want to dance with me, right?' She, with that look, you know, head tilted sideways and an eye roll, said, 'Right.' And then I heard her say to her girls, 'Puhleez.' At least they held back their laughter until after I walked away as fast as I could with my tail between my legs. It took me nearly a year to work up the nerve to even go to a party again."

Girls can be so hard on a brother. It's difficult enough for a young man to brave the walk across the room to face the unknown when it comes to getting the answer to the simple question "Would you like to dance?" A yes could set you on top of the world. A no can send you into the dark corner of humiliation. Max was especially vulnerable, and I wasn't sure how much his fragile ego could withstand.

After we delivered Max to the door, guarded with security to check for the names on the guest list and to tell parents, "Teens only," Moe and

I walked to the courtyard nearby, where we waited outside for hours. I wanted to be close by—to be the safety net to catch his woe just in case things did not go well. While I fretted, Moe feted me with words of encouragement and an ice-cream cone. "He'll be fine," he reassured me over and over. As we strolled past the shops nearby, he was unaware that I was pretending to window-shop while intensely looking at the reflections in the windows to watch for any signs of Max exiting from the building in distress.

More than two hours passed, and I was antsy. I was threatening that it was time to go retrieve him. Besides, it was getting late. Moe had done all he could to hold me back, but I couldn't stand it anymore.

As I approached the entrance to the club, I knew I was treading into sacred territory made exclusive only to the special guests inside for that one evening each month, off limits to helicopter parents. With a slight reservation, I knocked on the door. When it opened, I had to raise my voice over a Ne-Yo "Closer" party mix pumping the floor and the loud chatter of voices and laughter.

"Do you see a young man in there wearing a blue Hawaiian shirt and a fedora?" I asked the guy guarding the door. He immediately knew exactly who I was referring to.

"You mean Max?"

The door opened a little wider, just enough for me to spy him sitting on a barstool, a drink (nonalcoholic) in hand, holding court with not one but two girls!

As it turned out, Moe was right. Max was more than fine. He was loving every minute. He was in his element. All that worry for nothing.

"Is it time to go? Meet my new friends before we go." He introduced the two smiling young ladies, who seemed to be sad to see him go. As we moved to leave, the two young ladies both chimed, "Bye, Max. See you around."

I should never have underestimated his ability to charm the socks off anyone, especially girls. With those beautiful hazel eyes and silky lashes, he owns you once he gets your attention. Uncle Moe laughed at me and slapped Max on the back.

"All right, son. Not bad!" Max beamed and proudly pulled out two little pieces of paper with phone numbers. He's a player! That was the moment that Max and Uncle Moe were forever bonded. From then on, they were "boys."

He never called either of the two girls whose phone numbers he had gotten. He didn't need to. He had earned them. He had proved to himself that he could pull members of the opposite sex, and they were cute too! Mission accomplished, he was imbued with a sense of validation that he was attractive despite his obvious physical challenges. More than anything in the world, Max needed to believe that being differently abled would not stand in the way of him being able to shine as a desirable person. He needed the opportunity to affirm that his personality defines who he is, not his cerebral palsy.

It is what we all seek. Acceptance of yourself and from others is a defining moment for anyone and everyone. Uncle Moe, who is thriving while gay and black, understood this well. He and his partner have experienced a lifetime of breaking down barriers of acceptance, and proving himself through his achievements and obvious joy in living a rich and full life. Uncle Moe role-models a deep commitment to staying true to oneself and a determination to forge forward rather than to retreat from a world that can be brutal and judgmental.

Max and Uncle Moe share a lot in common as men who must bear the extra weight of overcoming societal pressure and challenge perceptions of human value. Part of the process of coming to understand and accept who you are is to discover your purpose and to live for it. That's when life becomes joyful. A joyful life is infectious and opens the door to beautiful relationships and meaningful impact on the lives of others.

Doc

I imagine that Dr. Nevin must be living a joyful life because of the way he has blessed ours with extraordinary compassion and kindness. We met him not long after the medical debacle with Max's hamstring surgery that he had when he was eleven years old. Turning thirteen meant a new lineup of specialists for his changing body, including a new pediatric neurologist for his teenage years. We were referred to Dr. Nevin, the man who righted Max's world back on its axis after he'd suffered such a devastating blow to his dream of being able to play basketball. "I'll never trust another doctor" was still part of his belief system.

When we first met our new doctor, I was skeptical. Dr. Nevin was awful young, I thought. After what we had gone through with medical "professionals," I was a bit skittish. But I must confess to my sin of reordering my priorities: because he's very good looking, I was inclined to give him the benefit of the doubt. I was eager when he invited me to join the two of them for Max's first exam. I was really hoping hard that he'd be great so that I could enjoy the eye candy while Max got good care. Lucky for us, we hit the jackpot.

Doc, as Max came to call him, was the first doctor to ever just sit and listen to Max spill his guts, which he will do easily with the tiniest bit of encouragement. Maybe it's because of his own personal background. Doc is Puerto Rican with two young sons of his own. So he knows what it is like to be seen and treated as different and he also understands the challenges of young boys who want to grow up to realize their dreams, just as he has.

After a visit to the examination room, Doc would invite Max into his private office so they could just talk like men. I didn't mind the extra time. In fact, I appreciated it. The best doctors are those who listen and understand how important taking a little extra time with a client is to the healing process. While Max unloaded his burdens, I sat outside in the waiting room reading old issues of *People* magazine, lost in the saga of the latest Hollywood breakup or the fashion reviews of "Who wore it better?"

They seemed to truly enjoy each other. Every time they emerged from that room, they were both laughing.

Doc nodded to me with Max in earshot. "He's all right. Max is a fine young man, very impressive."

It was Doc who actually helped Max walk with a little less pain by operating on his spirit rather than his legs. Doc helped Max feel so much better about himself from the inside that it showed outside. Max began to find his own stride.

Doc's dose of patience and compassion extended beyond office visits. He was instrumental in allowing Max the opportunity to have a universe-opening experience to go stargazing at the summit of Mauna Kea on the Big Island of Hawaii.

In order to take the tour, we had to fill out a health waiver. I didn't know this before we left for our trip. When I indicated that Max had cerebral palsy, they absolutely would not let him go on the excursion without a doctor's note. My heart sank. The tour was the next day. That meant we had a very short window to get permission, and the six-hour time difference was not in our favor. So with urgency, I called and explained the situation to Doc's assistant. In what can be described as a heroic act of kindness, he responded immediately with exactly what we needed to allow us to join the eight other fellow excursionists to experience a view that few get to see.

The next day, Max and I enjoyed the scenic road trip in a van up to the highest point of Hawaii, nearly fourteen thousand feet, to witness the grandeur of the galaxy in the midnight sky. It was much colder than we were prepared for at that altitude. Even with the parkas and gloves that the tour guide provided, it was freezing. As we cuddled and shivered together, it warmed my heart to be able to see the awe in his eyes.

"The world is so beautiful from up here," he said scanning the expanse above and below from his perch on a big rock in the shape of an armchair.

"How does it make you feel?" I whispered in his ear, careful not to interrupt the reverent quiet that enveloped our group of stargazers.

He whispered back to me, "Anything is possible," and smiled. He was quoting Uncle Kevin.

"Amen," I said, my head tilted upward in prayer toward the gods.

I prayed that he would remember that moment and that it would seep into his soul. Down on the ground, his view of life could often slip into a dark space. Years of bullying had taken their toll. Often, his words reflected a worldview focused on what he thought was impossible. Once, while getting a little fresh air and some exercise during a walk around our neighborhood of manicured homes on a jetty of land surrounded by boat docks, he bemoaned man's lack of humanity. I was struck by the dichotomy of the views of the beautiful outdoors and the pessimism he was expressing at a moment of obvious abundance. I made note of that to him, but my words seemed to fall at his feet.

"Just because you live in a nice house doesn't mean you are a nice person. Lots of people care only about their own selfish interests even if it means they trample on those of others," he philosophized quite eloquently, I thought.

I could not deny he had a good point. However, for someone so young who wants to change the world, I wanted to restore the optimism he found on the mountaintop.

After his rant about the downfalls of society, I countered, "Your worldview sounds a lot like despots who rule to oppress rather than to serve and protect people."

I knew that would get a rise out of him. He is totally an Obama man. He stopped dead in his tracks and looked at me in shock.

"I am NOT like them. I have a heart! I care about people!"

"Well, that's all that matters," I said to him. "What is in your heart is all that matters."

It is true. He does care deeply. As dark as society can seem at times, he can find the good in everyone as deep as it may be buried. That is his special gift. He can see the best in you and bring it out, like he did with Doc. On our next office visit, Max brought pictures of the summit at Mauna Kea to show him. He had signed one of them to give to him, the one of him standing on top of the rock where he sat to view the stars, in his signature pose holding the peace sign over his heart. Doc was pleased to see Max so jubilant as he recounted our big adventure, since many of their conversations were laden with the latest ill that was troubling him, physical or psychological.

"I'm glad to see you so happy," Doc said to him. "I'm happy I could help make it possible."

He proved to Max that there are people besides his Black Mitzvah mentors, his mother, his family and friends, who do care about others just as much as he does—one block at a time, restoring his faith in humanity. Anything is possible with a little help from a beautiful man, inside and out. The potential is even greater with the help of many more like him.

"Magic"

Max's potential is easily recognized by even the most uniquely exceptional.

As he often does, Max accompanied me on a business trip, this time to Schaumburg, Illinois, to attend a full-day corporate supplier conference. He was on summer break between ninth and tenth grades and had just been kicked out of the Ringling College of Art and Design summer arts program and so needed a little magic, and wouldn't it be great to get a chance to see the man who was nicknamed for having so much of it, Earvin "Magic" Johnson, who was the featured speaker at the event!

While I listened to speakers and networked with other minority business owners, he quietly camped in the cafeteria, where he completed the math homework I had given him for the summer and occasionally chatted up an employee on break. Then right in the middle of things, one of the event staff approached and whispered for me to step out of the room. I was a little nervous. What was wrong? What did he do? But when I saw him in the hallway with a great big smile, waiting for me to join him, I knew something special was about to happen.

"Is it okay if I take him to meet Magic Johnson?" the staffer asked.

"WHAT!!! Absolutely! As long as you take me with you!" I said a little too loud, and I had to gather myself to avoid embarrassing us all. I had hoped that Max would get to see him, but to meet him in person—priceless!

I followed along like a puppy as Max was personally escorted by the corporate brass, a senior management-level executive, to meet one of the NBA's most illustrious players in history and a billion-dollar business mogul. We merged into a private hallway, where Earvin "Magic" Johnson was on his way to take the stage to speak.

"Mr. Johnson!" she called.

He stopped and turned as if he was expecting us.

"I'd like you to meet someone very special," she said.

Magic seemed to take in the full measure of the young man as he approached. Standing six feet nine inches of pure mandinka—a term of admiration that I use to describe a proud strong brother—he was a literal giant beside Max, who had to nearly look straight up in the air to meet his gaze. It was comical to see them standing side by side, and they both knew it. After sizing each other up, they both laughed, then introduced themselves to each other.

"Hello, my name is Magic," he said.

Max, craning his neck, returned, "My name is Max. Nice to meet you. You play basketball. I always wanted to play basketball."

Magic raised his eyebrows in surprise.

"Yeah, I used to play a little ball," he said slyly. "You look like you might be a great ball player. You look like you could do anything you want to do," he told him. "What do you want to do?" he asked Max.

"I'm an artist."

"Wow, man, that's really cool. I can't draw a lick. But I admire people who have that skill," Magic responded.

I know that Max really wanted to ask him, "Do you like anime?" so he could get him on the playing field for a game that he would most assuredly win. But Magic is known for his fast moves and charging the lane, and so before Max could go in for the alley-oop, Magic chuckled again and stole his move and dunked on him with, "Nice tie, man. I like your style."

Swish. Max was toast.

"Thanks. I like yours too," he rebounded, as he straightened as tall as he could to take in the full, meticulously well-dressed stature of the larger-than-life man in front of him. We all did. Magic, just as his name implies, has seemingly supernatural powers. He motioned to the company's staff photographer to come over.

"Can I take a picture with you?" he asked Max.

He put his hands on Max's shoulders and leaned in. After a few minutes of posing, it seemed that Magic had taken a liking to the young man. Maybe he recognized something that he saw in himself—a sense of purpose, leadership, and a sensitivity to the strengths and weaknesses in others.

"I think you're a point guard like me," Magic told Max. "Your 'ball control' is your command of the world around you. I can see it in just the way you handle yourself, young man."

Max was visibly overwhelmed that this giant of a man thought that he was a boss.

"Can I have your phone number?" Max blurted out. He wanted more of this of kind of mentoring.

"Sure, here's my card. Call me anytime."

Max grinned so hard I thought his cheeks might cramp. Then, Magic grabbed a copy of his book, *32 Ways to Be a Champion in Business*, and signed it to Max. They shook hands again and we snapped more pictures like paparazzi.

Afterward, conference attendees were regaled by Magic as we listened to him speak in his unmistakable style, interspersed with chuckles of bemusement at his own expense. He waxed on about his basketball career and how it led to his journey to become a titan in business. Central to his success, he pointed out, was the role of mentors, especially when it came to starting his businesses.

"I had watched so many other professional athletes lose all of their money. I knew I didn't want to make the same mistake," he said.

He knew that he wanted to do something for his own community. He started buying Starbucks franchises in black and Latino neighborhoods, proving that underserved communities could produce a significant return on investment. With one success after another, he began building an empire known as Magic Johnson Enterprises. Today, it includes movie theaters, T.G.I. Friday's franchises, Sodexo food services, and Burger King locations in urban communities across the country. From a point guard to a point man, Earvin "Magic" Johnson has grown into an author, a motivational speaker, a businessman, and a billionaire.

A man who had risen to great heights because he was able to maximize his full potential, Magic wanted to affirm that for Max.

Max has not yet made that call to Magic. But I believe he will one day when he is ready. He knows his game and can run offense with the skills of a pro. His players include the friends he has cultivated into a carefully recruited creative arts team who look to him to lead production of their projects. He is the executive producer, overseeing quality and completion to ensure the final product fulfills the collaborative vision of the team. His players include his friends who coordinate their schedules to accommodate his very organized group outings and events. His players also include his family and mentors, who have come to know when it is time for them to step in and step up to take the ball to assist Max's team-winning drive for the score.

It was an esteemed honor for Max to meet Barack Obama, Allan Houston, and Earvin "Magic" Johnson, three giants among men. But there are men who are not so famous and may not have legions of fans but who, nevertheless, are of tremendous influence in their fields of industry. They were men I thought Max needed to meet. I leveraged every available resource I had to make that happen. I wanted to make certain that Max had a chance to make a connection that might open his world of possibilities and to benefit from the guidance, wisdom, and encouragement of those who are living his dream.

These were mentoring moments that have had a significant impact on his life and that resonated all the way to his soul.

Industry men

Max has the soul of a storyteller. By the age of seventeen, he had become a human Wikipedia of information about the history of animation and had an arsenal of opinions about what is good and bad about the state of the art. He has watched every cartoon and anime series, can give you the chronology and audience demographics, and knows every character and story line, the cartoon and anime creators, voice actors, music scores, and the animation techniques and who uses which. If you ask his favorites in any category, it is impossible to get one answer. There's just way too much to love. However, among his heroes in the industry are Butch Hartman, creator of *Jimmy Neutron* and *The Fairly OddParents*, and Rebecca Sugar, the creator of *Steven Universe*. He can talk for hours on end about anything and everything animated and does little else. He has accumulated way too much knowledge and it clearly would be a terrible thing to waste. It was time for him to get a deeper understanding of the business of entertainment media so he could turn all his passion and knowledge into a profitable career.

I planned an "interview" week for Max in Los Angeles so he could meet with a few professionals with successful careers in the world of animation. He met my friend Roland Poindexter, senior vice president of original programming for animation at Nickelodeon. He also got to meet Mike Carlin, director of animation for DC Entertainment, and Jay Bastian, senior vice president of animation at Warner Bros.

For Max, they are men with whom he shares a special bond. They have built substantial careers in the world Max desperately wants to live in. They each gave him the benefit of an inside look at the inner workings of the largest entertainment companies in the world.

As we entered each studio campus and drove up to the gilded gates, we had to go through strict security protocol to gain access into the world of Hollywood. His exclusive special visitor pass on each studio lot came with VIP access to co-workers and team members who offered additional advice and perspective.

Our first stop was Warner Bros.

"Very nice to meet you, Max," Mr. Bastian said with an extended handshake.

"Nice to meet you too, Mr. Bastian."

"You can call me Jay." Then he turned to me and asked, "Would you like to join us, Mom, or rather take a tour while the two of us chat a bit?"

"Come with us," Max said to me. He was clearly a little nervous about his first "interview."

"Okay, for a little while," I told him. "I'll be a distraction and I think he wants you all to himself," I said looking at Mr. Bastian, or as he preferred to be called, Jay, to assure him.

He did. "Let your mom have some fun while we talk business," he winked at Max.

As we walked the hallway on the way to his office, two men clad in jeans and T-shirts were padding around in their socks in what was tantamount to a playroom filled with more cartoon toys and genuinely seemed to be having a great time enjoying playful banter. Turns out they were the head writers for *Teen Titans Go!* on Cartoon Network, one of Max's favorite shows. Max was invited in, and the three of them enjoyed a raucous conversation about their favorite *Teen Titans* episodes and those they hated. Is this supposed to be work?

Jay's executive "office" was more like a marvelous cartoon museum, brimming with toys and collectibles from years of Warner Bros., Hanna-Barbera, and *Looney Tunes* original animated shows. *Star Wars* starfighters hovered overhead, suspended from the ceiling, and figurines of characters lined shelves that would normally hold books.

After we were both fully introduced to the man in charge of it all, I left Max to have some one-on-one time with Jay. While Max was in his meeting, I spent the time taking a Warner Bros. Studio Tour of the backlots to see the sets of famous movies and popular television shows such as *Casablanca* and *Gilmore Girls*. It was fascinating to see "New York Street," a set that is customizable for any big city scene as in *Blade Runner* and the *Superman* movies. And there was no mistaking the Gotham City Police Headquarters in the *Batman* television series. I could just picture the Dynamic Duo running up the steps. I think my favorite was "Hennessy Street" that looks like Brooklyn but could be St. Louis, which it was in National Lampoon's *Vacation* starring Chevy Chase. It still makes me laugh when I think of the Griswold family's wild adventure trip to Walley World.

I didn't get to complete the lot tour before Max texted me. It was time to get him back so we could resume our day of scheduled interviews. I met them back in Jay's office to meet some of Jay's team. The meeting continued with one of Jay's assistant producers who seemed impressed by Max's depth of knowledge and strong opinions and insightful critiques of cartoons, some of them created right in that very studio and immortalized in the colorful cartoon memorabilia that filled every space in the room where we sat. I was mortified when he was critical, even harsh in his views on some of their shows and about how they could be better, but she and Jay seemed totally cool about it. She advised him to start his own blog and said she'd keep an eye out for it if he did, assuring him he could be very successful with it.

Max was breathless from his first interview.

"What did you learn?"

"He does Looney Tunes and *Scooby-Doo*! Those are two of my favorites!"

Max waxed on about all his favorite episodes and characters they had shared.

"That's great, but what do you think it might be like to work here?" I asked him.

"Definitely cool. You know, like Jennie [Max's childhood physical therapist] would always say about my therapy: it's not work, it's play." We both laughed at fond memories of Max climbing on top of balls to stretch those hamstrings and reaching to ring the bell to get that arm extension. She was good at making her work and his so much fun.

"Yep, it's perfect for you," I said. "It's what you've wanted all your life. But you have to do more than work hard. You also have to work smart like Jay did to get here, and practice your craft every day like Mr. Jared tells you. Are you ready to commit to do everything it takes? There are a whole lot of folks who would love to work here and you have to compete."

"Yeah, I know. But what I think I learned from Jay is that he is like a big kid. He hasn't lost his inner child. I want to be like that," Max added with a deep longing. "I don't want just any job. I want to love what I do, like he does. I think that's what it takes. I'll love my job and all the people who I'll work with to do it!"

He's right. That just might be the key to his success.

The next stop was Nickelodeon.

With my friend Roland, he had a more down-to-earth conversation about the business side of entertainment, as he wanted to give him the real deal about how to survive in the industry, especially as a black man.

Max was anxious to show him his characters and storyboards and Roland looked and listened to Max describe each one. "It's great to see a young talent like yourself with so much creativity and enthusiasm. We need more people of color in the business. But just remember that entertainment is not just about creativity—it's a business," Roland told him. "That's what you're here to learn about, and I'm happy to answer any questions. So ask away."

Pow! Wham! Right at the start, he pushed Max's red button.

"It's not about the money! Not for me! It's about the joy!" Max was emphatic. Roland was patient.

"Yes, that's an important part of it. But what brings you joy might not be what brings joy to others. And if your product doesn't sell to a large-enough audience, it won't stay on the air. That's important to think about. I don't want to burst your bubble. I just want you to be realistic."

Max retorted, "I think it's sad that so many people become so greedy that they lose their creativity and their joy. That's the problem with lots of cartoons today. They're not good. They're not quality. They have no joy. They make lots of cheap jokes. I hate that. I want to tell better stories."

"That's important. We need good stories," Roland told him. "What's your favorite?"

At this point, it was time for me to leave. I knew the conversation would turn to spirited debate about Batman versus Superman and favorite episodes of *Jimmy Neutron* and *SpongeBob SquarePants*.

While Max visited with Roland, I went shopping at the studio store where I bought my copy of *The Secret Life of Walter Mitty* on DVD. It just seemed so perfect for the occasion of Max living his dream. Prompted by his text that it was time to go, I met up with them as they headed toward me outside the building. They were still in full conversation, with Max still arguing his point about creativity versus the business side of the profession.

As I got closer, I could hear Roland explaining, "But we also need money to be able to pay you and a whole team of people to create them. We have to pay the writers, the artists, the animators, the directors, and producers, like me, and all the people who help this studio run. I have to take care of my own family just as we all have to take care of our families. I have also earned my way to be here in this position to share my knowledge and experience with you today to help you get here too.

"Sorry, that's how business works. It's not about greed, it's about getting paid so you can afford to do what you enjoy most. You want to eat while you're doing your thing, don't you?"

Roland was making sense, but Max wasn't ready to think about that. That part is too hard.

Ending the meeting on a high note, Max grinned and promised his new friend, "I'll be back one day. I hope you'll hire me for my talent. I don't care about the money. I just want to work for you."

"I look forward to it," Roland returned.

Max still fumes about the power and influence of money over the joy in life. There is wisdom in his naïveté. He knows his own truth, pure and simple. The world of fantasy is a lot more fun than the real world.

Our next stop proved the point. The larger-than-life-size Batman, which announces DC Comics' might and glory right inside the doors to the corporate kingdom, has brought joy to millions for years. After we paid our due homage, the receptionist noted our arrival, and we were led upstairs to the office of one of the industry's kingmakers.

Max got to spend a couple of hours talking about DC Comics superhero history with Mike Carlin, the writer-editor of the iconic caped crusader Batman and the Superman series, also known for his work on Marvel's Captain America and Masters of the Universe.

"You are kind of like Superman's Clark Kent," Mike told him after he got to know Max a little. You've got this real-life nerd side, but you have the heart of a superhero.

"When are you going to put on your cape?" he asked Max, only half joking. "What kind of hero do you want to be?"

For effect, Max snatched away his glasses and announced, "Meet Max Zolo."

"That's pretty cool, man. What's your superpower?" Carlin asked him.

"I can see your aura. I can see who people really are inside," Max said.

"Who am I?" Carlin asked.

"You are the master of your universe," Max proclaimed.

Carlin laughed and said, "Well, I get to be when I'm telling stories about characters I love. I guess that's why I enjoy working here."

Max left that last meeting of the day fired up, affirmed of what he was born to do—tell stories that bring out the joyful child in people. After a day of adrenaline-filled activity and excitement, I asked Max what impressed him most about what he had seen and heard.

"I really like that they enjoy what they do, especially Jay Bastian," he said.

I asked him why Bastian in particular.

"He's got the coolest office."

Meeting Billy Frolick, a feature screenwriter for the hit movie *Madagascar*, was another one of our favorite moments of his interview week in Hollywood. The very funny Frolick is also a director of the noteworthy screenplay *It Is What It Is* and the author of *What I Really Want to Do Is Direct*, the definitive book on starting a career in the film industry, according to the Academy Award–winning producer Steven Soderbergh.

Through a personal friend, we arranged to meet up with Frolick for lunch at a small café in central Los Angeles. He had grabbed a table outside and seemed to know who we were as soon as he spotted us even before we did him, as he immediately stood up and extended his hand as we approached the restaurant. I guess Max's inimitable walk and my crown of loc'ed hair were the giveaway. We seem to stand out in any crowd.

Madagascar is one of Max's all-time favorite movies, and together we probably have watched it dozens of times. So Max couldn't resist greeting him with "This place is crackalackin'" in his best Marty (Chris Rock) voice. Frolick, quick on his own script, tagged him back with, "Yep. I like to move it, move it." Oh, this was going to be so much fun!

Max was anxious to show him his characters he had created for his own stories in progress. He carries them with him everywhere he goes. He has spent years with each one of them. They have backstories and interpersonal relationships, and each has facets of Max's own personality. Jack and Lily are siblings, Mary is their mom, Akira is a warrior, and Jezebel is a seductress. There are others, but these are the main characters who transition in roles and situations throughout Max's various narratives.

Max introduced each of them one by one as Frolick quietly followed along, interjecting with an occasional observation, but mostly just listening and nodding as Max turned each page, slowly presenting each creation with intimate detail. It was not lost on Max that Frolick is a master. His opinion mattered a great deal. When Max finished, Frolick took the portfolio from him, flipped back a few pages, and stopped on the one he liked best.

"This one," he showed him. "I like her the best," he said, pointing to Jezebel, a voluptuous beauty clad in tight-fitting clothes. We all burst out laughing.

As Frolick took over the conversation to share wisdom about the rules for great storytelling, Max sat quiet, riveted, which is rare. Getting and keeping his attention is like trying to nail Jell-O to the wall. But his ADHD was in complete check when the writer of a hit animated comedy film, a connoisseur of humor and wit, gave him insight and advice on how to hold an audience captive for an hour and a half with a simple story. Max's questions came rapid-fire.

"What inspires you? Who are your favorite characters? How long does it take you to write a full movie script?"

Frolick thoroughly enjoyed Max's unbridled enthusiasm.

"The first rule to remember is 'you admire a character more for trying than for their successes,'" he said, borrowing from a quote from Pixar story artist Emma Coats.

He stressed the importance of humor, vulnerability, and staying true to your beliefs.

"Come up with your ending before you figure out your middle. Endings are hard, get yours working up front," he said, citing another rule of thumb for successful storytelling.

At this point, he had my full attention as well. The points he was making were as if he was talking about real life rather than just a well-told story. We both hung on his every word. His words held wisdom for an important life lesson: deciding your destination up front will define the journey it will take to get there. The journey is the messy, down and dirty, juicy part. It's surviving the trials and challenges, peaks and valleys, setbacks and triumphs that determines the measure of a person.

It was time to wrap our meeting, and I wanted to take a picture of the two of them. Frolick moved in close and put his arm around Max.

"Please send me a copy. When Max is famous one day, I'll be happy to be in the history books alongside him, in the chapter 'Max, the Early Days.'"

We laughed again and I took several shots just to be sure we had the perfect one to preserve for posterity, or perhaps for the future feature in *Vanity Fair* alongside his portrait shots by Annie Leibovitz, the famed photographer for Hollywood's biggest stars!

After a week of mesmerizing, wide-eyed, real-life immersion in what his career of choice looks like, feels like, and smells like, Max was supercharged. He reported back to his mentors on what he gained from the experience of meeting successful men in his field.

Max especially enjoyed describing to Uncle Lawrence Jay Bastian's office filled with "dolls," as Uncle Lawrence called them, in defense of his own.

"So, you see, it's cool to collect action figures," he said defiantly.

"Yeah, but it's cooler if you're creating the product," Uncle Lawrence clapped back. "He's creating the marketplace and making money, while you're just buying the product and spending yours. Are you going to be a creator or a consumer?"

Max was caught in his crosshairs. He had to think hard and long about that.

But Uncle Chris wanted to know what Max intended to do with all that advice he'd received from the industry men he got to meet.

"So your mother has given you the opportunity of a lifetime to go to Hollywood and meet titans in the field of animation. Not everybody gets to sit in the executive office of a head of a studio or the writer of a hit animated movie. What are you going to do with all that good advice they gave to you?" he asked.

Max thought about his answer for a few minutes.

"I'm going to run my own anime studio one day!"

Uncle Chris smiled.

"You must be listening to your uncle Lawrence. I'm glad to hear that."

"I didn't need him to tell me that," Max said. "I've always known that. It's called Max Zolo Studio. When I win my Oscar for Best Story, I'm going to thank all my mentors and give it to my mom."

You already did, I thought to myself as my eyes welled up and a tear of joy slipped out.

Chapter 7

The Power of Motherhood

Besides the support of steadfast righteous men, I have also sought the advice, strength, and wisdom of other mothers, single and married, raising their own boys who are coming of age.

I have shared in their pride and joy as their sons have come home with trophies for soccer and football. I have seen scads of photos of young men in various poses of triumph, winning a chess or a debate tournament, in the starring role in a school play, or receiving an academic honor. I've listened to stories about getting a driver's license and driving a car for the first time, or a school trip abroad to discover the world, and working on an internship for a political campaign. Achievements appear in blog posts, on Facebook, or in an invitation to an event showcasing his or her special talent.

There were not-so-wonderful stories too. I saw bad kids transform into angels, and sometimes the reverse. There are struggles with divorce, difficulties in school, police encounters, or behavior issues that lead to serious problems. There was the mother whose son got into drugs. There were even the most tragic stories of death of a life too young.

We have all witnessed or experienced losses and triumphs. To some extent, it is not totally under our control. But all of it is our responsibility.

For as long as they live and breathe, the safety, health, well-being, and future of our children rests on our shoulders.

I could depend on the shoulders of strong women who have been there for me and for Max when we have needed them most. We received incredible life-saving support from the female doctors and nurses in the NICU for his first eighty-three days out of the womb. His therapists and caregivers taught me healing, acceptance, and how to manage expectations and push for more during his early years. His teachers, especially in the third and sixth grades, showed him patience and provided much-needed encouragement to succeed academically. But support from other women has also come from some unexpected places and in unpredictable ways.

The power of gratitude

From the time he came home from the hospital until he was three years old, Max was receiving services from a development center that provides pediatric and preschool therapy designed to teach social and life skills to children with disabilities. Its clients are children whose lives are complicated by myriad physical and mental impairments and chronic disease and their parents, who are constantly in search of answers, solutions, and small miracles.

While in the parking lot one day, I was in the middle of checking Max's leg braces, steadying him to walk, and making sure that I had everything in his bag that he would need for the day, when Steven's mom approached me. My hands full, I could only use my head to nod hello to her and to her son, waiting patiently right behind her.

"Good morning. Need some help?" she offered.

"No. I think I got it now. How are you?"

Steven also has cerebral palsy, but his is much more "involved," a term used to describe the level of a disability. He was unable to walk and could not verbalize. He could communicate only through shifting his wheelchair and making shaky head movements, and his shiny and alert blue eyes, which seemed to be in constant movement. He was a genius trapped in a body of extreme limitations.

"How are you?" hardly seemed a sufficient question. But it had to do for now.

"Where's Steven's dad today?" I asked her. She mumbled an answer that I couldn't quite make out. It was clear that she had something else on her mind.

Typically both of his parents were always with him because it took a lot of work to unload his wheelchair, secure Steven into his seat, and carry all the things that he needed throughout the day. I had always thought how wonderful for Steven that he had two remarkable parents who worked as a team to take care of him when I had to manage the care of Max all by myself.

This particular day, it was just his mom. What she said to me that morning I'll never forget.

"You are so lucky," she said.

I was shocked.

"What could you possibly mean?" I asked her.

Then she said, lowering her voice so that Steven could not hear, "You get to make the big decisions on your own. You don't have to fight and argue over what's best for your child. It's exhausting. I've watched you and Max, and I envy you. You are doing such a great job."

I was stunned. Here, all this time, I thought my life was so hard as a single mother of a child with a disability, second-guessing myself with every critical decision I had to make. There were so many. These were not just medical decisions about whether we should pursue another corrective surgery or a new therapy that required a new regimen, or the choice between behavior modification techniques or medication to treat his ADHD. There were also questions about whether I would be able to handle the postsurgery rehabilitation or medicinal side effects that would impact school, work, and travel. I also struggled mightily about what school he should attend and when it might be time to change schools because he wasn't getting the kind of support that he needed. One of the hardest decisions was whether he was ready to go away to summer camp at the UCLA School of Performing Arts thousands of miles away. Could he survive on his own?

I had never thought about what life might be like when it is complicated by the added stresses and strains of trying to negotiate serious and unplanned-for life decisions with someone who may not believe what you believe, know what you know, or be as strong as you need them to be.

That day, standing outside the little white brick building whose halls and rooms held the highest hopes for the potential of the little lives who entered them with myriad stages and levels of birth trauma, I felt my spirits lifted. Woman to woman, she gave me the gift of respect and confidence that I have the strength to do what I need to do in the best interests of my son—on my own.

She does not know it, but the power of her words "you are so lucky" made me realize how fortunate I truly am that she was there in my life to give affirmation when I needed it, and something that I could hold on to then and for many years to come.

The power of grief

Sometimes developing a sound mind, body, and spirit goes beyond what any mother or father figure can provide.

When Max was sixteen, he started his second semester of tenth grade at a new high school. It was the first week of January, the week before school started when the unthinkable happened. Max's best friend died in a horrible car crash. He was the only one in the car.

Mikey was nineteen, two and a half years older than Max, and in his junior year at the same high school that Max would be attending. He was tall and thin, with silky light brown hair and a quick smile that always made him look like he was blushing. Popular at school and at home, he was good with the ladies, was great in track, and loved fast cars. The latter, a little too much. But most of all, Mikey was the big brother that Max looked up to, and he was so excited that he would finally have someone to look out for him in the hallways, stand up to his bullies, and maybe finally Max would get some respect, because Mikey would have his back.

Max loved Mikey more than he loved himself. They had grown up together. Holidays, birthday parties, sleepovers, and lots of shenanigans had created the kind of bond that was one of a kind and forever.

Max was beyond devastated and, to this day, the wound is still open. Every now and then, still, he cries.

"What's wrong Max?"

"I miss Mikey."

"I know. He misses you too."

It pains me to know there is nothing that I can do, that only time can.

As shocking as it all was, there were signs that Mikey was troubled. To this day, we do not know what was going through Mikey's mind at the time of the accident. How could we? But before he literally crashed and burned, his mom, Diana, did everything she could to save her son.

Coming to the conclusion that you do not know what to do and being willing to admit that your child needs professional help is one of the toughest things a parent can face.

Typically, it's required that at least one parent has to be willing to participate in counseling with your child. In this case, it was Diana. Of course, those sessions are private and personal and so I cannot know what was shared, but I do know that she wore her worry like an open wound. But after time, it seemed to help and things seemed to get better for her family.

I have known of only one family member, a cousin, who was treated for a mental illness, and that was from something that happened with some really bad drug when he had gone away to college. Other than that, those kinds of things were never discussed, as if not talking about a problem meant it didn't exist. We have been taught for so long that because our ancestors were strong, we must be too. Thus, our inner struggles are devalued, or can simply be prayed away.

"You don't know struggle, young man. I had to work two jobs and take care of my younger brothers and sisters when I was your age. That's struggle!" is something you would hear from grown folk.

But there was no denying that after years of bullying, a self-identity crisis, and then especially after the death of his best friend in the whole world, Max was struggling to catch his breath, catch a break, to breathe. He was experiencing bouts of depression and fear of abandonment, problems that were outside of my expertise and that of his mentors. I had to acknowledge it when he stopped smiling. His grades began to suffer. He slept a lot. He complained a lot, and about everything.

Our conversations in the car on the way to school began to shift to strange subjects like "What would you do if it were the apocalypse?" or "What would you do if you were the last person on Earth?" It took a couple of months for me to recognize that these were survival questions. It dawned on me that he was afraid of going out on his own into the world. He knew that someday soon he would have to leave the safe and familiar and felt that leaving home was like leaving to die. The truth of the matter is that Max was scared as much as he was bitter. After all, if life is so difficult while living in the security of home with Mom, how on earth could he face independence?

Max finally confirmed his deepest fears when he confided to me that he didn't want to grow up.

"I don't want to live on my own. I'll be lonely," he moaned.

"No, you won't. You make friends easily," I said, trying to boost his confidence. "If you get a job, you can earn your own money and make new friends, meet a nice girl, and get out more often and enjoy doing new things."

"Why is everything about money?" he often lamented. He thought having to pay for things was annoying. That meant you had to manage money, something Max had proven to be no good at. He was always either losing it or spending it, and seemed to never have enough of it. Uncle Jay may love that stuff, but to Max, it was a source of anxiety. It was work.

He didn't want to get a job. No matter my constant nagging, as he thought of it, applications for part-time work at GameStop, the Regal Cinema movie theater, and the local Publix and Kroger were left unfinished.

"Everything is not about money. It's about what you do with it," I answered. "Wouldn't you like to be able to make your own decisions about how to spend your money? You could have sushi whenever you want!"

I thought that would tease him into at least half a smile. It worked a little. But that was only a momentary reprieve. He lived in the world of "NO."

It was unfathomable to me. His perspective on life at his age was vastly different from mine when I was his age. At sixteen years old, I was not only ready to break free from parental bondage, but looking forward to the new adventure of leaving home to go to college after high school graduation. I just took it for granted that Max would too. I never thought for a minute that he might be reluctant to strike out into the world on his own once he finally got his diploma in hand. He had worked so hard for it. He had overcome so much that in my eyes he had always been a fearless warrior, my hero. I had never once considered how he might be agonizing over his future independent from me. I had always been right there by his side, and he had grown to depend on that, perhaps too much.

Uncle Chris had pegged it early on.

"Max is sabotaging his success by underperforming in school to prolong being able to stay at home. He is imagining that what happened to Mikey might happen to him," he told me. "He's afraid and he wants to stay close to you because you've always taken care of him. It's easier than all that scary stuff that comes with being responsible for all your own shit," he said, summing it all up. In a word, "shit" might be the perfect way to describe what Max felt like.

Uncle Chris was right. He took up sending Max handwritten postcards that would arrive in the mail every now and then, each with words of encouragement.

Hope you are having a great school year. Stay strong. Aloha.

They helped a little.

But underneath, Max was still seething. He was bitter and confused, fearful, and, mostly, lonely.

I feared that without professional intervention, Max's inner struggles could present far more challenges for his full integration into society than any physical disability. A prosthetic or mobility device can return you to movement and freedom. However, without a sound mind to determine the direction you need to go or the will to even try, the world is inaccessible.

Diana gave me the strength and courage to ask Max about making an appointment to get counseling. It was soon after Mikey had passed, and Max's anger and sadness were amplified to a level that had grown beyond what I or his mentors could manage. I knew that he needed professional help and that, at sixteen years old, he would need to have a say in a very difficult decision.

Concerned that he might take offense, I took his hand in mine and asked gently and lovingly, "Do you think you want to talk to somebody about this? A professional?"

I was surprised when he responded without hesitation, "Yes, I do. I think I need help."

I nearly collapsed into tears with relief. All I needed now was to find the right help, and I didn't even know where to start. But I knew who would.

The power of the village

Ramona holds a PhD in child psychology. So I turned to her for support in an area that I was completely ill equipped to handle. She gave me clarity about what Max might be feeling, a healthy perspective about how to help, and a prescription for seeking the counseling he needed.

She was not unfamiliar with what had been going on, given her interactions with Max when he spent time with Uncle Chris. She was well aware of his pain.

"Max needs help, Ramona, and not the kind of help I can give him. I've tried everything I know to try to help him out of his depression, and nothing works. I think you would know better than anyone in our network exactly what kind of help he needs."

"I realize that it must be hard on you too," she said. "This is a very difficult moment in his life.

"Sometimes you need to find out how to transcend your life circumstances so that you can activate your potential, to bring you into the fullness of your capacity," she imparted to me like an oracle atop a mountain of pain. "Max is on the verge of a breakthrough into what he is becoming, and sometimes this phase of life can be confusing and difficult.

"He is in conflict about growing up and getting ready to soon leave the comfort of his home and your care. Add to that, Max is attempting to pioneer into a world that has not been accessible for people with disabilities, on top of the challenge of the societal pressures of living as an African American. That's daunting and scary. He wants to tell better stories because he has something to say, and he knows that finding his own voice and an audience willing to listen won't be easy. He knows that better than anyone," she said, dropping pearls of wisdom.

"Therapy might be just the lifeline he needs."

I was relieved. It felt good to be able to talk about it, especially to someone who not only understood but who could help.

"Finding the right professional is important," she said. "You should talk to several and compare their answers to some critical questions that you need to ask."

These questions included

1. Are you a licensed psychologist?
2. How many years have you been practicing psychology?
3. I have been feeling [anxious, tense, depressed, etc.], and I'm having problems [with school, eating, sleeping, etc.]. What experience do you have helping people with these types of problems?
4. What are your areas of expertise—for example, working with children and families? Specifically, have you worked with sons estranged from their fathers?
5. What kinds of treatments do you use, and have they been proven effective for dealing with this kind of problem or issue?
6. What are your fees? (Fees are usually based on a forty-five- to fifty-minute session.) Do you have a sliding-scale fee policy?
7. What types of insurance do you accept? Will you accept direct billing to or payment from an insurance company? Are you affiliated with any managed-care organizations?
8. Are you available for a brief in-person or telephone meeting so potential clients can get a feel for you as a clinician? What would you charge for this?

Diana showed me that it was okay to get help when you need it. Ramona gave us the process of identifying the right kind of help and the right questions to ask to be sure that we got the kind of help we needed.

Having someone on the outside look in and be objective, listen, and ask thoughtful questions helped Max get a grasp on his own world. A sound mind can level any playing field.

After a year of therapy, Max continues to struggle but less so. He has come to accept that, to some degree, he always will. Just as the old Cherokee taught his grandson about life:

"A fight is going on inside me," he said to the boy.

"It is a terrible fight and it is between two wolves. One is evil—he is anger, envy, sorrow, regret, greed, arrogance, self-pity, guilt, resentment, inferiority, lies, false pride, superiority, and ego.

"The other is good—he is joy, peace, love, hope, serenity, humility, kindness, benevolence, empathy, generosity, truth, compassion, and faith. The same fight is going on inside you—and inside every other person too."

The grandson thought about it for a minute and then asked his grandfather: "Which wolf will win?"

The old Cherokee simply replied, "The one you feed."

Therapy has helped Max find his own voice, rewrite his script, maintain course, and move forward in the right direction. He has learned that he has unlimited potential to do anything he wants to do as long as he stays positive and focused. He has learned that he can achieve any goal he sets his mind to when he feeds the "good wolf" inside him.

The power of letting go

I have seen men as fathers and as father figures come and go. And I have seen those mothers who stand strong through it all.

Sheila is one of the mothers who have suffered through a difficult divorce. Oh, there had been drama, like the time after their separation when her husband stalked and smoldered outside their house after she was forced to change the locks on him. He had begun shouting and making a spectacle in the neighborhood. There was also the madness that ensued when he insisted that his new girlfriend come live with them. Oh yeah, he did that! All of her girlfriends came to rally around her, just in case some extreme intervention was necessary. And then there were the lawsuits resulting in the loss of their vacation home, where we had just enjoyed visiting with them the year before. Shame. It was a beautiful house on the Vineyard with a big yard for the kids out back.

The best interests of their son, Jesse, became the one single consensus between a contentious battle of wills.

Jesse was the kind of child who needed lots of discipline. Sheila recognized that and understood that despite their personal relationship issues, her little boy needed to be raised under the percussive tenor of a male parent who could penetrate and mitigate his hyperactive mind and spirit. In a courageous decision of love, she gave his father full custody and became the parent who got only weekends and weeks during summer vacations, and paid child support.

That took guts.

Sheila's journey may have been one of the single-most important factors in helping me understand the value of the Black Mitzvah. Her rambunctious five-year-old son needed a forceful father figure in his life more than he needed a doting mom in order to give him what she could not. Though a hard-driving professional, she is lenient when it comes to her son and can easily be taken advantage of. But that's not the case with his father. He wasn't having any of it. Jesse required a firm hand and his father had two. Understanding that, she was able to summon the strength and courage to put Jesse above her own feelings about a man who was not a very good husband and who had caused her so much pain. She knew what was best and did it for her son. I don't know many women who could or would do that.

When she first told me of her jaw-dropping decision, before thinking, I blurted out, "What! He's crazy!"

"Yes, he's quite something. But one thing he is, is a good father. Jesse needs him. They are close and he can give him the discipline he needs. That is not my strong suit. He knows how to take advantage of me, and he can't get away with that with his father."

I had witnessed Jesse's high-energy antics, so I did understand what she meant, but still!

"Is it hard to pay child support when you know that he's got a girlfriend—who he wanted to move into your house!"

"There's nothing I can do about it. But I do know that he's a good father and that's what Jesse needs, so I'm focused on that. I have to do what's best for my son."

There is no way to convey the amount of respect and admiration I felt for Sheila at that moment—and still do.

I understood exactly what she meant and why she'd made the very difficult decision to let go. Just as I'd realized that I could not know or conceive of what to do for my own son beyond a mother's protective love and instincts, we both knew that a man could easily recognize and handle the tough stuff in a way that validates his son's sensibilities and adds a notch of respect on his belt. Some boys need more tough love than others.

Matters of ego, pride, self-control, and freedom require a tightwire balancing act of mothering and fathering to ensure that a young man arrives at his destination with sound mind, body, and spirit. Sometimes there is a need for more weight on one side over the other in order to keep him centered.

Sheila let her son go to let him grow with the kind of nurturing that Jesse needed. It took guts, but it also took a great deal of trust. It paid off. When it was time to get ready for college, Jesse was back on Sheila's turf. In this world she reigns queen.

"He was a knucklehead. Now he's a mature young man with achievements that we are all proud of. Now he listens to me, and I can take over now. We can all focus on his future, and I can take the lead."

The time will come soon when I know I will need guts and trust to let Max go when he is ready to strike out on his own to grow into the man he is still becoming. But I take comfort that I won't be the only one who will feel the pangs of parental anxiety—his mentors will be right there with us.

Chapter 8

Defining Moment

We each travel a different path on our own individual journey to maturity, to reach the pinnacle of clarity in our mission and purpose in life. The amount of time it takes to get there differs for each and every one of us.

On the day of Max's high school graduation, when he was eighteen years old, with diploma in hand, the mentors all agreed, "Now the real mentoring begins." After six years of fathering, brothering, friending, and loving, they have all doubled down to help Max channel his many gifts into a force that he can use to change the world in his own way so that he can be the hero he wants to be.

"Now, more than ever, you have to always be mindful of your choices and your time. They both have limits. When either one is wasted or invested poorly, it can limit your possibilities," Uncle Chris advised Max. "With that diploma comes more responsibility. There is still a lot to learn. You must still be a student of life."

Uncle Jay underscored that message, focusing in on Max's Achilles' heel when it came to taking care of business.

"Be careful of spending too many hours in chat rooms or just watching videos. That is not the best use of your time. If you are serious about your career and are firm in your commitment to your desire to change the world, then think about and do what you need to get there. I have built my financial practice into a successful business, and I am still investing much of my time learning all I can to be better. Learning and seeking knowledge are things you should be doing every day for the rest of your life."

Max enjoyed the celebration and all the back-patting and attention, but underneath it all, he felt the weight of his future in front of him and it was scary.

After the festivities, after everyone had left to return home, knowing him as I do, I sensed that something was wrong. I sat down with Max for one of our mother-son check-ins.

"So what's up?" I asked him.

"I'm not ready yet."

"What do you mean?"

"I plan to go to L.A. next year, and I need to take care of a few things. I need to work on me. I don't want to get a job right now, not here in this city. It's not who I am. When I get a job, I want it to be what I want to do. I'll get a job when I get to L.A., because that's where I need to be," he explained.

I felt he was preparing me for his gap year. I listened carefully, since I knew I had to be mindful of whether it was thoughtful strategy or just fear talking.

His words made me take stock of my son in a way that I never had. Max was all grown up! As I sat watching him talk, taking in the full extent of the man in front of me, with mustache and goatee, his legs stretched out in front of him, I was suddenly aware of how grown-up and mature he has become.

Max continued, "I'm going to keep taking classes and try to earn my degree like Jay Bastian said I need to do."

I remained silent so as not to interrupt his train of thought. He was earnest about what he needed to share, and I knew that he needed me to just listen.

"Tomorrow, can we go for another driving lesson? I need to know how to drive in L.A." He paused. "You know I'm scared to drive." There was a longer pause. "I'm not yet confident that I can control my fear."

At this point, I interrupted, wanting to lighten his load.

"You know you don't have to drive. You can use public transportation or a car service. But let's just work on getting your license so you have that as an option when you are ready," I assured him.

He nodded and continued with his pronouncements.

"The world is different from what I had expected, hoped. I wish I wasn't so sensitive. My friends say I'm naive because I want to trust people. I've been disappointed so many times. The bullying has really impacted me. It is still painful. My therapy has helped me understand that's not healthy and I need to get right, and until I do, I fear that I will not be able to do my best work. I have no inspiration right now and I need to get it back."

He pointed to the sketch pad where a new character was waiting to be born.

"I want to be great," he said.

"What does that mean?" I asked.

"I want to achieve my goals, but I'm not sure I can," he said.

"What's standing in your way?" I asked him.

Pain. He didn't have to say it. I could hear it in every word he spoke.

"You know, it was not the boys. They're just stupid. It was the girls. They said mean things to me. I even hit a girl who was my best friend because her sister said so many mean things to me and I just lashed out. I'm still ashamed of that. I'll never forgive myself for that, hitting my best friend. I've been raped by another girl, and because I am too nice, I refused to tell. One girl even slapped me. Then in high school, a girl used me to go to prom to make the boy she really liked jealous. I'm so tired of being bullied by girls. It all happened because I'm different. I have a disability. I know it. No matter how nice I tried to be, not one of them has ever taken the time to get to know me. It hurts."

As he spoke his truth, I came to understand that perhaps he did need a break, a time to rediscover himself and renew the self-confidence he felt when he declared, "I know who I am," at fourteen years old, when others had attempted to define him because of how he wore his hair, his disability, or the color of his skin.

For our youth, as members of a global community accessible online and in an instant, the path to a mission and purpose has become riddled with confusing and complex messages. While limitless information and communication have enhanced learning and opportunity, social and moral influences that used to be controlled by home, school, and church are now invaded by those that escape even the strictest parental-control software. A generation ago, one mistake might be forgotten in time. Today, it can go viral in twenty-four hours and can devastate a young life in the same amount of time.

After he graduated from high school, he had more free time, and I had more to worry about. I had despaired about an online relationship that he developed in a chat room with a girl. Their conversation went offline to FaceTime every day. I could not understand or condone the inappropriateness of the relationship with someone who spent as much time online and in chat rooms as he was doing. Then he explained what that relationship meant to him, and I understood something about Max that reminded me of myself at that age.

"The reason why we talk so much is that she listens to me. She accepts me for who I am."

No matter whether she was real or fake, there was no competing with that. She had him. Whatever happens, she is the result of the years of bad experiences with the girls in his life. And until he learns to love himself, he'll take it from wherever it flows freely.

In the past year, many things turned clearer about the man Max has become.

Writing this book has been an extraordinary experience and provided me with a tremendous gift. I have gained many new insights and perspectives about parenting, and have thought long and hard about things I could have done better and things that I'm most proud of.

Looking back, I would have spent more time playing with Max and less time mothering him. There was always so much to work on between nursing and rehab, physical therapy, homework, tutoring, piano lessons and violin lessons to improve fine motor skills, and bedtime stories, that there wasn't much time left over for just play.

Max could have used much more playtime.

I remember when I was a kid and we would come home from school, the first thing me and my brothers did was drop our books and run outside to play until the streetlights came on. We usually did homework after dinner. Those three hours of freedom to let loose and discover our bodies, minds, spirits, and our relationship to the world around us were some of the best times of our lives.

Maybe if Max and I had played more hide-and-seek . . . maybe if we had more sleepovers . . . spent more time dancing and less time exercising . . . Maybe if Max had spent more carefree time just running . . .

What I am most proud of is allowing Max to be who he is. I have been determined to not define or limit what he can or can not do. What we may have missed in play, we made up for in exploring new opportunities, something that he continues to do. Today, Max is a man determined to make a difference in the world.

His face still lights up whenever he talks about his favorite cartoons that he grew up with: *Courage the Cowardly Dog, Codename: Kids Next Door, Foster's Home for Imaginary Friends, Dexter's Laboratory,* and many more.

"That's when cartoons were funny. They helped me cope. If I can't still enjoy them, I don't want to grow up. I want to tell stories that make people laugh. People need to laugh," he said.

He constantly laments that the current industry suffers from a lack of originality and complains about the lack of quality in animated shows.

I don't want to get into the business of animation just for money, like so many production companies today do. I want to do it because I love it. I have a lot of respect for Maurice Sendak, the author of *Where the Wild Things Are.* He says that he writes stories for himself because he enjoys them. That's the point. If you create a story from the heart, from your own truth, that's what makes it good.

"But I also want to teach," he added. "The world needs a reality check. People need to know the truth about what real people are feeling. I have been treated like I'm different all my life, and it hurts. And I don't want pity. Don't you dare pity me! I just want respect. We all need more empathy. If we had more empathy in the world, there would be no boundaries between race, religion, and other groups that people get lumped into.

"There needs to be more diversity in animation, without the stereotypes of black people and people with disabilities. People need to learn to treat each other with respect. That is going to make the world a better place. I want people to know that no matter what the odds, deep inside you are special. I love the classic stories like *Romeo and Juliet* and *Beauty and the Beast*, and the superheroes of *X-Men*. I want to tell better stories and introduce the world to more characters that have depth, beauty, and courage, and have the power to overcome whatever challenges are in front of them."

He will. In fact, I believe that Max has already changed the world in many ways.

For years, so many people have often said to me how smart, amazing, and confident he is. And, as his mom, always picking and tweaking, paying more attention to the things that we want to see our children do better, I sometimes overlooked the many gifts that are easily visible to others. There was the stranger who sought me out during intermission at a Cirque du Soleil show to come tell me what an extraordinary young man Max was after just a ten-minute conversation with him in the hallway; and the mother we met in an airport who was so dazzled by Max's encyclopedic knowledge of anime that she took his e-mail so that she could stay in touch and connect him to her son who also wanted to pursue a career in animation; and the auto service manager who wanted to buy one of Max's art pieces right out of the trunk of my car—a self-portrait and definitely not for sale. Despite the constant affirmations of his unique gifts, I had somehow grown to perhaps take them so much for granted that I had not really taken in how magnificent he really is.

Most important, while writing this book, Max and I have had much more time together because I've been home in our shared space, which has afforded me the opportunity to observe and interact with him in a way that has allowed me to get to know him all over again.

"Remember that you told me when you were just four years old that you are going to be great?"

"Yeah, I'm afraid that I might let you down," he said.

"Never. Besides, you made me a promise. With just those few words, you changed my world. You gave me hope when I was afraid to hope. Not only am I going to hold you to yours, but you can hold me to my promise to support your greatness. I have spent all these years completely invested in helping you achieve anything you wanted to. I am still here and will always be. I promise," I told him.

We talked a while longer and shared more personal revelations that we will just keep to ourselves.

When our talked lulled to a relaxed tête-à-tête, he closed with, "I love you because you are not a generic mom. You listen and you care." (Sniffle)

At nineteen, Max is a man who has started believing in himself again. His proclamation at age four that he is going to be great has resurfaced in the way he carries himself. Filled with opinions, ideas, and plans for his future, he has the principles instilled in him by his mentors.

From Uncle Lawrence, he learned "boot camp" discipline in hygiene, etiquette, and social skills.

From Uncle Chris, he learned the values of living in community.

From Uncle Kevin, he learned entrepreneurship and humility.

From Uncle Jay, he learned financial stewardship.

From promise and purpose to propriety and a plan of action, Max IS great!

His Black Mitzvah still continues because they have all decided that the commitment to mentoring is every day for the rest of his life.

I know that someday soon he'll strike out on his own to make his mark, conquer the world, and raise his own family. I look forward to that day with pride and joy, and sadness. I'll miss my baby boy, holding him, caring for him, protecting him, picking him up when he falls, wiping tears, making his favorite home-cooked meal of noodles with salmon, baking his favorite molasses cookies, stocking the refrigerator for him and his friends, going to opening nights of Marvel films, and dropping into his studio to see his latest project in the works.

It warms my heart that his special bond with "Uncles" Lawrence, Chris, Kevin, and Jay will keep him in good stead.

It takes a village to raise a child, but it takes a circle of kings to raise a gentle warrior, including the four we chose as mentors from the start and the many others the universe has sent along the way. Max has emerged from the jungle of adolescence a gentleman and a warrior.

Epilogue

Creating Your Own Black Mitzvah

If you are interested in creating a Black Mitzvah for your own son or daughter, I recommend that you start with your own available resources. The three basic tenets that we established for a solid youth-development support system are faith, community, and accountability. It does not matter whether you are married, what religion you practice, where you live, or what your circumstances are, your child can have his or her own Black Mitzvah, or whatever you want to name their rite of passage. All it takes is a little imagination and the commitment of a few men or women who role-model the values that you believe in and would like to develop in your child.

The following questions and guidelines are the same ones we used to begin:

1. What are the goals of the Black Mitzvah? What is the vision that you have for your child's future?

2. What tenets/teachings will be the foundation for your child's growth and development?

3. Who are the men and/or women in your family/community you most admire, trust, and respect? These are individuals you know personally and feel that your child is completely safe with. Once you have your list, it is important to make the decision together with your child about whom you would like to invite to be a mentor. After all, it is your child who must be open to the relationships and who will determine how successful those relationships will be.

4. What are other considerations for selecting a mentor?
    a. Time commitment: How many hours/days per month, in person and/or via digital communications, can they commit to?
    b. Reliability: Are they willing to be consistent and responsive?
    c. Confidentiality: Are they willing to keep the relationship private? This is important so your child can trust that what is shared is between him or her and the mentor, and that any discussion of what is shared, is by permission only.
    d. Profession: If your child is interested in a particular career choice or has a particular aptitude, it may be a good idea to ask someone you know who is experienced or knowledgeable in that particular industry. This can be invaluable along the way to help with motivation and educational counsel.

5. How to make the ask is up to you. I called each one personally and just simply asked, "Would you be willing to be a mentor to my son?" and then described our goals for my son's future. After a yes, I asked why they agreed to do this and wrote it down for reference in the celebration.

6. Once all the mentors are secured, then it's time to plan the celebration. There are a number of preparation activities to consider:

    a. Ask your son or daughter to write a letter to each mentor telling them what they most like or respect about them, stating what they hope to learn from them, and, most important, thanking them.

    b. Ask your son or daughter to prepare for the moment spiritually. No matter what your faith, whether it's the Bible, Quran, Torah, or any other source, is there a particular verse or story that your child feels is important to them at this moment and would like to share during the celebration?

    c. Ask each mentor to think of a gift that is particularly meaningful and appropriate for a thirteen-year-old to create a teachable moment during the celebration. Examples: a watch, a book, seeds, an heirloom, a pet (with a parent's permission). Ask each mentor to prepare a thought or choose a particular spiritual verse to share during the presentation of their gift.

7. Include mentor-mentee bonding activities during the celebration. The celebration can last one day, two days, a weekend, or however long you wish. The goal is to make this important rite of passage a memorable and symbolic occasion. One example is to create an activity for mentors and mentees that the mentors did when they were thirteen, which is great for bonding and credibility. Other activities could be teaching a favorite recipe in the kitchen or learning to tie a tie, something that can come in handy for girls too. The idea is to be creative and have fun.

8. After the celebration, be sure your child writes a thank-you note to each mentor for their gift and their time. This is also a good time for your child to ask when they will see or hear from them next. We have to train the mentors too.

9. After each visit with a mentor, be sure your child writes a thank-you note, and it's a great idea if they also mention what they learned or maybe include a question. This helps prompt a response from a mentor.

10. For the parents, it is important to keep the mentors up to date on any important moments that they should be aware of to say "congratulations" or to just check in. I was always careful to not interfere or ask too much. I learned that it is very important to let the mentee take responsibility for the relationship. That way the relationship of trust is natural and unfettered.

11. Don't hyperventilate if your child doesn't want to talk about a visit or a conversation with a mentor. Occasional check-ins on how they're doing or feeling about life in general are very revealing and can help monitor any issues that may arise that you should be concerned about.

12. Encourage mentors to provide tasks for your child to teach a skill and accountability. It is up to them to decide if it merits a reward or not, since we all know in life that sometimes the best reward is self-satisfaction in a job well done.

13. The Black Mitzvah is a development support system for children from age thirteen to eighteen, but I have found that once the relationships are established, the mentoring will likely not stop there, but can continue lifelong.

Feel free to add to this list, and we'd love for you to share your own experiences and suggestions. The possibilities are limitless. If you would like additional support or help customizing your own Black Mitzvah, please visit blackmitzvah.org.

Acknowledgments

To write this personal memoir, I had to go deep. I had to tap into my reservoir filled with the good will of people who poured their faith into my first endeavor to find my own voice and to use it to inspire others.

Thank you, Jim Ed Norman, for insisting, "You have to write the book!" My respect for your wisdom, guidance, and friendship led me to a point of clarity that the next chapter of my life is about continuing our honest and open conversation about raising our children. If *Warrior Rising* has only a fraction of the impact that your legendary contribution to the music industry has had on the world, it will be worthy of every agonizing moment of labor, every rewrite, every tear, and every fear I had to overcome to marshal words on paper.

Thank you, Geoff Howland, Stephen Blessman, Kyle Donovan, and Glen Wright for saying YES with unconditional love to participate in a human experiment that required courage, gut instinct, and a tremendous amount of time and patience with no guarantees. It takes a warrior to raise one. Good on you and your own circle of kings—and queens—who made you who you are. The ancestors are proud.

Thank you, Dr. Frank Boehm of Vanderbilt Hospital, and all of the NICU doctors and nurses at Baptist Hospital. Precious few understand what you experience every day: babies in crisis, parents facing their worst fear, prayers and last rites, and tears of profound joy when a family gets to go home with their bundle of high hopes. Your fight on the front lines as the life line between heartbreak and heart lift is worthy of the gods. Thank you to Dr. T. S. Park at St. Louis Children's Hospital, Jeannie Vraciu, and all the medical professionals, pediatric physicians, therapists—angels on earth—whose acts of divine intervention are to you routine, but little miracles to the families you serve.

We have been blessed with a few extraordinary teachers who taught with a level of love and kindness that turns a learning experience into a lesson about the celebration of human value, dignity, and respect. Thank you, Chris Dudgeon, Victoria Stacey, and James Dittes for seizing the opportunity to innovate inclusive solutions that made learning fun for a bright student who learns differently. His success is your success too.

Willing protagonists and divine inspiration provided the tools for writing my first book. Mastering them was not easy. Trained to write professionally for clients, I have spent years learning to listen well, and to distill thoughts into corporate communications. Rediscovering my own voice was a process. I have to thank Gail Larsen, guru of Transformational Speaking, for helping me embrace that I am a "Beautiful Queen" and bringing focus and force to my mission as a change agent.

Thank you to my incredibly thorough copy editor, Maureen Klier, and the entire production and marketing team at Penguin Random House who set the bar for the best reader experience and persisted in extracting the best from me in every way. The idea that my book will publish out of the same house as Pulitzer Prize–winning author and fellow Nashvillian Jon Meacham is a breathtaking honor. Thank you, Sara Carder, for believing that "it's more than a book, it's a movement." As a chief editor at one of the largest publishing houses in the world, your belief in the message and me as the messenger, from the very beginning, when I was just a soon-to-be author, still astounds me. However, now I see how you weave your own creative genius into the projects you love, and just hope that every author has their own dedicated book project maven to shepherd it into being.

It was, in fact, serendipity that led me to Serendipity Literary Agency. Thank you, Greg Campbell, for being my friend, the kind of friend who wants to see others be successful and acts on it. You are the real deal. Who knew that lunch at a restaurant in New York with your friend would turn out to be an introduction to my book agent, a game changer for a mother who simply wanted to share her story about trying to do the best for her son. Thank you, Regina Brooks, and your team, Jodi Fodor and Karen Thomas, for your valuable input in navigating the process from proposal through to final manuscript. And to Nadeen Gayle, thank you for wanting to give agency to this book. Your passion fueled mine. I look forward to your son's Black Mitzvah.

Thank you to all of my mentors, past and present, especially Toni Faye and Betty Adams, for role modeling elegant excellence, and my ride-or-die posse of badass "aunties," Patricia Jones Blessman, Michelle Richardson, Kathy Johnson, Rachel Christmas Derrick, Regina Barboza, and Lenore Washington-Graham.

Thank you to all of the incredibly generous men who have been a part of our journey: Joe Charles, Joe Steele, Glenn Tunstull, Chip Davis, Jamie Hathcock, Michael McBride, Walter Searcy, and Stuart Lycett. Your spirit is woven into the fabric of this story in a way that you will surely recognize.

And finally, I must thank my literary sheroes, Zora Neale Hurston and Nikki Giovanni. Because of them, I did.

In Loving Memory of My Mother

Only a month has passed since my mother transitioned at the age of ninety-two, a few months before this book will be published. While the manuscript was coming to life, she began succumbing to death, losing her intellectual acuity and growing more frail day by day. Clinging to every opportunity to create a new memory or to jog her own, I read to her from the pages I had written to fill the space our banter used to fill. She seemed to be content to just listen, to not have to speak, her eyes trained on my every facial expression. Every now and then, I would get a chuckle or a smile out of her. I was uncertain if it was from something I said or from a place inside her own private memoir of a time long ago. Quietly, I yearned to know. A master wordsmith herself with a quick-witted sense of humor, I was not able to benefit from her ability to turn a prosaic sentence into a clever turn of phrase. Was she laughing at my own awkward or inadequate sentence structure? Or was she simply enjoying listening to the recounting of so many stories of her own daughter and her grandson she had already known—many of them she largely helped to write through her wisdom in words and deeds imbued in my own motherhood? Though she will never be able to hold a copy of my first book in her hands, or display it prominently on her shelf, I want to believe my story is also part of hers, one that she is proud of.

As the matriarch of our family, her story is of a simple midwestern girl with extreme skills as an entrepreneur, business professional, artist, musician, seamstress, and community servant. In short, she role-modeled phenomenal womanhood. She taught me the virtues of strength, fortitude, and independence. It made me fearless in my confidence that I am, therefore I can. Even her weaknesses and imperfections provide insight and acceptance that we are all simply doing our best with our blessings. What more can one ask of a mother. I am truly blessed.

Thank you, Mom, for the wonderful life you gave to all of us.

Her legacy of community service lives on at the June Irene Howland Legacy Fund at the Cleveland Foundation.

Index

About the Author

First and foremost, MaryAnne Howland is a proud mother and advocate for persons with disabilities. She is a communications specialist and the owner of a portfolio of social enterprises that fan the mission of equity, inclusion, and sustainability. They include Ibis Communications, Global Diversity Leadership Exchange, and THIS!, a new fashion line for all body types. In pursuit of advancing understanding of cultures and our common values, she has also worked as a travel writer/researcher for Fielding's, Open Roads, and *Black Enterprise* magazine. A servant leader, MaryAnne sits on the board of the American Sustainable Business Council based in Washington, DC. She also serves on the corporate board of ABLE, beautiful products made by women who have overcome. With this book, MaryAnne has founded blackmitzvah.org to fuel the movement to traditionalize rites of passage for boys and girls, and to support a community dialogue about parenting and mentorship. Born in Cleveland, Ohio, she is a graduate of Boston University School of Communication, and serves the world as a global citizen from her current residence in Nashville, Tennessee.

MaryAnne Howland is available for speaking engagements. To inquire about possible appearances, please contact Penguin Random House Speakers Bureau.

Please visit her website at ibiscommunications.com.